A True Story

About

A Girl Named

Connie

This book is a true story. The characters, incidents and dialogue are drawn from the author's research, interviews, and observations. Some of the names have been changed.

Copyright ©2016

All rights reserved. Printed in the United State of America. No part of this book may be used or reproduced in any manner whatsoever without written permission except in the case of brief quotations in critical articles and reviews.

To my husband Guy I dedicate this book because of his support and faith in my abilities.   Carol

I dedicate this work to my parents, Bill and Cloteel Wilson, who gave me a life of love and opportunities, and to Aunt Hazel for reminding me that I was "one of them."

                                             Connie

Acknowledgments

Thanks to my writer and dear friend, Carol Perkins, who put my story on paper.

Mother and Dad who provided a good life and all the opportunities a girl might want.

Aunt Hazel for her making sure I was always treated as, "One of them."

My Smith family-all of them (around 70) - I continue to give my love.

My Mona Rae who is kind and loving. I thank her.

My longest friends for seventy years, Carol Perkins and Judy Wallace Irvin-what a great "ride" we have had, and it's not over.

My friends I call my "home girls"-I love them all and they know who they are.

Peggy Hourigan-thank you and the Hourigan family that I love. They gave me a family when I lost my own and have kept me close long after Peggy's death.

Dr. Peggy Stephens and Charleen Stephens Allen-thank you for giving me a place to live, and the love I have always needed from others.

To those with whom I taught who brought me out of a deep depression and forced me to "get back into life," I thank you.

My half-sisters-I love you and wish we had grown up knowing each other as sisters.

Wanda, my "go to girl" for the Smith family- I thank you.

To those who proof read for us, especially Susan Chambers who was my high school English teacher, thank you for taking the time to do so.

There is much to this story I will never know because all of the parties involved are gone, but I have as much as I need.

A True Story

About

A Girl Named

Connie

CHAPTER ONE

MY DAD SAT QUIETLY at the kitchen table, reading the *Courier-Journal* just as he had done every morning as long as I could remember. His chair faced the window overlooking the huge magnolia just beginning to bloom. It was a nuisance to him because it blocked his view of the street. He enjoyed watching passing cars and neighbors in their yards, but each time he suggested cutting it, Mother would say, "Bill, you're not cutting my tree." She meant business.

In a little while, he would get into his car and go "over to town," as he put it, where he would spend the day at his store, which had been at the same location for over sixty years.

The rural town of Edmonton, in South Central Kentucky, with a population of only a thousand or so, was dependable and predictable. Although active for its size with county fairs, softball games at the park and trail rides on weekends, its main attraction to newcomers was that it was frozen in time; not moving forward or backward. It had come to a halt sometime in the 50's, and not much had changed since, even the population.

A Girl Named Connie

That is the way Edmonton was in 1946 when I was born, and the way it remains.

Dad looked tired as he stirred his coffee more times than necessary without looking down at the cup. His large hands were painfully wrinkled and covered with age spots. Thinner than usual, his broad shoulders slumped as he read. He was aging and because I didn't see him as often as I should, I had not realized how quickly this was happening. I wanted to look at him for a long time as we sat together, soaking up this rare moment with just the three of us in the kitchen, but I did not want him to notice.

Mother, as slim as she had been all my life, fried his eggs at the same avocado-colored stove she had been using since we moved into this house in 1958 when I was twelve. Without speaking, she set the plate in front of him. After sixty plus years of marriage, words were unnecessary. Very little had changed during the time I had been away.

What had once been the height of style in my childhood home sadly looked dated. The traditional couch covered in brocade, the matching chairs with a table between them at the picture window, and the console TV pushed against the back wall were straight out of the fifties. The wallpaper had been stripped and redone a few times in the living room, new coats of paint spread on the other walls, a room added where the carport once was, and Dad had the back porch screened in, but that had been done before I left home. The gold leaf mirror over the couch reminded me of how many times I stopped to check my hair or my clothing before leaving the house. The piece I loved the most was the portrait of me hanging over the television, simply because of how special it was to Mother.

"Sister, would you like some eggs Benedict?" I had been sitting quietly as the morning news filled the room.

My father peered over his newspaper after a long silence. "How's school?" He had been asking me that question since my first day of elementary school. The conversation between adult children and their parents is often awkward, especially since the years of being out of each other's lives are usually more numerous than those that are spent together. After moving a hundred miles away, I had shared a few weekends and holidays over the years but not stayed for any length of time.

"I think I am going to retire at the end of this year." I opened the dialogue.

"That's what your mother told me. Are you sure that's what you want to do?" He laid aside his newspaper. He might have been trying to talk me out of my decision. I was only fifty-one and, in his eyes, far too young to quit working. After all, he had not retired, and he was in his eighties.

"I'm not quitting exactly. There is a position for a few hours a day at my school that I'm going to take for some extra money, but I am going to retire officially from full-time teaching. I'm just tired."

"Well, you need to do what you think is right." That was my dad's answer for most things. If I did what I thought was right, I could always live with my decisions. He went back to his newspaper, and I watched him read it.

My mother busied herself with my eggs, and I waited for her to speak first about what we needed to do, but instead she fidgeted around the two of us, waiting for me to lay out the plan. Undoubtedly, she was as nervous as I.

This trip home was a difficult one because I had not come to visit; I came for a purpose, and one that would affect the rest of my life.

My greatest challenge faced me across the kitchen table, and I was losing my nerve.

CHAPTER TWO

I WAS BORN IN 1946, but not to Bill and Cloteel Wilson. When I was twelve, the truth emerged from an unlikely source on a busy elementary school playground. Not that I hadn't had my suspicions, but on this day a girl named Lisa confirmed them.

Edmonton Elementary was a short distance from the main part of town. Actually, there was only one part of town, and a person could stand on one side of the public square and see across the courthouse yard to the other. Our school consisted of the "big" building as we called it, which stood directly in line with the only road that led to the school, but surrounding this three-story brick structure were dozens of clapboard-sided buildings. Many had been one-room country schools hauled in on the back of oversized trucks and set on foundations surrounding the school ground.

These dozen or so buildings faced a gravel playground laden with weeds growing through rocks, and there were a couple of swing sets, a slide, a merry-go-round, and a seesaw. A thick forest area behind these buildings with paths leading to a creek enticed us to follow it at recess, even though we youngsters were warned to stay out of the woods.

"Don't ya'll go down there. You don't know what might be hiding from you," our teacher cautioned, but she knew where we were headed in spite of her threats. Back then teachers could scare kids, but most of the time we knew they were bluffing, so we sneaked away to brave the forbidden territory beyond the boundaries of the playground.

When we heard the bell ring for class, we were slow to climb the hill to begin our lessons. Often our shoes were wet from slipping in the creek and squeaked across the wood floors. The boys could make their shoes sound much louder than we girls could.

Our school was small compared to many elementary schools in other areas. As a matter of fact, each grade level was divided into two groups according to the alphabet, and I never had classes with anyone from "A to M." Therefore, my friends were in the last part of the alphabet for those eight years, and I knew very few of the other kids until we reached high school.

Each teacher taught all subjects, including art and music. If I had a bad teacher, I was stuck with her or him for nine long months.

Carol Sullivan, Roberta Reece, and I were in the same "room" for eight grades, and we were always best friends. They were first cousins and lived just a half a mile out of town, side by side, and I don't remember life without them. Our bond would remain intact the rest of our lives.

A new girl named Lisa Miller joined our sixth-grade class not long after the year began. Lisa's family moved to Edmonton, which was a rare occurrence for anyone to do that had no family in town, and she was interesting, if not a little strange. Her Northern accent enthralled us, and she found ours to be "country." By the end of a few weeks, we students realized that intellectually she was advanced, but socially she was lacking.

"Move over; I want to sit with Connie," she would order a kid sitting next to me in the cafeteria, and usually the kid did what she said. Because she was an avid reader and wanted us to know it, she felt superior, I suppose, by complaining about the lack of books in the library.

"Don't you have any new books?" she would ask our librarian who would then say, "Which ones do you have in mind?" None of us would have had the nerve to make such a remark to our librarian.

However, our sixth-grade teacher encouraged us "town" girls to befriend her since she knew no one. Unwavering in her pursuit of our friendship, she inserted herself quite aggressively, moving in on conversations and tailing us on the playground. Her bossy, confrontational attitude moved us away from her as often as we could escape. However, if she couldn't attract our attention one way, she would find another.

If I turned around to ask another student for help, she joined the conversation. "I don't think that is the way to work the problem. You're going to miss it if you do what he says," referring to the boy who was helping me. She was probably correct, but I didn't like the way she talked to him.

She was also an authority on whatever subject arose. If we talked about skating, she had been the best skater in the last place she lived, a fact we could not prove or disprove. If we talked about our school projects, hers would always be more complicated than ours. There was no area that she wasn't one step ahead of us, so she thought. She prefaced every sentence with, "My dad said." Therefore, we tried to maneuver her away from us, but she was going nowhere.

One day when the bell rang for morning recess, Carol and Roberta lined up at the water fountain just outside our classroom door. "Hurry up or they'll leave us," I said, rushing them so we could get outside before Wallace and Larry ran off to the woods and left us behind.

We hiked with them down the narrow trail behind the school to the creek almost every day. Even though I was normally as brave as any of the boys, I was not ever courageous without them in the thick of these woods. I don't know what I thought they could have done to protect us. I was taller and probably stronger than either.

Just as we bounced down the steps, skipping a couple at a time, and raced out the front door, Lisa fell in behind us. We were already in the rear of the group, and she was having a hard time moving through the undergrowth. I could hear her yelling, "Will you slow down?" It was more of an order than a request.

I didn't want to slow down. I wasn't focusing on her but on keeping the boys in sight. Then out of nowhere I heard this bellowing scream echoing through the trees. "STOP RIGHT NOW!"

We didn't.

Then I heard, "You better STOP NOW! I know something you don't know."

She had found a way to stop us after all.

I stopped because I wasn't sure to whom she was speaking or what was wrong with her. Here was a twelve-year-old girl stomping the ground like a bull after his matador, one foot after another raising the dust. When we finally made eye contact, she had me.

I moved slowly back up the hill toward her, wondering what she intended to tell one of us, but before I was close enough to ask her what she was talking about, she burst forth. Clenching her fists at her sides, she looked directly at me and started singing and swaying her plump body in a musical rhythm, "You're a-dopt-ed; you're a-dopt-ed," stretching each syllable into a singsong chant as her hips swayed from side to side. Over and over she sang, "You're a-dopt-ed; you're a-dopt-ed." When I was certain she was addressing me instead of Carol or Roberta, who had also stopped for this outburst, I ran.

A Girl Named Connie

I'll never know why I ran, but as fast as my legs could carry me, I turned away from the woods and circled back up the hill to the playground, darting and zigzagging around the swings and the slide with her pursuing me close behind, still chanting, "You're adopted." She was deranged.

I was fast on my feet, but at this moment so was she; consequently, every direction I turned, she closed in. Following behind her, Carol and Roberta were shrieking, "SHUT UP! SHUT UP!"

To the kids and teachers on the playground, we might have been playing a game, but this was no game. I rushed far ahead of her, and looped around to the front door of the school, sprinted up the steps, and scurried back into the classroom, thankful the bell had rung.

Out of breath, she soon slid into her desk. Her smirk signaled she thought she had won the battle or at least crippled her opponent. In fact, that is what she did. Sweating from exhaustion, I laid over on the desk, pondering her words and wishing to beat my head against the surface to stop hearing, "You're a-dopt-ed; You're a-dopt-ed.

Every time I glanced up, she smiled a know-it-all despicable smile. By now, I was struggling not to jump up, leap across my desk to hers and punch her in the face. Whipping her would have been easy, but not wise because I would have had to explain to the principal why I hit her, and he would have then called my mother.

As I sat quietly, I devised a plan to attack her after school. Before I could digest what she had said, I had to make her pay for saying it. As soon as the day ended, I was going to gouge her in the eye, plunge at her knees, knocking her to the ground, and then paralyze her with fear. That thought provided momentary satisfaction, even though doing so was unrealistic. My getting in trouble would not have pleased my dad.

As I sneaked a peek at her across the aisle, the more irritated I was that I had run; I never ran from anyone. I felt weak. I had spent most of my childhood with town boys, playing ball and climbing trees, so I was conditioned to defend myself. Dolls and playhouses bored me, and no matter how much my mother tried to steer me away from "boy" things, she did not succeed until I was a teenager. "Connie, it is time you acted like a lady."

However, verbal confrontations made me nervous and anxious, so that was almost certainly why I ran. If she had hit me, then I would have socked her a good one.

The rest of the day when our eyes met, she cocked her head and grinned with her thin, tight lips. I wanted her to fear me; she wanted me to know she didn't. I didn't hear the teacher's voice because Lisa's was ringing over and over: "You're a-dopt-ed. You're a-dopt-ed." I hated her for taunting me, but more importantly for saying what I had suspected since I was seven years old: I was adopted and if she knew, who else did?

I glanced around at my classmates pouring over their lesson; the friends I had gone to school with for six years. Did they know? Did my teacher know? If this newcomer knew about me, then all my classmates likely did, too. Betrayed. That is how I felt. Totally betrayed.

CHAPTER THREE

EACH AFTERNOON, those whose parents worked near or around the square meandered down the unevenly paved road that led to and from school. We dodged potholes and vehicles leaving for home, then turned a left corner, passed Ms. Hughes' Restaurant (where we were not allowed to go because of its reputation for rowdy behavior of the patrons on weekends), and headed the short distance to town. The school was so close that kids were allowed to go home for lunch.

Another turn took us past the Presbyterian Church with its stained glassed windows and impressive history. However, neither my friends nor I went to church there. We were either Methodists or Baptists.

Because her dad had an office in town, Lisa usually walked with us, but not this day and not ever again. "Let's walk fast," I said to my friends.

"Come on Judy; let's get out of here," Carol said as she picked up speed down the road."We'll fill you in later."

Judy was a year younger and had no idea of the events of the day, but she rushed along the road with us just the same.

"Is she behind us?" Roberta asked without turning around to look.

"I bet she is, but she sure isn't walking with us today," I said.

I had already made up my mind before leaving school that the sun was not going to set without my finding out what my best friends knew and had withheld from me.

When we neared the church, I stopped them, "We need to talk." Both Carol and Roberta knew what was coming, but Judy did not.

This conversation was to be our first and last for many years about my alleged adoption.

I took the lead toward the church steps, and they followed. "Ok, what do you know?" I said standing in front of them, taking charge of this interrogation.

"About what?" Judy frowned, looking at the other two for understanding.

"Am I adopted or not?" Always known for getting straight to the point, I foolishly thought they would tell what they knew. Instead, they squirmed.

No one replied for several seconds. "I don't know. I just heard it," Carol finally said fiddling with her notebook. A peacemaker even at a young age and somewhat of a people pleaser, she would never want to tell me anything that might hurt my feelings, but I wanted answers and assumed that if Lisa knew, so did my best friends.

"I don't know; I just heard it, too." Roberta echoed with her nails easing toward her mouth. She quit biting people when she discovered her nails.

"Judy, you have got to know. Your family has known Mother and Dad long before I was born, so surely someone has mentioned it?" Ruby and Gilbert Wallace were witnesses when my parents got married.

A Girl Named Connie

"I don't know anything for sure." That's all Judy would say. Selfishly, I could have drilled them further, but they were uncomfortable, and so was I. They could have told me that their mothers had told them the truth and made them promise not to tell it, but they didn't. One day they would, but not for many years.

"Well, I'm not going to ask you again, but if you know anything you owe me the truth." They said nothing.

We strolled on down the street in silence passing Shirley's Hardware Store, the Cozy Inn Cafe, Metcalfe Furniture and the Corner Restaurant until we stood together under a highway sign pointing right toward HWY 68 & 80, the main road out of town. We then crossed the street in the opposite direction and turned toward the drugstore. Nothing looked the way it did on my way to school that morning. I was not the same person; I was not happy. All this time I was not Connie Wilson and no one told me. Suddenly, I felt self-conscious and uneasy. For years, I would wonder what others knew. It would be years before anyone told me.

CHAPTER FOUR

THE FIRST STOP ON THE WAY to the drugstore was for my daily dime, which I took from the cash register in my dad's dry goods store. Wilson's Dry Goods was the third building on the north side of the square. The Edmonton State Bank sat on the corner and an insurance office was next to my dad's store. A small grassy plot of land between the bank and the insurance office where I played with other town kids was the town playground.

While they waited outside and probably talked about what to tell me and not to tell me, I slid behind the counter, pushed the cash register button and heard the familiar clang of the money tray as it shot out. This antique cash register had probably been my grandfather's, but my dad would see no reason to invest in a new one with features he didn't need. I took the dime and shoved the tray back into the machine with a little extra force.

"Did you have a good day, Sister?" my mother asked as she refolded one of many stacks of jeans in the back of the store. She had called me "Sister" since my brother learned to say that word. I called him "Brother" until he was grown.

A Girl Named Connie

"It was fine." I had the urge to tell her what happened, but I didn't have the nerve.

"It was the worst day of my life! There you are acting like this is an ordinary day and I'm supposed to act like nothing happened. I just found out for sure that you have lied to me all my life! Who are you? I don't even know you!" That is what I wanted to say, but instead, I said, "It was fine." I couldn't get out of there fast enough.

The four of us claimed an empty booth at the drugstore and ordered Cokes. Metcalfe Drugs was in the business of prescriptions and over-the-counter medicines, but to the young people in Edmonton, it was all about the soda fountain and three booths. By three o'clock, a group of teens, mostly girls, rushed to claim one of them. Not enough room? Move over one more inch. Guys didn't go there, which gave teenage girls a chance to talk about them and we listened. "Oh, he's so cute. I heard he is taking HER out Saturday night."

Would any boy ever want to take me on a date now?

Adults were also patrons of the fountain, but they knew to avoid coming near it after school. The menu wasn't extensive, but the ladies who worked there made all sandwiches and desserts from scratch. Malts and sodas (not soft drinks but sodas) were only thirty cents. Fountain drinks were either five cents or a dime, depending on the size.

Early morning coffee drinkers lined the stools smoking cigarettes, and workers in town ate lunch if they could find a place to sit. Metcalfe Drugs was the focal point of the community.

Shortly after we arrived, Lisa strolled up to the counter and sat on one of the swirling stools just a few steps from us. Normally, she would have been sitting beside one of us. I was facing her but looked away and pretended she wasn't there. "What will we do if she comes back here?" Carol whispered over her glass.

"She wouldn't dare," I said, but I didn't feel confident. If she had made her way back to our booth, I don't know what I would have said or done. My emotions had gone from fear to hurt to anger, but creating a scene in a public place, just steps from my family store, was not in my best interest. Dad was a stickler about public image.

"She isn't going to push me into a fight because she knows I would win," I whispered. I was tall and thin, and she was neither. I was street smart; she was not. However, at this moment, she had the emotional upper hand because she knew too much.

She bought her Coke, glanced our way, flipped her stool around and left. From that day forward, I never spoke another word to her.

"What will you do if she says something to you tomorrow like she did today?" Roberta asked as she held her blond hair away from her straw. Roberta would be nervous about the possibility of a fight. Among all of us, she was the one who was slow to anger or voice an opinion. If pushed, she would stand her ground but not as readily as the rest of us.

"I don't know yet, but I won't take it like I did today." It was easy to talk big to my friends, but in truth, I had no idea how to handle her.

The three of them would go home that afternoon and tell their mothers what Lisa had done, and their mothers would say, "Don't tell anyone else about this and maybe it will blow over," or "It was just a matter of time." They would have been right-it was just a matter of time.

Small towns can't keep secrets well, but evidently mine had been the exception. If not for Lisa, I might have gone through my adult life without knowing the real truth, but I wasn't feeling grateful. She shamed me in front of my friends, and I was vengeful. This was not her secret to tell.

A Girl Named Connie

At home, I acted no differently, but that night I wore out the sheets, twisting and turning and rehashing every word she said, changed the end scenario to suit myself. I replayed how I reacted and what I should have done instead of running. Then my thoughts went to what she knew and how she knew it. What led her to say that she knew something I didn't know? How did she know I didn't know? Who told her it was a secret?

Her family had been in the community less than a year, so had someone made a point of providing the story of Connie Wilson? Did this person say, "She doesn't know, so don't say a word."

What prompted Lisa to tell me? Why was she mad at me? What had I done to her?

At first, I was more vengeful toward her than I was inquisitive about myself. That would come later. Retaliation was crucial to my pride.

I formulated a plan for revenge during those restless hours, and by morning, I was armed and ready for her. My parents, sleeping as if this were just another ordinary night, were oblivious to what I had been through that day and furthermore, they would continue to be.

If Lisa said one word, I was going to coax her behind the building at recess and beat her up. My new strategy was to bloody her nose and kick her a few times, leaving bruises and maybe a black eye. Although I had never struck another person, I had seen girl fights at school and in the courthouse yard, so I had an idea of what to do.

Immediately, she would tattle to the teacher, the teacher would tell the principal, and when he called me to his office, I would tell the truth and take my punishment. This scene played out as clearly as one from a saloon fight in a western where the ladies jumped on the gun slinging men. From the perspective of a twelve-year-old, my strategy was flawless.

The next morning on my walk to school, confidence walked beside me. From my desk, I waited anxiously and watched for her to enter. Would she have the courage to show up after what she had done? I wished I never had to see her again, but not only did she show up, but she also came into the classroom with the same silly smirk she had left with the day before. I hated this girl.

"Hi, Connie," she said, swishing her way to her seat and tucking her lunchbox inside her desk. She was always on a special diet that kept her from eating in the lunchroom.

I was confused. She was not supposed to speak to me. She was not expected to act as if nothing had happened. I didn't respond and purposefully snapped my head so as not to look her way.

Maybe while I was formulating a plan during the wee hours, she was doing the same. Realizing she had likely jeopardized her chances of ever being friends with me again, maybe she wanted to make amends. Too late. Her honey did not melt in my mouth. I blackballed her from the Wilson Circle.

I glared at her with venom eyes. This little bitch was going to pay. In a way, I was relieved not to have to pretend to like her any longer. Not only was she rude, but she also thought everyone in the class was dumb and backward, yet she smothered my friends and me. The weight of dragging her along was lifted, but a much heavier one would soon replace it.

Her gushy attitude was such a disappointment that by recess my plan was slippery, and I was no longer feeling combative. Beating up someone who was acting like Shirley Temple would have been useless in redeeming myself. I could hear my teacher saying, "Poor Lisa, what on earth made Connie do this to you?" as she dragged me to the principal's office.

"Connie, what made you do this to Lisa?" the principal would have asked. He would have called my mother. "What is the matter with you, Sister?" she would have questioned. Was I willing to recount the scene from the previous day, or should I keep it to myself and move forward as if nothing had happened? I wanted to whip her, but I couldn't summons enough rage to carry out my original plan.

As I abandoned one idea, another formed. I was going to ignore her; pretend she was invisible. Give her no attention and no feedback. I discovered a depth of loathing I didn't know I had. As a result of her antics, she found herself a group of one. Roberta and Carol would never soften toward her again.

Finally, she made a new friend and left us alone. If she ever told her parents what she did, she certainly made no indication of it. There was no apology. For the rest of the school year, she was nonexistent to me. Yet, she was never out of the corner of my eye.

CHAPTER FIVE

IN ALL THE DAYS AND WEEKS that followed after Lisa's confrontation, I never asked my parents or anyone else about my alleged adoption or told the story of what she had said. I say "alleged" because I had no proof. Not that I wasn't tempted to ask, but I was scared.

Some kids would have rushed home, slammed their books on the counter, and demanded answers. I could not do that. I feared that if I told my dad what Lisa had said, he would have marched across town to her dad's office and had a showdown. The thought of my dad being hauled off to jail because he knocked out Lisa's father petrified me. If Bill Wilson knew, there would be hell to pay. I didn't want anyone to pay hell.

In the meantime, after discovering what I had viewed as a perfect life was not even my life, I sank into a private darkness. Nights brought intrusive thoughts of the playground, the words, Lisa's face, and the running.

Who gave me away? What was wrong with me? Why did my real mother not want me? Where was I born? How did I get to Edmonton? I had questions but no one to ask, so I did the worst thing for my emotional health; I buried this newfound information. However, it wasn't resting in peace. My detective work began immediately.

On the surface, my mother was the same woman she had been the day before, but what she didn't know was that I could see the hidden side of her; the one that kept secrets and pretended to be my mother. She likely never considered keeping this secret exactly a lie, but I did. Would I ever trust her again?

Mother wasn't the only one I viewed differently; I once had looked at my dad as sturdy as an oak, but was he as vulnerable as the weakest branch? If he found out I knew the truth, I feared the branch might break. He was not as emotionally sound as my mother, yet I had no sympathy for him. My dad should have told me the truth. Of all the people in my life, I had trusted him the most.

It wouldn't have been in his nature to tell me. He would have given this job to Mother. Any corrections or suggestions as to improving my behavior came from Mother but many times indirectly from Dad. "Mother, you need to tell her to …" Dad shifted unpleasant tasks to Mother. I knew this about him.

He was not an effective communicator, but he was a good showman. This man I thought was an example of the moral high ground was a man without integrity? I went from high opinions of them to low and back and forth.

I wanted to yell at him, "You owe me the truth. Tell me who I am. You've never lied to me," but I didn't. Just as in a Shakespearean play, I was now going to be an actor on the Wilson stage. They were already stars, but I would soon learn my lines to perfection.

At the age of twelve, I decided to assume the role of a visitor named Connie living with Bill and Cloteel Wilson. I was a traveler through their lives who had no known previous residence and would dwell here until I left home. Just as guests do not want to intrude nor do they want to be too much trouble, neither did I.

I resolved to be kind, obedient, and grateful. If I were perfect, I would not run the risk of my parents sending me back. Back where? What would keep them from deciding that they didn't want me? I had to be careful within the family unit not to upset the routine of eating, working, going to school, and sleeping. Play nice, Connie. Be a good girl. Don't mess up.

Foremost, being a perfect child meant pleasing my mother who would be delighted if I helped more around the house, which meant keeping things straight and orderly. She valued that. "Connie, stop throwing your clothes on your bed. Hang them up." That was my worst habit.

My room became so neat it looked as if no one slept there. It was almost like a hotel room. There was a bed, a dresser, a chest, and a desk with a lamp. My friends had posters of Elvis and James Dean on their walls, but mine were sterile. I doubt they had to seek permission to hang them, but I would never have taped anything to our pristine walls and risked the tape pulling the paint off.

When my friends came over, which wasn't often, we stayed outside or in the den and shoes came off at the door. My mother insisted on everything in its place, and I decided that included me.

Slumber parties at my friends' houses were chaotic, so I never asked to have an overnight party. I could have one friend for a sleepover at a time, but not three. My friends would beg their mothers to give in to a last minute slumber party, but that would never have worked with mine.

The only time I had a party was one New Year's Eve when I was in high school. My parents had just closed in the carport and made a den, so we teenagers played music, danced and ate. Kids came in and out the sliding glass doors and every time they did, my mother was looking out the window. The worry of someone messing up the carpet or breaking a piece of furniture stressed me so much I never asked to have another party.

From the time I knew I was not their child, my home did not feel as welcoming or as comfortable as it had been. I can't explain the difference except to say that nothing felt like home and I was growing homesick.

CHAPTER SIX

ALL I WANTED TO KNOW was where I came from and who gave me to them? This had become a game of "fill in the blanks." If someone like Lisa, with no ties to the community, had known, then the entire town must have been privy to this secret.

At the most unexpected times, childish thoughts cut through my mind like a chainsaw. Quite ridiculous to think of now, but I wondered when or if some strange woman or man might drive up to my house to take me back, and my mother or dad hand me over to them. I pictured myself looking back at Bill and Cloteel through a car window as these strangers drove off. Could this happen? I had seen this play out on TV when an adopted parent tearfully relinquished her child after the mother changed her mind. I didn't want that to happen to me.

Consequently, I became whatever anyone thought I should be so my parents would not send me away.

In the meantime, I continued to look for clues and listen for hints. For weeks, I recreated incidents and played back conversations, mostly from

A Girl Named Connie

customers. Becoming obsessed with my origin, I allowed the investigation to consume my life.

One of the first clues came from a farmer smiling down at me as he stood in the doorway of the store. It was my birthday, and Dad was proudly telling him about how old I was and what I could do at such an early age. The man patted me on the head and said, "I can't believe you are six already. I remember when Bill and Cloteel got you." Dad rushed him out the door. Neither of us mentioned the moment.

"Got me?" I wasn't born; I was "gotten?" I kept that memory but was so young I didn't dwell on it, deciding the man misspoke. I had a knack for avoiding unpleasant truths.

Unlike the accounts my friends told of when and where they were born, I knew nothing. I found nothing hidden in drawers among my parents' belongings that gave any indication of my birth. Where I was born was never mentioned even among my extended family. No one ever said, "I remember when you were born." The only item from my young years was a bronzed set of baby shoes.

The earliest picture I have of myself was when I was about a year old. I was a blonde-haired little girl with ringlets and wore a fancy dress and a bow in my hair. I ditched the dress and the bow but not the blonde hair. Where were my baby pictures? Someone surely snapped a picture of me. As far as I knew, I could have been born in California or Alaska, or my mother could have been living right under my nose.

I did not want to be adopted. No one wanted to be adopted. The stereotype of adopted children during the 40's and 50's was that they were unwanted and usually wound up with less than enthusiastic relatives or in orphanages. Did I come from an orphanage?

I assumed most adopted children were born out of wedlock, a term I had heard from adults. I didn't want to be born out of wedlock. I became fixated on my birth mother and envisioned her in the worst way. Honestly, I never thought too much about my father. Fathers are often insignificant in an adopted child's search for identity.

I concluded that this woman was a whore that didn't even know who fathered me. I was the illegitimate daughter of a prostitute. Mother had no idea what I was reading tucked down in a chair waiting for her at the local beauty shop. True Story Magazine even though off limits to my friends and me, educated many young girls and in this case, led me to the wrong conclusion about my birth mother.

My investigation uncovered some facts I didn't know, but reaffirmed some I did. At the time of my birth in 1946, my parents were living in Louisville. That much I did know. Mother would have been around twenty-seven and my dad thirty. This period would have been just after WWII, and a time when money was not plentiful but my parents were prosperous, so why would they leave their business to move to Louisville? I also knew that they returned to Edmonton with me when I was around six weeks old. What happened in between would require more time to unravel.

How did I learn this? Months after the schoolyard incident, I asked one of my dad's sisters, Aunt Mag, about that time in my parents' life because she knew everything about my dad. Aunt Mag was a stout woman and the youngest of the three Wilson children. She was also the kindest.

I dropped by her house several times a week, so when I saw her sitting on her front porch one afternoon, I made my move and after a bit of chit chatting, I asked, "Aunt Mag, who ran the store when Mother and Dad lived in Louisville?"

She looked at me as if to ask how I knew they lived in Louisville but replied, "Why, I did."

What kept me from asking her why they went? I wanted to know but was afraid to know at the same time.

"Aunt Mag, do you remember when I was a baby?" I was fishing.

"Why, of course, I do. You were a doll with your blonde hair, and your mama pushed you around in a fancy carriage." Aunt Mag kept the front porch swing moving back and forth as I sat on the stoop in front of her. She and Uncle Lawrence, an insurance agent, lived on the south side of the square in a white-framed house. He wasn't a tall man, but I thought he was a giant.

"How old was I when they came back home?" Maybe she would ask me what I meant about "come back home." She didn't.

"Oh, I don't know. Maybe around six weeks." She was not as forthcoming as I had hoped, but I was formulating a timeline with what I did know.

They left town and came back with me. Did they want others to think my mom had delivered me while they were gone? Assumptions were all I had.

"You know, Connie, I had never seen your daddy as happy as when they brought you home." I knew that was true. He loved me dearly. "Seems like he couldn't show you off enough. Your mama dressed you like a little doll and loved showing you off." She had opened a window, but I chose not to go through.

I concluded that my parents couldn't have children, so they adopted a baby from an orphanage in Louisville. I don't think they tried to pass me off as their own; I think they didn't expect anyone to ask about my birth, and as far as I know, nobody did. Some people don't respond to or open themselves up for nosy questions, and my parents were like that.

I could not imagine anyone having the nerve to ask intrusive questions about my adoption or my birth parents. To outsiders and sometimes within the family, my dad could be intimidating, and certainly quirky. Back when I thought only sailors and criminals had tattoos, my dad had one of a naked lady on his arm, which was embarrassing for a young daughter to see and worse yet, her friends. In addition to that, a long scar ran down his neck that I heard much later was from a knife fight long before he married. What kind of man had my dad been before I arrived? Not one person ever told a story about growing up with my dad.

When I was a teenager, I mustered up enough nerve to ask him about the tattoo. "It was a dumb thing to do. When I was single, I got out with a group one night, drank too much and we all got tattoos." My dad always wore a long-sleeved white shirt, and only the family knew why. As for the scar, that was never mentioned. Not even I had the guts to tackle that subject.

My mother was a strong woman with a volatile temper. I heard a story about how one night when Dad had a poker game at the apartment (long before I arrived) someone drank too much, so she pushed him out the door and down the steps. I never knew *that* couple because when I arrived, there would be no more card games in the Wilson home.

He never completely stopped gambling, often running a poker game in the basement of the store one night a week that they didn't know I knew about, but he turned more toward betting on horses, which in Kentucky is a more acceptable activity. My mother did not object, or I would have heard them fighting about it. Whatever money he made at the track was more money for her to spend. They complemented each other.

My dad's love for horse racing took him to many tracks throughout the state, and although my mother went with him on occasion, most of the time he traveled with a couple of men from town. They picked Dad up at the house, and he left with his clothes in a brown paper bag. Why didn't he take a piece of luggage? I never asked. Dad had no qualm about carrying that paper bag, but my mother would never have done that. She would have used her Samsonite luggage. They would be gone a few days and come back either happy or not. On those times when Dad was not happy, we stayed clear of him until the fog had lifted. Dad was addicted to gambling.

He also gambled on the stock market. The only time my dad came close to having a nervous breakdown was when he invested in a railroad stock and lost $10,000. "I lose $10,000 and they notify me with a postcard." He never got over that. For months, Dad moped around the store, the house, and paced the street in front of the store. His temper flared, and even Mother could not pull him out of this hole. In time, he moved away from investing in the stock market, but kept his gambling to what he could better control.

In spite of how I came to be in Edmonton, I lived a life of excessiveness from my mother and adoration from my dad. But that was also before the birth of my brother.

One afternoon when I was only seven, my family was visiting my mom's sister, Aunt Jewell, in Glasgow when I overheard something quite disturbing and immensely confusing.

Even more so than my mother, Aunt Jewell valued possessions and a prosperous life. Being around her made me feel pleasing because she always admired something about me. Her home was in the country club section of town and filled with "important" people and endless social events. At Christmas, I longed to have her ten-foot tree decorated to the nine's with a train running around the base as one might see in the window of Macy's.

She served dinner in fine China to her proper husband, her proper children, and her proper guests. Although she put on airs with her family and friends, she did not with Mother who still saw her as the Haywood girl who didn't have two nickels to rub together.

I understood Aunt Jewell. She thrived on being noticed, and since she was a beautiful woman, she turned heads. A local doctor even named a racehorse after her. She married well (twice) and lived well with her three children, with whom, for no particular reason, I would have limited contact during my life.

Both my mother and her sister used appearances as a measuring stick of importance. I would tend to do the same until I knew better.

Aunt Jewell owned an upscale ladies' boutique that catered to wealthy ladies from all over the state, and Mother often had first pick of new items.

On one visit to Aunt Jewell's house, she and my mother sneaked off into the dining room and sat at her lovely table that was set with her fine China as if someone were coming to dinner. They intended to have a private conversation, but there was just enough of a crack in the door that a curious child could overhear. I hid and listened.

My mother said joyfully, "I have good news. I'm pregnant."

My aunt was shocked, "Oh, my word, after all this time you're finally pregnant. How could this be? I didn't think you could get pregnant."

"I don't know but I've been to the doctor, and he told me I am pregnant!"

They were giddy! I ran away from the door and sat on the couch. When they came out, I was sitting alone rather than outside with the other kids.

"Why aren't you out with them?" Mother asked motioning to the front door.

"It's too cold." The cold I felt was the blood that had turned to ice in my veins. Frozen in fear about what I had heard and how that would affect my life, I said nothing. What could I say?

Obviously, Mother had not been pregnant with me so where did I come from? Even at this young age, I knew what pregnant meant and if she wasn't supposed to be able to have a baby, how did I get on this earth? I pretended not to have overheard their conversation and had no idea how to find out how I came to be their daughter.

The three of us rode toward Aunt Hazel's for another afternoon visit in silence. As I sat between them, tears were trying to come, but I knew if I cried, I would have to tell why. I didn't want a baby in our family. That I knew for sure.

Predictably, I never mentioned what I had heard and filed it away. With the impending birth of this child, my mother was wrapped up in planning for the baby but never talked about the fact that I was going to have a sibling. Were they planning to appear with him without saying a word ahead of time? When they put up the baby bed, and she grew more rounded, they finally had to tell me. Naturally, I acted thrilled, but I was far from it. Whether I wanted to be or not, I was going to be a sister.

My reaction was not an unreasonable one for a child, but it went deeper than jealousy. I didn't want this baby because it would be theirs and evidently, I wasn't. I was wise enough to figure this out, so what would be my place in this family now? If they could have one of their own, would they still want me?

When my brother was born at a Glasgow hospital, my dad took me to the Buster Brown Shoe Store on the square and bought me a brand new pair of brown and white saddle oxfords. The pattern of buying gifts to assure love was not typical of my father, so I assumed my mother had told him to do this.

Mother was confined for several weeks, as all women were back then, so she didn't go to the store with Dad every day. When I got home from school, she was always tending to my brother. I don't think I was jealous of him, but I didn't know how to react to this tiny being. My friends had siblings, and they played and fought, but I was seven, so we would miss those opportunities. Both of us were like "only" children. My mother doted on him, but Dad didn't seem to know what to do with him either. When my brother was born, Dad and I grew closer, and Mother and I farther apart.

After they brought my brother home, I spent even more time outside or visiting neighbors because I didn't like watching Mother coddle James. When she looked down at him, she saw part of herself and my dad. What did she see when she looked at me? In my mind, my home now consisted of a family of three and Connie.

CHAPTER SEVEN

F ROM A VERY EARLY AGE, the town of Edmonton provided me with an enormous sense of security. We lived less than a block off the town square in an apartment over a store building, which my dad owned and rented to a family who operated a grocery store. This apartment was enormous. Along the entire front was the living room with windows all along the front and sides. The main piece of furniture in that room was a used piano my dad bought when I started taking piano lessons.

The other most impressive room was the kitchen. Cabinets lined three sides of the walls with a dinette set in the middle of the floor. This room was almost as large as the local skating rink. As a matter of fact, I would often put on my street skates and make my way from my room across the kitchen floor and out the back to the covered porch.

From the porch were steps leading to the backyard. I used these steps as a type of clubhouse. When my cousin Wanda came to visit each summer from Smiths Grove, we created many adventures on those steps. Wanda was six years older than I was and the youngest of Aunt Hazel's children. She often told me I was spoilt, but I didn't think I was spoilt simply because I didn't let her have her way! We made good playmates and I dreaded to see her go home each time she left.

Growing up with a panoramic view of Edmonton connected me to the town because I was never without it. The town was mapped out like other small rural communities with a red brick courthouse in the middle of a grassy courtyard where kids played baseball on one side, and older men sat on benches, whittling and swapping gossip, on the other.

On all four sides of the square were businesses with private dwellings dotted among them. The appearance and the owners of each might have changed over the years, but the structures are still the same.

Looking out the front and side windows from the upstairs, I could see people walking into one of the several grocery stores, going to the Strand Theatre to watch the latest Doris Day movie, or entering the Corner Restaurant or Miss Bessie's. At night, a car of teenage boys, long after stores were closed, might "mark off the square," which meant waiting for the local police to make their rounds out of town, then "burning rubber" on the street. When I had nothing to do, I watched the town.

Across the street from the store building was a Ford dealership. Back in the late forties and through the fifties, car choices amounted to only a few designs, and the unveiling was a monumental event. My love for cars has persisted since the early days of standing outside the showroom window looking at the new models. My dad bought a new car every three years, which was a mark in the community of being "somebody." The need to be "somebody" rubbed off on me. I never owned a car that wasn't sporty and fast.

A Girl Named Connie

Occasionally, I asked Mother for a nickel to go downstairs to the grocery store to buy a piece of candy. My purpose for going was to talk to the lady who worked there or to play with the owner's son who was a little older than I was. If he were in town, we shot marbles in the side yard or climbed trees behind my house and played Tarzan. He lived in the country, so I had to keep a lookout to see when he might show up. We would later go to the same college.

If I conjured up enough nerve, I stood outside John Moran's Store, (an empty lot separated it from our store building) and looked at the elegant bolts of lace and the variety of specialty boots and hats. His wife would later be my fifth-grade teacher and wear my hand out with a ruler for talking too much, but she was seldom at the store. Because he didn't appear to like children, I didn't go inside very often. If I saw him looking at me, I ducked and skipped around the corner to the "cream station." Not thinking that my dad and Mr. Moran were in direct competition, he might have accused me of spying on the enemy.

Mr. and Mrs. Moran were prime targets for Halloween pranks long before my time. He was so contrary that some teens did ornery things to his house, which just made him more intolerable.

The "cream station" was where farmers and their wives brought fresh cream to sell for making butter, and fresh milk that suppliers from area processing companies came once a week to buy. I observed farmers unloading silver milk cans, usually rolling them from side to side because they were so heavy, as I sat on the edge of the porch and talked to their wives who sold fresh eggs just snatched from the hen. Sometimes if they brought their children, we wandered off to the vacant lot next to my house for a game of hopscotch, tag or marbles. I was always looking for someone with whom to play and pass the otherwise lingering and lonely days.

The courthouse yard, just steps away from our apartment, gave some of the older men a place to be during the day, and sometimes I veered off from my friends to watch them whittle while sitting on the iron benches conveniently placed in a circle.

Mr. Williams was one of the men who came each day with a piece of cedar and his pocketknife. I was only about six when he started carving objects for me. One of those was a cedar knife with two blades. I watched him whittle on this knife, letting me touch the ends, knowing they were not sharp enough to hurt me. He made many items for me including a bird and a frog, and I kept them in a shoebox in my closet.

When I was in college, a girl in my dorm was giving a presentation on the art of whittling and while listening to her talk about her paper, I told her the story about the items Mr. Williams had made for me. "Could I borrow them for my presentation?" I didn't think I would have a problem by loaning them to her, but I was wrong.

I made a special trip home to get them, and she was thrilled at these treasures. "These are perfect. How can I ever thank you?" As evident throughout my life, I went out of the way to please others. I wish I had been more selfish.

After the presentation, I assumed she would return them promptly, but she did not. When I asked about them, she always had an excuse. "I can't ever remember to bring them to you," was one I heard often. Finally, after harsh words and hurt feelings on my part, she admitted she didn't know where she had put them. I never believed her story.

It wouldn't have surprised me if she had given them to her teacher. For whatever reason, I did not get them back and for whatever reason, she appeared not to care.

A Girl Named Connie

I could hear my mother saying as she had done so many times, "You cannot give everything you own away." To this day, I resent this woman for taking my precious items and betraying my trust, but I never completely learned not to be such an easy mark.

In today's society a little girl might not be safe in the presence of elderly men without an adult present, but back then times were different. I was never out of my dad's view and many times he walked over and watched as they carved, standing beside me and admiring what Mr. Williams or old man Jamison was creating. Our town was trusting, and it hasn't changed since I left.

CHAPTER EIGHT

BECAUSE I WAS around them so much, business owners were like aunts and uncles. Mr. Albright, the shoe man, taught me how to manipulate leather and tack a sole on a boot. Ruth White, one of our beauticians, taught me to tie my shoes.

One person, beyond tolerant of me, was Miss Bessie and her cook Beulah. Miss Bessie owned a family style restaurant in a small storefront not far from the old Presbyterian Church. Her place was always busy because of her fabulous food.

Beulah was a happy, robust black woman whose first words to me when I frequently dashed through the door and headed directly to the kitchen were, "Child, are you hungry?" I spent lunchtime in the summer eating at Miss Bessie's when I wasn't at my grandmother's house.

In the early fifties, before integration and segregation were hot issues in our country, we didn't have civil strife in our town because we had few black families. Looking back, I don't think any of us ever thought about how black families felt about eating at the back door or drinking from "colored only"

A Girl Named Connie

water fountains. I never attended school with a black student until I was a senior, but I was never prone to discriminate. I was not brought up that way; one of my dad's good friends was a black man who often asked Dad for a ride somewhere. He didn't have a car.

In addition to the good company and food, a fascinating thing about that restaurant was a little hole in the floor in front of the curtain separating the kitchen from the eating area. I pondered about what made the hole in the first place. A gunshot? Did someone shoot through the floor? Many times, out of curiosity, I dropped my extra marbles down it, hoping they would roll out through a secret tunnel in the back of the building. Even though I searched, I never found those marbles. No one asked me what I was doing or indicated that I might need to move; they walked around me. I never asked what caused the hole to be in the floor.

When I grew bored with the hole, I darted back to the kitchen where Beulah was cooking over two wood cook stoves. The heat was sweltering, but she never complained. The largest pot on the stove held the pinto beans, and she often fixed me a bowl, added a piece of cornbread, and poured a tall glass of milk.

Black people ate on the back porch at Miss Bessie's because they couldn't eat with white folks, so I sat on the back steps and ate with them. Miss Bessie, a white lady, never asked me to pay for a meal and it never occurred to me to offer. I must have thought I was eating a family dinner with relatives. I became friends with Beulah's son and his daughters and remained close to them until I left for college.

Looking back, I believe Beulah and I sensed a kinship. Long after I heard the words from my classmate, "You're adopted; You're adopted," I sat with Beulah on the back porch and saw through her eyes how it felt to be an outsider. I was part of a family but not really. She was part of a community, but not really. If I had asked her about my being adopted, she would have known, but she would have been afraid to tell me. I always knew Beulah loved me, and I loved her. Our souls were colorless.

Another of those whose company I sought was a lady townspeople called Miss Cynthie. She ran a small short order restaurant on the upper side of our apartment. The place was so small that a counter with stools was all it offered, but business was always booming, especially at lunchtime. She drew customers from the garage across the street, and business owners who had only a small window of time to eat. When I appeared at her back door, she usually had a fried pie ready. Pressing my face against the screen, I would barely see her outline, but I heard her say, "Just give me a minute and I'll sit with you." When the last customers went out the front door, she came out the back with the fried pie, and we sat on a concrete block and talked.

After pondering for so long about my life and the mysteries it held, I looked up from my fried pie one day and blurted out, "Miss Cynthie, can you tell me if I am adopted?" I had never asked anyone that question and I'm not sure why I chose to ask her.

With no hesitation, she responded, "Why, yes you are." She continued to sip on her glass of tea, and I took another bite of pie. I said nothing more and she said nothing further. Obviously, she wasn't afraid of my dad or mother. It was easier to ask a stranger than family.

I had come to the conclusion that the truth was now obvious, but the details were difficult to uncover. Did anyone know to whom I belonged or from where I came? I would eventually ask those questions, but I had to be patient so as not to alarm my parents. What would they do if they found out I knew the truth?

CHAPTER NINE

WHEN I WAS TIRED OF hanging out at the store or looking for something to do, I became intrigued by a group of boys playing baseball in the courthouse yard. I wasn't interested in the boys; I was interested in playing ball. Girls were supposed to play with dolls and make playhouses, but I wanted to run bases with the guys. However, the likelihood of that happening was slim. I was, after all, a girl.

Girls did not play sports with boys except at recess at school, and that was only because our teachers made the boys share the field. No guy was thrilled having a girl on his team, and when it came to choosing sides at recess, most girls were chosen last. I was the exception. However, in courthouse yard, guys didn't have to share their space so they didn't. I devised a plan to entice the big shot town boys (as I saw them), to let me play.

I figured that if I asked Dad to buy some equipment, I might be more attractive to the fellows. I had promised myself not to be a bother to my parents when it came to money, but I was desperate.

I sat on the stool behind the counter at the store until the final customer left. I needed to talk to Dad.

"Dad, I have a problem," I said as if this problem was akin to sickness or death.

"What kind of problem?" he asked with a slight sound of alarm in his voice.

"I want to play ball with the boys over in the courthouse yard."

"Then why don't you?" He probably felt a little relieved that my problem was not an emergency.

"They won't let a girl play, but I have an idea how I might get them to let me."

I suggested that if I could add some value to the team in the form of equipment, they would break the rules.

"Ok, I can do that," he said, so Dad agreed to buy me a glove, a bat, and ball from the Western Auto Store. I recognized from watching them from the sidelines that the boys had one bat and just a few gloves, so I was in the position to barter.

Having never played ball on a team of this magnitude, I practiced. There was a grassy yard between the store building where we lived and John Moran's store, so I pitched my baseball up and hit it, over and over, until I could place it where I wanted. Fortunately for me, but unfortunately for John Moran, I used his brick wall for my batting cage. I must have driven him mad, even though he never complained, but Dad did. "You need to use a rubber ball." That was his way of telling me I might be bothering Mr. Moran or damaging his building.

To preserve the sanity of the owner, I changed to a rubber ball and threw it against that same building until I could catch it at every angle. I caught fly balls, grounders, and pretended I was throwing back to home, all against that brick wall. Occasionally, a boy would come by that I could coax into practicing with me; one who wasn't on the team and didn't care that I was a girl. After weeks of preparation, I was ready to make my move. I didn't tell my mother because she would have said, "Girls don't play ball with boys."

Armed with my brand new equipment and ready to make a deal, I marched to the courthouse yard and waited until the inning changed. With as much confidence as I could fake, I walked up to the two leaders and asked, "Will you let me play?" They laughed. These were boys I had known all my life but were not going to play ball with a girl.

"Look, I have a new bat, a new glove, and a new ball that I will let anyone use if you will let me play." I held the bait in front of them.

They looked at each other, smiled arrogantly, and said, "OK." They thought I wouldn't last an inning, so they put me in at shortstop, hoping I would be wiped out; but when I caught a grounder hit directly to me, threw it to first, and got the man out, they didn't know what to think. From that time on, I played ball with the boys until my mother announced it was time to act like a girl, which would have been when I entered high school.

Our one and only doctor, whose office was across from our playing field, took his lunch break to watch us play. He sat on the railing, (once a hitching post for horses) and gave me pointers. He had played ball as a young man and must have found my ambition to equal the boys impressive enough to help me. It could have been because he had two daughters himself.

He was the same man who had delivered almost every baby in town including my brother, and would be yet another to know that I was not the child of Bill and Cloteel Wilson. I envied my friends who could tell of Dr. Dunham delivering them.

Some of these boys became outstanding high school baseball players, and if softball (now a high school sport for girls) had been sanctioned at that time, I know I could have been a competitor. However, it would be in the 70's before girls were given the same opportunities as boys to play high school sports.

Many times in the future I felt the only way to gain attention or become a necessary part of something was to buy it. That ball, glove, and bat were my leverage. I always needed leverage.

CHAPTER TEN

IN THE CENTER of this massive courthouse yard sat our historic courthouse. This red brick two-story structure with concrete steps leading to the front entrance reminded me of how times must have been back in colonial America. Behind the narrow front doors was the courtroom where an iron pot-bellied stove, which had sizzled more than once from tobacco spit slung at it, dominated the middle of the floor. No more than fifty people could find a place to sit during proceedings, and many times there was standing room only. One of the most famous murder trials drew large enough crowds that the courtroom overflowed onto the courthouse yard. My mother never missed a session. The townspeople dressed up for this occasion.

Every inch of that courthouse fascinated me, but one of the most intriguing was the liberty shaped bell that hung over the entrance. As a means of communication long before I was born, a designated person would reach outside the upstairs window, grab a string and ring the bell until the town came alive. It clanged like a dinner bell and warned of impending storms or fires or any trouble. One of the most famous times the bell rang was to signal the end of WWII. Another more recent one was when Judy's dad, Gilbert Wallace, died. He was a long-time resident and vital member of our community. I longed to be that designated person when I grew up. I needed to have an important task.

Tucked between brick and wooden buildings around the town square were quaint cottages. Some had indoor plumbing, but others had outhouses as far away from the main house as possible. By early afternoon, ladies sat in porch swings and waited for neighbors to drop by or for something exciting to happen within view. All had front porches, but few had air conditioners. Aged oak trees cooled the town.

Without invitation, I sat with many of them to pass the time. My parents thought I was playing with other town kids, but I often sought the company of the elderly. Older people liked to talk to me because I was a good listener. Sometimes I thought I knew more about other families than I knew about my own. Later, I would wonder if they let me occupy their time because they were hoping to find out something about me. Did they have a motive? Some of their grandchildren didn't spend as much time with them as I did.

Another explanation for my affinity with older people might have been because they gave me an extended family. Unlike my friends who had dozens of aunts and uncles and cousins with whom to gather on Sunday or for holidays, my dad's family never spent one day together that I recall. I had two cousins on the Wilson side, who were both twenty years older than I was. I sought these older ladies because I was lonely for companionship, and so were they. One of those ladies was my grandmother.

Just a few steps from the square out on Hwy 68/80 lived my somewhat cantankerous grandmother Pampy Wilson. Her stately two-story white house sat a few steps away from the main street, and sometimes I would drop by for lunch or just to sit with her for a talk. She frightened my friends and most of the citizens of Edmonton with her gruff voice and robust personality. To some, she looked much like a witch and acted the part, but not to me. She was a tall, sturdy woman who wore a white, starched apron that could stand stiffly in a corner by itself. Her shoes were always shiny, so when I complimented them, she taught me how to shine my own (primarily with spit), which was useful when I wanted to look at different views of my face in my patent leather shoes on Sunday morning instead of listening to the preacher.

Once I found out I was adopted, I could have asked her to tell me the truth, but I didn't want any awkwardness between us. Even as a child, I was aware of the impact my knowledge might have on others. She would have summons my dad and said, "I told you to tell her. Now look what happened." I avoided drama and knowing her; she would have given an Oscar-winning performance.

Her lunches consisted of mashed potatoes and peas, hot water cornbread, and hot water to drink. I never met anyone else who drank hot water. She was also the only person I ever knew who could scrap up a knife full of peas and not drop one of them before getting them to her mouth. I tried to mimic her, but couldn't keep one single pea on my knife. When they splattered to the floor, she would say, "That's all right; when you get a little older, you'll be able to get the peas to your mouth like I do." I never did.

Loud and boisterous, she cursed like a sailor, swearing at those who walked on her grass, stepped on her porch, or threw rocks at her house when they thought she was not looking. She chased pranksters with a broom or gun or whatever she found handy, and they fled for their lives. Indeed, she was a cranky old woman, but she loved me, and I felt her love. When I knew the truth, I assumed she treated me so well because she felt sorry for me. I came to replace the idea of genuine kindness coming from others with their sympathy.

Ironically, she had the fear of God in her soul and attended the Baptist Church every time the door opened. At the time, this church was located on one corner of the square near some of the houses where I sat with little ladies on their front porches.

Mammaw positioned herself in the "Amen" corner, and often embarrassed her children and even me by her moments of "getting the spirit" and shouting at the top of her lungs about her love for Jesus. Then she would walk out of that church, hat on her head and gloves on her hands go home and become as sinister as she was the other six days of the week.

As an adult, I realized that when I knew her best she was probably going through menopause. She was the only woman I have ever seen with a full beard who shaved every day. When she could no longer shave, Mother did it for her. At the time I didn't think this was strange; I thought it was just Mammaw.

She didn't get along exceptionally well with her three children or with her other grandchildren and certainly did not like my brother, but catered to me, maybe because I did not have Wilson blood. She treated my dad like he was a child. However, she loved my mother, and they were kind to each other. Even though my memories of this are dim, I know that Mother and Mammaw often went shopping. Early pictures of her showed a stylish young woman with a mink collar around the neck of her coat. This was certainly not the woman I knew.

As I grew older and went a few days without seeing her she would say, "I've been so hungry to see you." No one else would have believed she had any goodness in her. She was quirky and very eccentric, so it is not surprising that my dad had the same qualities.

When she died, the only thing I wanted from her estate was the picture of Jesus kneeling in the Garden of Gethsemane that hung over her bed. She kissed that picture every day. Those kisses eventually wore a hole in the middle of Jesus' face. I never knew what happened to it.

My dad's other sister, Aunt Kathleen, was difficult and most of the time a little too high and mighty for the rest of us. Occasionally, when she saw me playing in the alley behind her house, she yelled out the back door, "Want a piece of pie?" I cut across the gully and charged up her backyard and into the kitchen, which was the only room I was allowed to step foot inside. Before moving an inch, off went the shoes. Not that I wanted her company, but I wanted the pie and to try to get beyond her kitchen. That seldom happened.

She lived in a new brick home with wall-to-wall carpet that also had a full basement and a garage. My mother would one day want the same type of home. From an early age, I witnessed Aunt Kathleen's arrogance in the way she treated my dad and her mother, but especially strangers in whom she had little interest. She was my dad's sister, so I tolerated her.

Truthfully, the only positive thing to come out of Aunt Kathleen was her son, Louie. Although he was quite a bit older, he was like a brother to me. He married a wonderful town girl, and when he graduated from college, they moved to the western part of the state where he was a noted optometrist, a fact Aunt Kathleen bragged about to most people who asked her how he was.

He and Stella invited me to visit them during a summer break when I was thirteen, which was the first time I had been away from home.

I did not trust Aunt Kathleen well enough to ask her about my adoption. She would have been indignant that I was asking and appalled that I knew. Frankly, having an adopted child dangling on their family tree probably embarrassed her. If I had mentioned what I knew, she would have run straight to Dad. Quite unexplainably, she was married to a gentle man, so perhaps the aunt I saw was not the same one he knew. I was thankful that I was not related to her.

My relationship with Aunt Kathleen was guarded but not with her sister, Aunt Mag, the one I sat with on the porch and fished for answers. She was outgoing, personable and witty. Unlike my dad and his sister Kathleen, she was social and enjoyed visitors. I never remember any visitors coming to my house.

Aunt Mag and Uncle Lawrence had one daughter who was much older than I and married after high school. As a matter of fact, she married the same man twice. They would have two children whose ages were not too far from my own. Later, she would be my first grade teacher.

Periodically, my parents took my brother with them to Arkansas to the horse races (Arkansas Derby) and left me with Aunt Mag and Uncle Lawrence because I was in school. Those times were vacations for me.

Aunt Mag and Uncle Lawrence took me to the Shriner's Circus in Louisville each year when I was young, which was a major trip because this was prior to I-65, so we traveled back roads, which took hours. Back then, cars were not air conditioned, so that made the journey almost unbearable with me riding snugly between them. Aunt Mag fanned us with her Butler Funeral Home fan, pushing the air mostly in my direction.

I specifically remember sitting under the circus tent and the lion trainer bringing out the lions. They were roaring and pawing at him, so I turned to my uncle and said, "What are we going to do if they get out and start to eat everybody?"

He said, "Don't worry. By the time they get up here, they will be full."

That made perfect sense.

After the circus, our tradition was to stop at White Castle's Hamburger known for mini burgers smothered in onions, pickles, and mustard and for leaving a lingering aroma inside the car if eaten on the run.

A Girl Named Connie

Each time we stopped, Uncle Lawrence asked, "How many White Castles do you want?"

"How many can I have?"

"As many as you want."

I ordered twelve and ate two.

Aunt Mag was a comfort to me when I could find no peace within myself. When I was approaching seventh grade and had suppressed the incident with Lisa, a few of the town girls and I were hanging out just as we had done on many Saturday afternoons. We were waiting for the movie to start when a girl named Jane Lynn said, "I guess you know you're not really a Wilson, don't you?" I could hear the same tone in her voice that I had heard in Lisa's not long before.

Not responding was the only way I knew to respond. I didn't go to the movie with her but instead drifted away from them and walked toward Aunt Mag's house where I was spending the night.

That evening as I was sitting in front of the TV, I asked bluntly, "Aunt Mag, am I adopted?" She turned to me sharply.

"Why would you ask that?"

"A girl told me I wasn't a Wilson."

"What girl?" I gave her a name. She frowned.

"You just need to ask your mama and daddy about that." I never did. This incident taught me that no matter how little other girls had in the way of material things; they felt superior because they had real parents and I was adopted. There would be other girls like Jane Lynn in my life.

CHAPTER ELEVEN

WHEN I WAS A BABY, my dad owned a drugstore. Before that, he had worked in Louisville on the WPA program because he wanted to do something in the war effort. He tried to join the Army but spots on his lungs kept him from serving. Louisville is where he met Mother. His drugstore venture was short lived because finding a dependable pharmacist who would drive to Edmonton for the job was difficult. At that time we had no one qualified within the county for the job. Mother often said that owning that drugstore gave my father the idea that he knew almost as much as a doctor.

I knew very little about my dad in his younger days, but one thing I did know was that Aunt Mag was the reason he was able to go into the dry goods business. Long before he married, Dad wanted to open a dry goods store like his father had once owned in Edmonton. When his father died at a young age, his mother sold the store.

Two store buildings on the square, side by side, became available, and Dad saw an opportunity. The problem was he didn't have enough money, even though he had saved from his drugstore venture for the down payment. He went to Aunt Mag and asked if she would loan him the difference, which amounted to about ten percent. "I don't want to loan you the money, but I will give you the money if you will take me on as a partner." Before his death, Dad owned six storefronts and rented them to other business owners. Aunt Mag co-owned many of them.

Dad thought Aunt Mag's offer was fair, and even after she died, he paid her daughter the same monthly percentage that would have been due his sister.

Aunt Mag worked alongside Dad when he needed her and as long as she was able. If he wanted to go to the races, he trusted she would take care of the store as well as he did. If he wanted to take his family to the Smokey Mountains, she was his backup. Theirs was a perfect union.

What my dad never knew was that while he and Mother were gone, Aunt Mag dragged out boxes of merchandise and marked items down before he came home. "Let's get rid of some of this stuff," she declared.

Her curly hair was often all I could see as she bent over to pull boxes from under the counters, dusty from years of being untouched. My dad never had a sale and didn't believe in one. I kept quiet because I was having fun looking through the mountain of boxes and scheming with Aunt Mag. Dad was always impressed by how much money Aunt Mag took in while he was gone. "Maybe I need to put you in charge." If he had only known the truth!

Shoes, dresses, gowns, housecoats, farming clothes, boots, notions, thousands of yards of material, stacks of thread boxes, men's shirts, rows of men's pants, and box after box of buttons made up Wilson's Dry Goods. My dad loved buttons. Behind the wooden counter were, at least, a hundred bolts of cotton material usually used for quilting, and when ladies laid their patterns on the counter, one of the clerks would help match pieces for their designs. Most women quilted during the long winter months.

Men's dress hats were on top of the material shelves that ran almost to the ceiling. Back then, a well-dressed man never left the house without his hat. Caps were for baseball players and farmers.

Unlike most department stores, there was only one rack in the store and it held ladies' dresses. They were wedged so tightly, looking through them was almost impossible. One of the ladies brought a few samples in the right size to the front of the store and laid them on the counter until the customer found what she wanted.

The wooden floor creaked as customers edged their way from the front to find an item in the back. Most of the time, my dad or one of his clerks retrieved items rather than allowing customers to look for themselves. Self-serve was not available at Wilson's Dry Goods.

Another problem was lighting. Dad was so frugal he would buy low wattage bulbs that made the store look very dim. The lights turned on with a pull string from in the ceiling. When a bulb burned out, it was a long time before it was replaced. A customer might think he was buying a blue shirt but in the light, it would be green. "Let's take it to the door to make sure what color it is," I often heard my dad say. He was also colorblind.

Down the wooden stairs with a rickety rail to hold on to was another floor of merchandise. In the early days, going to the basement was a clear path, but each year it became more treacherous. Men's bib overalls, work pants, work shirts, four buckle boots, dress boots, cowboy boots, and insulated jackets were plentiful in the basement. When a lingering snow covered Edmonton, parents knew they could find four-buckle rubber boots for their children at Wilson's Dry Goods.

A Girl Named Connie

Some of those boots had been in boxes for years, so Dad often sold them for a dollar. The dry rotted ones he reluctantly threw away. Ladies boots were also in the basement. Those with fur around the top and zippers on the side were very popular in the 60's, and he had enough of these for every woman in town. The rest of the items were for men. An ironing board and a sewing machine were in the very back where my aunt occasionally altered men's pants.

In later years, the path down the stairs grew narrower because Dad bought more boots and had nowhere to stack them except on the stairs. Going to the basement was an ordeal, and customers could not go down just to look around. Dad or a clerk would pull the sting of the single light bulb at the top of the stairs and then say, "Watch your step, young lady. Be careful with that rail because it's not sturdy." The "young lady" could have been older than he was.

When the customer went back up the stairs, Dad turned the light off behind her. I was in trouble many times for forgetting to turn off the light.

The main part of the store was primarily for women. Stacked in tiers of boxes that stood higher than my head were Nancy King bras, slips and panties. When I was working one day, a lady came in and wanted a half-slip. "I know where they are; can I get it?" I asked. For some reason, Dad said "yes."

My dad had taught me how to pull a box out from a stack without the others falling. This day something happened and I wasn't as quick on the draw as I should have been, and hundreds of boxes of Nancy King fell, leaving me up to my knees in ladies' underwear and slip boxes. The magic trick of sliding out the tablecloth and leaving the dishes didn't work on these slick boxes.

"Is everything okay back there?" he asked from the front of the store.

"No, I have a problem." My dad found me in the middle of the lingerie. He looked at me with a grin and said, "Do you have the right size?" I was holding a slip. For the next few hours, the clerks and I restacked and sorted the sizes. Thankfully, he did not scold me.

If a customer needed to try on an item, there were no dressing rooms. A makeshift curtain hung in the back, and one of the two clerks would guard the back door to make sure no one came in.

From the outside, the show window was covered with a metal awning and a handy bench for whittlers and smokers to sit on. If they chewed tobacco, Dad wouldn't allow them to spit on the sidewalk. Often he would stand outside with them and shoot the breeze, so to speak, but he was never away from the store.

At the end of each day, I was in charge of sweeping the sidewalk in front of the bench. I earned twenty-five cents.

The background of the storefront window, which was at least fifteen feet wide, was dotted with colorful bolts of material stacked higher than my head. Polyester was popular then, and each bolt was heavy. I tried when I was older to climb over the bolts to get to the platform inside the window to dress the mannequins that had been wearing the same outfits for decades, but one time was enough for me.

Years after I left home, a water line broke and flooded the basement, ruining dozens and dozens of shoes that had lined the walls, and boxes of unopened merchandise molded in the muddy water. Dad assumed the city would have insurance to cover his loss; the city denied being responsible, so he refused to pay his city taxes until he calculated he had saved enough to compensate for his loss. No one pressed him for that money.

A Girl Named Connie

This store was the center of my childhood. I knew most people, but everyone who came in seemed to know me. Even as an adult, I identified myself as Bill Wilson's daughter. If a stranger came into the store, my dad would bring me to the front and introduce me, and I would shake hands with him or her. Being respectful of elders was a necessity, and I was going to make eye contact and know how to address them properly. That was part of my training. With my parents, I seemed always to be in training.

Periodically, customers' comments about me and my father's lack of a good defense initiated a comeback on my part.

I was in high school when an old man who smelled of liquor and stale cigarettes came in the store one day and said, "I remember when your daddy got you." My dad was standing behind the counter with me, and I must have looked puzzled. The man didn't stop there. "You know your daddy ain't your daddy, don't you?" I stared at the man and then at my dad and then replied, "He's the only dad I've ever known." Did Dad suspect I knew the truth? Wouldn't that have given him a clue?

My dad was speechless, but I sensed his blood rising, so my goal was to diffuse the situation. He could have used this incident to explain things to me, but he didn't. Once again, this was a missed opportunity.

Every other Thursday my family went to Nashville to a wholesale house to buy merchandise. During the summer, I lived for these trips because this was a time when the three of us were together alone and happy. My brother stayed with Aunt Mag.

Dad always bought too much fabric. "Bill, we'll never sell all this," my mom would say, and she was right, but he loved it. He carried a list of requested goods and tried to find what people wanted.

Mother was good at choosing ladies shoes and dresses. Women did not wear pants, but they did wear jeans, so she was in charge of them. Many women in our county worked on the farm alongside their husbands or fathers. They cut tobacco, stripped tobacco, raised gardens, and cleaned out chicken houses, and did not do these chores in a dress; so Wilson's had just what they needed. Dad chose hats and boots, along with the fabric and buttons. They made good business partners.

When we headed home loaded down with goods, Dad could barely see out the side or the back windows. I rode in the front seat between them and often fell asleep on Mother's shoulder. My parents were not overly affectionate people. Putting my head on her shoulder was a rarity.

I was as much a part of their business life as I was their personal one, and probably learned more about life, finance, and social graces working alongside them in the store than I did in school. There was no technology, not even a phone in our store and no such thing as a calculator, so learning to count change was a must if I were going to work there.

The cash register only went to ten. If a customer bought twenty dollars worth, I would strike the ten twice. I knew I better not mess up a person's bill. My dad was so good at math that he could quote a price and then quote the price with tax. How many could do that today?

When I was having trouble learning my multiplication tables, my dad took me to the back of the store and handed me a set of dice. "Throw those against the door," he said and I did. Up came a three and a six. "What is three times six?" I learned how to multiply by throwing dice.

Those dice didn't just happen to appear. After I was grown, I was told how Dad ran a daily "crap shoot" against that same door. Fellows laid five dollars on the floor and high roller took the pot.

A Girl Named Connie

Dad hired two ladies to help run the store on a daily basis: Ruby Garmon, a quiet, reserved woman, and Dorothy Franklin, a gum popping, friendly lady who was best friends even to those she didn't particularly know, made up Dad's employees. Frances Pemberton would also work there in the early days. There would be others, but these two worked at Wilson's the longest and were like family. Dad was loyal to his employees, and they were faithful to him. I am sure; however, that he paid them not nearly what they were worth.

Amazing to me, Dad had a little box in which he put IOU's on note cards. Many customers couldn't pay for what they bought until they sold their tobacco, so Dad gave them credit. Very few didn't pay their debts, but some died before doing so. "Why do you keep the debts of dead people in this box, Dad?" I asked when I was an adult.

"You never know who in the family might come in to pay it." He never gave up on the honesty of others, yet he avoided being honest with me about the most important aspect of my life.

CHAPTER TWELVE

DURING THE TIMES when I was alone and didn't see or hear anyone within earshot with whom to play, I sought out kids a short distance away from the square. Many of them were very poor and what some might call "needy." They might have been needy, but I was the one in need.

Long before factories came to the county and social programs developed, poor people did whatever they could to make a living and often barely did. Men worked as farm hands or handymen; and women ironed, babysat, or cleaned for people when they could. From a young age, I knew my life was very different from many of the kids in town, and I often felt embarrassed by those differences. I didn't want them to play with me because I was Bill Wilson's daughter, but because I was just another kid.

There was a section of town called Dog Street named for the many dogs that roamed freely in the neighborhood and consequently, through the streets of Edmonton. Many kids lived on Dog Street, but I was not supposed to go that far off the square.

A Girl Named Connie

Red Row was another area of low-income homes where many kids lived. Rows of houses that originally had been painted red lined this street that led to a beautiful creek. Across that creek was the stockyard. Kids living in these homes could also cross the road and be at the elementary school in five minutes. I thought that was "cool."

I was not allowed to go to Red Row because it was also too far from my parents' view, but I disobeyed, and when they couldn't find me quickly, they knew where to look. My mother spanked me many times for my visits to Dog Street and Red Row. This was before my vow to be perfect.

The one incident that made my mother demand I stay away from that part of the town occurred when a little girl from Dog Street, along with her mother, came into the store one Saturday wearing MY new coat. I knew I was in trouble.

Mother didn't say a word to the girl, as she looked her up and down, and I was grateful she didn't make a scene. When the girl left, I expected Mother to lash out, but she didn't. However, she had merely put her anger on hold until we went home.

"Why was that girl wearing your coat?" Mother was not happy.

In my defense, I said, "Mother, she asked me for it. She said she didn't have one."

"Now YOU don't have one," she said, "and she does! Does that make sense to you?" I had an older one in the closet, but Mother had just bought this one before the season began. Each year she bought me a new coat because I grew out of the last one or she wanted me to have the latest style.

"You can't give things away just because someone asks you for them," she insisted. At the time, I didn't understand why she would care if I gave away my coat, but she thought the girl and others to follow were taking advantage of me. I hadn't hesitated to give it away even though I didn't have another one as good. I never thought the little girl was taking advantage of me; I just thought she needed a coat. I continue to think she needed a coat. I had to wear my old one the rest of the year even though it was tight through the shoulders and came above my dresses. Coats always had to fall below the hemline of a girl's dress to be in style.

I must have been a slow learner because there was yet another memorable time when she protected my interest, and it had to do with a game of marbles. I was playing with an older boy who was quite good at this game. He was a professional by my standards, but that challenged me to play with him. We were shooting in my side yard behind the old icehouse and were playing for pennies. I lost all my pennies, which amounted to twenty cents. I went upstairs to ask Mother for some more.

"Why do you need pennies?"

"I lost all my pennies playing marbles."

"Who were you playing with?"

When I told her, she wanted to know the rules of our game. By the time I finished, she had grabbed my hand and marched down the back steps to the yard where he was waiting.

"Are you two playing marbles for pennies?" she asked with her hands on her hips.

He nodded.

"I'm pretty sure you have just cheated her out of her pennies. Am I right?"

"Yes." He didn't mess with my mother.

"Give them back. She is nine, and you are at least twelve. You should know better!" He handed them over and then she told us that we should play together without playing for money, and we did. That was that.

A Girl Named Connie

What he didn't realize and neither did I was that my mother was an expert marble player and knew the rules backward and forward. I never quite learned the art of not being gullible and continued to give away things. In my subconscious, giving things to people would make them accept me. Never did I feel accepted the way my friends were. Even though this might not have been true, I felt a little "off" when it came to my relationships. That was my life. Slightly off.

CHAPTER THIRTEEN

As EARLY AS FIRST GRADE, which was in 1952, I sensed I was not going to be like everyone else. I couldn't conform to rules the way my classmates did. Maybe I was spoiled or maybe I needed attention, but for whatever reason, that was a difficult year.

Before many days went by, I discovered that sitting at a table with other six-year-olds and reading or adding was not what I had anticipated or enjoyed. Where was the fun? Not being able to talk was stifling, so when I blurted out answers or asked a question without permission, I stood in the dreaded corner for my transgressions. Aunt Mag's grown daughter was my teacher, and she usually whipped me once a week for an infraction. One night she took the whipping to a new height; she visited my mother.

"Aunt Cloteel, I hate to whip Connie, but she is going to have to learn not to blurt out whenever she wants to. She talks too much!" The classroom was designed, in my opinion, to encourage talking, which consequently made my actions the teacher's fault. The long wooden tables with chairs on each side gave me an audience. Sometimes one of the other kids said something funny and I laughed. The only laugh my teacher heard was mine, so off to the corner I went again. Being the first cousin of the teacher was crimping my style.

My mother said, "That's all right, and if you need to whip her again, you do it." I had been whipped at home many times and now I was going to be whipped at school. How fair was that? I was listening from the bedroom and praying not to be called to face both of them.

After my teacher left, Mother ordered me out of the bedroom. "What is wrong with you? You have to behave at school." Her face was red.

I had no answer then, but now I realize I wanted students to focus on me. I was quiet at home and should have been more respectful at school, plus I was annoying my cousin and my mother.

Honestly, I had been accustomed to being in charge when I was with other children in town, so when I started school, I thought I could still be in charge. It took me a while to find another way to lead.

Thinking about how much trouble I caused my teacher and myself in first grade, perhaps it was a type of rebellion against my parents for having this other child. If I couldn't be the center of attention at home, I would make sure I was at school. For whatever reason, I soon learned that negative attention was as good as positive attention.

Focusing had always been difficult for me, and I didn't quite know why my mind would wander away from whatever the teacher was saying and toward any distraction in the classroom. While she was at the blackboard, I wasn't necessarily listening to her, but I was longing to write on it the way she did with sticks of white chalk. I wanted to take the chalk marker that held six sticks and go from one side of the board to the other, listening as the chalk scrapped against the slate. Then I would have stood at the board alone and filled in my ABC's. I drifted into that world while my classmates were following directions. My daydreams easily distracted me.

While we "blue birds" were reading to our teacher in our reading group, I envied the "red birds" coloring pictures from store bought coloring books or the "black birds" drawing on their arms. No matter where I was, I was never content. I wanted to be somewhere else.

However, I had no choice but to follow along with the bluebirds or I would be disappointing my parents and falling below my friends if I didn't. I was too competitive not to be smart.

In first grade, kids from the poor homes continued to make up the majority of students, but this time, they weren't just town kids. They rode buses from outlying farming communities where their one-room schools had been closed or moved to town.

Our county was one of the poorest in the state, which was evident in the faces of many of these children. Some walked out of their shoes, most of the girls washed their hair maybe once a month, and their clothes had been handed down until they showed wear and tear. Some lived on tenant farms and moved often. Many of the homes had no running water or inside plumbing. I had only lived in one place and never known what it was like not to have either. I felt sorry for them, but I think I also had a plan I wasn't truly aware of at the time to take advantage of their situation.

Soon, I was giving away my crayons and my glue and passing out pencils, paper, and construction paper. Back home at the end of the day, I announced that I needed more supplies and Mother would question me about what happened to mine. "You can't furnish half the supplies in the room!" Mother would once again try to explain the necessity of not being taken advantage of, but her soft heart wore her down, and extra supplies appeared in my school satchel.

A Girl Named Connie

The more supplies and milk money and snacks I gave them, the more attention they gave me, so I became very popular with my peers. If I ran for a class position, they voted for me. If I drew a picture, they chose mine as the best. A part of me had to know I was buying their loyalty, and even though it is embarrassing to admit, this is an issue I continue to address. Once again, I was the "leader" among these kids.

I was creating a Connie Wilson that classmates would admire and want to be with both in and out of the classroom.

As I was easing toward the end of first grade, I was feeling good about school and my friendships. Then life took a turn.

As I grew older, I became obsessed about my birth mother and wondering if I might have other siblings and if so, would I ever know them? Would she have kept them or given them away like she did me? Each time I was playing with my brother, I thought about what little boy or girl might never know me.

Even when I didn't realize she was in my mind, I often had reoccurring dreams about my birth mother. In these dreams she was a desperate woman, struggling, down on her luck, and gave me up because my parents paid her. They bought me. I didn't want to have a bad woman for a mother, and I didn't want to be bought. Many of these misconceptions came from movies.

By the time I was old enough to go alone, I went to the Strand, a movie theater just off the square, while my mom was home with James and my dad was working. It was a haven for all ages because the lady who owned and operated it was a no nonsense person. She hired teenagers to sell tickets, pop popcorn and run the projector. I thought those jobs were more than desirable and hoped she would hire me when I was older.

The balcony was for blacks only. This section was for Beulah and her sons, but not for me. I could sit with them on the back porch at Miss Bessie's, but we were not allowed together in a movie theater. Once or twice I would sneak up the stairs just to see what it looked like up there. The owner would be right behind me saying, "Connie, you can't be up here. Come back down with me." Honestly, I felt as if I should be up there.

I never questioned her.

Westerns were my favorites. I wanted to be a cowgirl and carry a gun in a holster. In these shows, there were always saloon girls flitting around in their skirts and drinking with customers. I even visualized my mother being one of the girls who had taken up with a drinker. I never thought of my birth mother as Doris Day or Sandra Dee.

At times I became envious of my friends because they had real parents; mine weren't. They came from their mother's; I didn't. When we were adults, they told me about how they feared being adopted, too. Carol said that when she learned I was adopted, she just knew she was too. "I worried my mother to death asking her if I were adopted. Later my mother would wonder if I wanted to be since you had so much more than we did! No, I didn't want to be adopted."

That was how much a child did not want to be adopted. Carol looked just like her parents. I did not. Roberta looked like her mom and dad. I did not. Judy was just like her parents. I was not. No one ever said, "You look just like your mom." I was fair skinned and blonde. She was olive skinned and brunette. My brother looked exactly like my dad.

To an outsider, I might have appeared to live a Cinderella life. However, the clock always struck midnight before I found the prince.

It is difficult to explain, but as I aged, I could never be at peace and was more often than not dreadfully miserable. However, no one would have guessed. My cheery outward self was a cover up for the sinking feeling of loneliness. I couldn't explain why I was lonely because I was never alone.

"Why would she be sad? She has everything?" They would have been right, but the "everything" I had did not replace knowing that somewhere was a woman who gave birth to me, and a man who was my father, and I might never know them or might never be able to reveal that I knew the truth about myself. This was a heavy burden for a child to carry.

As for my brother, I grew to love him and took care of him when my parents were working at the store. One day when I was watching James in the side yard next to the store, he began to cough the way a choking person would do. I grabbed him and ran into the store, yelling for dad. "Cough it up, Brother," Dad said as he beat him on the back, but whatever was stuck was not coming out; so off Dad ran with James down the street to the doctor's office.

"Bill, you've got to take him to Louisville. Specialists there are the only ones who can do this surgery because this penny is sitting up on its side and if it tilts, either way, it could kill him. Don't let him throw up." I thought about how a person could keep someone from throwing up.

We had no ambulance service in town, so Dad, Mother (who held James), and I headed to Louisville as fast as Dad could get us there. Even though he wasn't supposed to, James threw up and this terrified us so much that Dad stopped and bought a long thin rubber hose, like one might find on a hot water bottle, so we could get it down his throat to give him air if he stopped breathing.

Dad, after running a drugstore, felt he was somewhat of a doctor and, this time, his knowledge could save a life-my brother's.

First of all, as I rode the hundred-mile distance, I prayed for God to save him. At ten years old, I prayed the prayer of a seasoned prayer warrior.

"Please don't let him die," I said, over and over. I felt this had happened because I wasn't watching him closely. Where had he gotten a penny and why hadn't I seen him put it in his mouth?

By the time we were within thirty miles of Louisville, peace and calm overcame me. "Mother, he is going to be okay."

"How do you know?" she asked.

"God has answered my prayers."

She said, "That is good, but I'll feel better when this penny is out of his throat."

I have never had that assurance of an answered prayer since then.

Once at Jewish Hospital, our hometown doctor had already notified a doctor there and within an hour the penny was gone, and James was fine. They never yelled at me, never blamed me, and said, "It's just one of those things." I, however, blamed myself. What if I had done something to cause their child to die? How could I have been so careless?

When I was in my first year of high school, James was in the second grade and refused to go to school. "What's the matter with you? What is wrong that you don't like school?" Mother asked when he would beat her back to town before the bell rang.

"Sissy's not there anymore." I was unaware of how much my presence meant to him. That was the first time I realized that I did make a difference in his life.

After Mother told me this, I sat down with him and explained that I was not too far away. "All you have to do is tell your teacher or your principal that you need to talk to me and they will call if anything is wrong." By then we had driven to the new high school to show him where I was. That seemed to satisfy him, and he went back to school.

CHAPTER FOURTEEN

EVEN THOUGH MY PARENTS pampered me with material things, I was brought up by two of the most explosive parents in the community, so I thought, and was disciplined far more often than I deemed necessary. Having a new baby did not keep my mother from knowing my whereabouts.

I'm not sure how many of my spankings were from wanting to teach me a lesson or from my mother's quick temper. She burst forth like fireworks at the least expected times, so I had to watch myself.

Mother used her hand or a switch to strike me. No matter what the infraction, she "let me have it." My wandering off infuriated her, so when I heard her calling, "Connie Allen" I knew I was in trouble. "How many times have I told you to let me know where you are?" Out came the flyswatter. These spankings came more often after my brother was born. In retrospect, she was probably worn out from dealing with both of us, and he was too little to whip. He would get "his" later.

Another example of harsh punishment, in my estimation, came when I climbed her "precious" mulberry tree in the backyard and fell out. I was breaking her rules of not climbing that tree, but it was too tempting. As I felt myself tumbling toward the ground, I grabbed every limb to break my fall, but none of them did. Instead, I took some with me. I hit the ground like a rock and promptly ran up the stairs to show Mother my scrapes.

Instead of sympathy, she said, "You weren't supposed to be in the mulberry tree. I have told you my last time to leave that tree alone." Then she ordered me to go after a switch and whipped me for disobeying her. I danced around the kitchen as she swatted my legs. The lesson I learned was not to tell my mother everything I did.

If she were bristling mad, sometimes the punishment waited for my dad. He pointed to my room, shut the door behind him and removed his belt. "I'm going to hit you two times. It won't be very hard (he was wrong), but it is going to hurt." The welts formed on my behind within minutes.

I assumed my friends also were whipped with a belt but they were not. I should have lived at their house.

Throughout my time at home, I witnessed violent outbursts that would have terrified my friends. Whether or not I had company, an audience did not stop them. My mother threw things, cursed, and stormed through the house. My dad was not as volatile, but he had a mean streak that I had seen a few times. His words could cut like a knife. Most of the time their anger was over as quickly as it started, but I never knew when they would go to war and never grew accustomed to these fits.

Most of my life I have seldom lost my temper and have learned to weigh my words before speaking. Words could lead to trouble. I learned that one Thanksgiving Day around 1963 when I spoke too soon.

A Girl Named Connie

Mother had been up before the rest of us preparing one of her prime meals. When the four of us sat down to eat, my dad simply asked, "Where's the deviled eggs?" My mother had forgotten to make deviled eggs, so when I saw how deflated she looked, I came to her defense. Determined that he was being terribly inconsiderate after all the food she placed in front of him to question the deviled eggs, I defended her.

"Mother, we are fine. We don't have to have deviled eggs." The next thing I knew I hit the floor. Contradicting my dad was a poor decision. Before I could pick myself up, she had grabbed the carving knife from the turkey plate and held it over his head. "If you lay a hand on her again, I'll kill you." Dad left the table, and the rest of us ate turkey in silence. James never looked up from his plate. I should have kept my mouth shut.

I went out to the front stoop to wait for dad. He had driven off, but I knew when he came back, he would want to talk to me.

His first words when he came up the steps were, "I guess you know you ruined our Thanksgiving dinner, don't you?"

"Dad, I'm sorry. I should never have said that." Naturally, he was not to blame. Blaming me was much easier.

I never said anything out of line to my dad or mother after that.

They had a way of irritating each other with jabs of insults or not-so-subtle criticisms. Each time they had a battle, I thought it the end of their marriage. Dad's way of fighting was to leave home. Even though I worried that he wouldn't, he always came back, and they acted as if they had never said an unkind word to each other. In the meantime, I was left to wonder what had just happened.

One morning I woke up to find my mother throwing plates at him. He left for work without his breakfast. I was sure they would part that day. When I asked my mom what the fight was about, she said, "Nothing." Those fights scared me when I was little, so I quickly learned to stay out of the line of fire. Another reason I never brought up the topic of my adoption was my fear of a "spree." I didn't want to be the cause of conflict.

On their sixtieth wedding anniversary, I half-jokingly said, "You and Dad have fought your way through sixty years of marriage."

She quickly responded, "Your dad and I never fought."

I then realized that from their perspective, they didn't consider it fighting at all- it was a way of life.

CHAPTER FIFTEEN

MY SCHOOL HOURS provided very little drama compared to being at home. One day blended into the next, and none of them were especially significant until the sixth grade.

My observation of what I had and what other kids didn't have become increasing bothersome for me. I might have been spoiled, but I cared deeply (and still do) about the less fortunate. For example, during recess students with a nickel could go to the candy room and buy a Baby Ruth or a Milky Way. Those without a nickel went straight to the playground. Sometimes I would have a few extra nickels and bought bars for those who didn't get to buy candy. Without being obvious, I slipped them to these kids. Their appreciation was immediate and my personal satisfaction humbling.

When these classmates were young, they were not embarrassed to take the candy, but as they aged, they would no longer see this gift as a kindness but more like charity. That is when I stopped.

So much about being in elementary school developed my personality. Playing in the band, cheerleading, singing in talent shows, and being in clubs gave me confidence. I did these without my parents hovering over me.

I never remember either of my parents attending a ballgame, but I didn't mind. They dropped me off outside the gym and picked me up at the same spot. Other parents were lined up waiting, too. Mother and Dad didn't know a thing about basketball or care. They supported my involvement, but that didn't mean they had to be involved, too.

Mother might not have cared about the game, but she was aware of what I was doing and if I made a misstep, she knew it. One of those missteps occurred the day of basketball homecoming during my eighth-grade year.

Our cheerleading uniforms were royal blue and gray. The heavy wool sweaters and long circular skirts were such a contrast to those of today. Because of this special occasion, our principal said, "You girls go on out to Fanny's Beauty Shop and let her fix your hair; she knows to send the bill to me." This must really be a big night for him to have let us out of school for this!

Carol, Roberta, and I walked across town to Fanny's, and along the way decided how "cool" it would be if we had our hair sprayed gray to match our uniforms.

"Think how good we'll look with our hair matching our sweaters," Carol said.

"Won't he be surprised!" said Roberta.

We thought our principal would be so proud of us because this was a special night for the entire school, and he had announced that he had "important people" coming to see the game. As far as we knew, it could have been the governor. It wasn't.

A Girl Named Connie

The ladies worked on our hair, heavily spraying each of us gray with sprays used for plays. Maybe they should have known better, instead of listening to three-eighth graders, but they did what we asked.

Walking back to school and admiring ourselves in store windows along the way, we should have noticed we looked like our grandmothers. As we walked up the wooden steps into the corridor of the big building, our principal must have been watching us from his oversized office window because he met us at the top of the steps. "Stop right there!" he ordered.

He grabbed my shoulders and proceeded to examine me. "WHAT HAVE YOU ALL DONE?" We thought we would share our genius idea, but as soon as I started to explain, he exploded. "YOU ALL GET BACK OUT THERE AND GET THAT MESS OUT." All hell broke loose.

By then, a crowd had gathered, and one of the seventh-grade teachers whispered, "I'll pray for you all." She was the same lady whose pumpkins we teens stole almost every Halloween. Suddenly, we were thirteen-year-old sinners with sprayed gray hair.

In humble humiliation and total shame for being chastised in front of our peers, we left for the beauty shop once again. "We have to get this out," I told Fanny the details of our encounter as an audience of local ladies listened carefully while appearing not to.

It took at least an hour and a half to redo us, and the shop was full of customers who had to be pushed back. Within that time, the story had spread.

It must have reached my mother because she charged right into the principal's office that afternoon and I was summoned. I had seen my mother irate before but not in public. With the door open so anyone within earshot could hear, she lambasted the principal for his temper fit while she was engaged in one of her best; but what I remember the most was her shouting,

"You paid for the first one, and YOU will pay for the second." She meant the hairdo. Was it about the money?

In reflection, we did look ridiculous and would have been an embarrassment with our gray-sprayed hair, cheering in front of a packed gym (which actually held only a few hundred people), but he didn't have to make such a spectacle of us in the hallway. Come to think of it, we did that on our own. My mother was my ally in public even when she didn't agree. As long as Mother was my ally, I was safe; so I kept giving her reasons to rescue me.

I was feeling smug about her attack on my behalf, but I should have known what was coming. Once I got home she said, "Don't ever do anything different to your hair anymore without MY permission." I didn't. However, this incident might have paved the way for my many hair experiments in the future.

CHAPTER SIXTEEN

MY MOTHER'S FAMILY was totally opposite of my dad's. Dad's was close in distance but distant in their closeness. Mother's family lived in Barren County around the Haywood community of South Central Kentucky. Her dad died in his forties, so my grandmother went to work to support her five children.

Mother told stories about how each child took care of the one below in age. Her oldest sister Hazel took care of my mother, and then she watched her brother Joe and on down the line. By the time she was a teenager, Mother had left home to work in Louisville, and that is where she met my dad. I wish I had asked about their courtship, but the past doesn't matter to young people until it is too late.

My dad always told me not to marry anyone unless I couldn't forget about him. "After I met your mother, I tried and tried to forget about her, but I couldn't get her out of my mind, so I asked her to marry me." That lasted for sixty-five years.

My mother was devoted to her brothers and sisters although we didn't visit any of them as much as we did Aunt Hazel. Almost every weekend we went to her house, and I thrived on those visits because there were cousins in the yard, women in the kitchen, men on the porch and non-stop talking.

Aunt Hazel's house was bustling with her seven children. She had eight, but her oldest son was killed during the Korean War, so I never knew him. She owned and operated a restaurant located in downtown Smiths Grove (Kentucky) right next to the railroad track. We didn't have trains in Edmonton so each time I heard the whistle, I ran out the back screen door.

As her daughters grew older, they also worked in the restaurant. She and the girls did all the cooking, which was mainly short order, and this bustling café was overwhelmingly popular.

Smiths Grove was a small town so everyone knew Aunt Hazel and her family. She managed to squeeze enough money out of the business to take care of her family, but never enough to enjoy the luxuries of life like my mother and my Aunt Jewell did. At least, that was the way I saw it. Actually, she might never have wanted the fancy clothes and brick home.

Uncle George was a good man when he wasn't drinking, but his drinking continued throughout most of their marriage. Aunt Hazel finally divorced him and he left town, remarried and had other children, but that was not until Wanda was in her preteen years. Life with Uncle George was not a happy one because when he was drinking, he was ornery.

My mother was a fierce defender of Aunt Hazel, and this might have been because Aunt Hazel had practically raised her. One Christmas when my uncle had been drinking too much, the rest of the family was in her living room enjoying the spirit of the day when he said something loud and obnoxious to Aunt Hazel, and she told him to be quiet. He put his hands on her shoulders supposedly to move her out of the way, but this turned into a shove and when she saw it, my mother turned into a linebacker.

He was standing in front of the couch, so she tackled him, flipping him over the back of it. His head appeared from behind the couch and just as he was about to say something to her, she screamed, "Don't you ever touch my sister gain!"

This scared everyone but me, and the silence that followed was eerie. His children didn't know what to say. His grandchildren were speechless. I was so proud of my mother and just as I was about to say something like, "Merry Christmas, Uncle George," I held myself for fear I would be next. One thing was for sure; anytime my mother was present, he never touched her beloved sister.

If anything ever happened to my parents, Aunt Hazel was my backup plan.

Although my mother was a constant visitor at Aunt Hazel's home, their other sister Jewell was not. Jewell was too busy with social affairs or whatever seemed to make her happy. Unlike my mother, she did not gather too much with her siblings and their children.

Because my mother and I spent time with Aunt Jewell, I did not view her the way others in the family did, but I could understand their assumption that she thought she was better than they were. In fact, most of them thought my mother and Aunt Jewell were both "uppity."

In contrast, Aunt Hazel was a gentle soul who never showed disapproval of anyone or judged others, but that trait didn't rub off on some of her children. Most of them resented Jewell for not paying more attention to her oldest sister who had taken care of the family in their mother's absence. There was no excuse for her lack of attention or affection.

Therefore, when Aunt Hazel gathered the family one Thanksgiving afternoon after all of us had arrived and announced, "Your Aunt Jewell is coming for a visit," I didn't know what to think. I feared fireworks!

"Oh my gosh, AUNT JEWELL! Why is she coming down here? What are we supposed to do?"

Mother scolded them. "Now Aunt Jewell is just Aunt Jewell. That's just how she is. She is as nice as she can be."

I heard a, "Yeah, right" coming from somewhere behind me.

Maybe she was as nice as she could be because she couldn't be nice.

Most of the fifty people in the house were puzzled by Aunt Jewell's reason for coming and not too thrilled about seeing their elusive relative. When the doorbell rang, Mother and Aunt Hazel were in the kitchen, and the rest of us scurried away from the door so as not to answer it.

"She's here," one of the sisters whispered into the kitchen.

Aunt Hazel said, "Well, did you let her in?"

"No, we aren't going to the door."

No one wanted to be the first to invite her into a house where she had seldom been.

Aunt Hazel, smoothing down her apron, walked back to the living room and toward the door, while a few of us followed like baby chicks and waited for Aunt Jewell's grand entrance.

Aunt Hazel opened the door and embraced her. "I'm so glad you're here."

"Me, too," said Mother, embracing her baby sister.

I was the only other person to greet her. The others would probably not have recognized her on the street.

She swept through the door with her second husband, Mr. Loper, behind her. He helped her off with her full-length mink coat, and Aunt Hazel took the coat and tossed it on the bed in the next room on top of the rest of the coats. Aunt Jewell would have frowned.

I could hear my cousins, who had sneaked back into the kitchen after the grand entrance, whispering about the mink coat. It wasn't in envy.

There she stood in the middle of the room in a lovely red dress and gold jewelry dripping from her neck and wrists. Aunt Hazel, wearing her housedress covered with an apron, seemed not to notice the stark contrast. After all, she knew the real Jewell and not the society icon she spent a lifetime creating.

By the end of the day she had warmed up to the family and taken the chill out of the room. I don't think she ever won over the hearts of Aunt Hazel's grown daughters because too many times Aunt Jewell had ignored their mother.

On Aunt Hazel's ninetieth birthday, the family gathered in a facility in Smiths Grove for a huge celebration, which Aunt Jewell attended. I could tell by her thin frame and overall demeanor that she was not well. Within a short period, her mind was slipping, along with her health, so she was soon placed in a nursing home, but not in her hometown of Glasgow but in the mountains of West Virginia. I never knew the details of why she ended up in another state other than her son lived in West Virginia, but her sisters and brothers were deeply hurt at how she was going to live out the rest of her life. After one visit they could not shake the paradox of how she lived and how she was going to die.

According to Mother, this nursing home was pathetically dirty and a far cry from what Jewell would have found acceptable even for a night's stay. She lay in a hospital bed in a white cotton gown, her eyes hollowed out, and her hair in disarray. Mother was heartbroken and thankful her sister was not aware of how her life was ending.

The mink coat and the fine home no longer mattered. Aunt Jewell stayed in that home for two years and most of the time knew nothing. She was brought back to Glasgow for burial, and I found it quite puzzling that for all fine clothing, prestigious home and country club friends, she had the smallest tombstone in the cemetery. Aunt Jewell would have been devastated.

Our family didn't visit Mother's brothers, Joe, Earl and Todd, very often, but that didn't mean my mother didn't adore them. What I remember most about Uncle Todd was his frail condition. He was in and out of hospitals and during his last years, suffered from lung cancer. His blood type was RH Negative, so Mother, Dad and I knocked on doors throughout the county and surrounding ones, searching for blood donors as he lay in the local hospital dying.

I said, door after door, "I am Connie Wilson and my uncle is dying of lung cancer and needs blood, so if you have RH negative blood would you go to TJ Samson Hospital and donate for him?" Door after door, I repeated my plea.

We found a few donors but not enough to save his life. He died at the age of forty. My mother was not going to allow her brother to die without trying to save him, but he did in spite of her attempts.

Of all the children, my mother was very much like her mother. Mom Bybee, as I called her, was high strung and a ball of energy. She could fly off the handle in a heartbeat, so we all tried to keep her peaceful. No one would ever have guessed she struggled during her life because she made the best of whatever she had. Her coat was not mink, but she wore it was if it were.

A Girl Named Connie

She remarried when she was sixty-nine and moved to Florida to be near her youngest son Earl. My mother now had a longer distance to travel to see her mother, but there was never a year we didn't make the journey.

She lived near the beach, so Mom Bybee took my brother and me to swim and pick up shells, and even in her eighties, she put on her swimsuit without hesitation. My dad, however, never joined us except to walk in the sand. His long-sleeved shirt and dress pants looked odd as he strolled along the edge of the water, but that was Dad. The last time he took off his shoes and waded up to his ankles something attacked his feet and bit him so badly he had to nurse them for a few days. I remember how my mother coddled him, keeping him in a good mood so we could stay longer.

When I was old enough to drive to Florida, Mom Bybee called me to come to get her. I would pick her up and sometimes Earl, her son, would come with her. "You drive like a truck driver," Uncle Earl said one time as I was cruising a little too fast and taking curves sometimes too carelessly. My daredevil spirit amused him.

When she was very ill, Mother, Aunt Hazel and Aunt Jewell went down to help Mr. Lloyd care for her. She called them to her bedroom, so the story goes, and said to all of them, "See that lamp on the dresser? I want Connie to have it. Cloteel, you take that home with you as you go."

Mother brought the lamp back home and kept it for a long time. Out of all her many grandchildren, I was not one of them.

It was in Florida she died in her nineties but was brought back to Glasgow for burial near Aunt Jewell. I would one day know why she left me the lamp. I thought it was because I had been the one to drive down to get her and bring her to Kentucky to visit, but I was wrong.

CHAPTER SEVENTEEN

SCHOOL CONTINUED to be my comfort zone. Mother and my brother were at home, Dad was at the store, and I was away for at least a few hours where I could be on my "stage." While I thought life revolved around my brother, I sought what I needed from my peers. I never told Carol, Roberta or Judy what I had heard my aunt and mother discuss at that dining room table or what Ms. Cynthie corroborated.

I didn't get the chance to ask Lisa how she knew about me because by the time we were in the seventh grade, and I might have had the nerve, she moved.

Connie Wilson continued to seek perfection.

The one area where I knew I could improve concerned money. My dad was frugal, so if there were things I wanted to do that cost more than a few coins, I decided to forego them. My childish reasoning hindered me from many opportunities that I later regretted, but I stood stubbornly firm.

A Girl Named Connie

For example, during the summer when Carol, Roberta, and Judy went to 4-H Camp, I stayed behind because I didn't want to ask for the money to go. I didn't tell my friends that was the reason; they assumed I had no interest in camp. I was a good actress.

My parents never mentioned the camp, and I guess they thought I wasn't interested, but I ached when the school bus pulled out and I wasn't on it. They came home a week later with stories of canoeing, singing around the campfire, swimming and making new friends and left me feeling sorry for myself. They never were aware that I wanted to go. My parents knew nothing about 4-H Camp. If I had asked, I would have been on that bus.

To earn my "keep," I worked alongside Dad as soon as I could see above the counter. Saturday was the busiest retail day in town and certainly for Wilson's Dry Goods. If my dad wore a suit to work, I knew I had to "dress up" and be presentable. It was important to make a good impression, according to my dad. I never fully understood the need to dress better than the customers, but it was his way of dignifying the business of selling coveralls and boots.

When I was in college and came to the store one Saturday wearing nice jeans and a blouse, he later told my mother to tell me he preferred I dressed a little better in front of customers. He didn't want to tell me himself. I never really understood his eccentric personality, but I respected it.

During the summer between my sixth and seventh grades, my parents moved us out of the apartment above the store building, even though it was as large as a regular house, and into a new three-bedroom brick home in an upscale subdivision. It was the only subdivision. A local doctor, new to the town by then, one dentist, a few teachers, and several business owners lived on this street that was within walking distance of town, but not in direct view. My days of watching the town were over.

Every summer day and after school, kids from all ages rode bikes, roller skated, jumped rope, played tag and hide and seek or threw the ball to each other in Muncie Court. I was living in a real neighborhood. I missed the square, but I was proud of my new home with its wall-to-wall carpet. Often I would feel guilty about having this home, knowing that somewhere was my birth mother who may not even have a home. Being satisfied with my good fortune was never easy.

This is where I would dwell until I moved out on my own in 1969.

Hour after hour, I played in the backyard. It was my new courthouse yard even though I still went to town and played ball on Saturdays. Dad made a deal with a local carpenter to construct a wooden swing set for my brother and me. This was the Cadillac of swing sets in the 50's, and I was thrilled that he had let go of the money for something not exactly necessary. Mother probably said, "Bill, Connie needs a swing set, and you can either buy one or have one built." That was usually the case.

While Carol and Roberta were building playhouses and pretending with their baby dolls to have a family and dinner and tea parties, I had other ideas. One day I built a store out of concrete blocks and planks left from construction materials stacked at the back of our lot. Moving those heavy blocks was no picnic, but with the help of a couple of neighborhood kids, I set the foundation. Fashioning it after my dad's store, I created counters and covered them with old tablecloths or lengths of material I had found in the house. Each counter displayed whatever cast-off items my mother loaned me, or toys from my collection, and soon I had a store. I "sold" half bottles of make-up, pencils, vases, pillows, and of course, material. If this had been during the time of yard sales, people might have stopped by.

A Girl Named Connie

Playmates showed up every day. I would be the clerk, and they would buy things with rocks, and then we reversed roles. I had to let them be the clerk, or they wouldn't have played all afternoon.

One day I was in the kitchen ready to go out to play when I saw two older boys, who were around fifteen, walking through the back yard, which wasn't unusual for kids to do. While I stood in the shadows of the kitchen window, I watched them kick down my store, scatter bottles and cans and planks across the yard and demolish what had taken me days to create. If I had been older, I would have rushed out and stopped them, but I was afraid of them; most of the younger kids were.

Why would they do that? I had never done anything to them. Every bad thing that happened to me, I thought, had to be because of some action I had done. In this case, I never had any connection to them. If nothing else, they should have been afraid my mother and dad would come after them.

I was crushed. This store was my source of entertainment, and they had destroyed it. The only things they didn't move were the blocks. I hated those boys.

I sat on the back steps and surveyed the damaged. Did I want to build it back or finish what they started? *I will not let them get by with this. I will build it and if they tear it down, I'll build it again.*

When other kids saw what happened, they helped me. Our new store might have been even better than the first one, but it didn't feel the same. One thing I did differently was to keep my BB gun loaded and on the back porch.

A few weeks later, I was home with my mother and I heard a knock on the door. When I peeked out, one of the boys was standing on the stoop. Reluctantly, I opened the door.

"Can you come outside?" he asked.

My mother was listening.

"I want to tell you I am sorry for tearing up your playhouse."

"All I want to know is what made you do it?" I asked.

"We were just being mean." I forgave him but never forgot what potentially mean boys can do when together.

On the far end of my street lived the only adopted children I knew, and we played endless hours together both at their house and mine. When I first moved to the subdivision, Lanny, who was two years younger, came by one day when I was in the yard and introduced himself. "I am adopted," he included along with his name.

"How do you feel about that?" I asked.

"Doesn't bother me." His parents, the Nunns, had never kept his adoption a secret, so he didn't flinch if someone mentioned it. I think he told me that so I would come back with a "me too" and I should have confided in him. He could have given me advice when I dug myself into a hole of depression with dark thoughts about my existence, but I feared he would tell his mother, and she would tell someone else, and soon my mother would know that I was aware of my adoption. I couldn't risk the aftermath.

One Sunday after church my family was driving home, which took us past their house. Seeking a reaction that might indicate how they felt about me I said, "Do you think Lanny and his sister Stephanie are as loved as they would have been if they had been the real children of Mr. and Mrs. Nunn?" My mother didn't miss a beat.

"I think their parents might even love them more because they chose them." She might not have known I was baiting her, but she gave the answer I wanted to hear.

Twelve was also an age for many other changes. I never missed Sunday school and church, so making the decision to turn my life over to God and be baptized was inevitable. Because we didn't have a baptismal at the Edmonton Baptist Church at the time, my preacher, my parents, and anyone else who wanted to attend went to Glasgow to a Baptist Church that did have a baptismal. That was one of those days a person never forgets.

My dad was a churchgoer, a valued member of the Edmonton Baptist Church, but had never been baptized. There was something in his personality that could not get up out of his seat and go down front in the presence of others and make a public profession. However, this troubled him.

When he learned that a Billy Graham Crusade was going to be at the fairgrounds in Louisville, he wanted to go. "We'll all go with you," my mother said. My brother was only five or six but they didn't leave him behind. Once in the stadium with thousands and thousands of others who came for a once in a lifetime chance to hear the most famous TV preacher of all times, I was overcome with the spirit of the moment and evidently, so was my dad.

As soon as George Beverly Shay began singing "Just As I Am," Dad looked at us and said, "I want to go down there." This was so out of character for him.

I said, "Dad, so do I. I will go with you." The chance to comfort my dad did not happen often. We made our way down to the stage along with several hundred other believers and stood in the presence of this great man. When he asked who accepted Jesus, Dad raised his hand. I was so proud of him and happy he had made his profession of faith. When I saw my father crying tears of joy, I could not contain my excitement, so I cried with him. That was the last time I saw him cry.

We made our way back to Mother and my brother and on the way Dad said, "You do know I can't go back home and do this in front of the church."

"I know Dad, and Jesus knows your heart, so nothing else matters." That was a defining moment in my relationship with my dad and with the Lord.

My parents were faithful churchgoers until a member made an innocent remark that kept my dad from ever going back to the Edmonton Baptist Church.

Bill Wilson wore a full suit to work every day, removing his coat and hanging it over the back of the stool at the cash register. I never saw him in a sports shirt until he retired and when I did, my jaw dropped. He was wearing a plaid, short-sleeved shirt that was so out of character I could do nothing but stare. One hot August day, my dad came to me as we were getting ready for church and said, "Sister, do you think it would be okay if I didn't wear a tie today?" He was very cautious about changes.

"Dad, many of the men don't wear ties, and you'll be fine without one." In all probability, he felt self-conscious without his tie.

Coming out of the church after the sermon, a long-time member casually slapped Dad on the back and said, "Bill, I can't believe you don't have on a tie." It was not meant as an insult, but my dad took it that way. As typical of him, he did not respond, but he never went back to church. The man likely never knew that he was the reason Bill Wilson quit going to church. My dad was odd.

It was a silly incident, but he was embarrassed and there was no talking him into going back no matter how many visits the preacher made. We left him each Sunday sitting in his chair reading the Sunday paper. Mother came home, cooked a delicious lunch, and church was never mentioned.

CHAPTER EIGHTEEN

LONG BEFORE I WAS OLD ENOUGH to think about dating, I became infatuated with a much older guy. My dad was not happy about it. His name was Pete; he was nineteen and very handsome in a leather jacket kind of way. His blond hair swept over his left eye and he swaggered. I lingered around the icehouse while he worked, and I mistook his friendliness for "liking me." Back then, "liking" someone meant as a girlfriend or boyfriend. I was far too young for him to see me the way I wanted to be seen.

The ice house was a place where farmers, among many other people, bought blocks of ice for their cattle or to use as refrigeration. When Pete lifted huge blocks of ice with oversized tongs, I was impressed with his strength. He was my idea of the perfect boy.

He never had much to say to me, but allowing me to be in his presence was all I wanted. I sat with my legs swinging off the porch of the little house and waited for him to finish with customers so we could talk. Our conversations were never personal. He did ask me what I wanted to be when I grew up. He didn't realize that I thought I was already grown up.

Dad, however, did not want me sitting on the ice house porch talking to him. "It doesn't look good," Dad said.

"But Dad, he has never been anything but nice to me. He doesn't say bad words or anything like that," I protested when he told me to stay away from him. I thought Dad was being unreasonable.

I stayed away and soon moved on to other things, but I couldn't resist the urge to go by the icehouse just for a glimpse of him. Pete was my first crush, and I was flattered by his attention. I will never know why, but Pete disappeared from the icehouse, and I have often wondered what my dad might have said to him about staying away from me. I can't remember ever seeing Pete again, so I assumed he either left town to work or joined the Army. Many boys during the 50's and 60's enlisted.

When Dad was unreasonable, I thought about what my real father might have done in situations as innocent as this one. I was doing nothing wrong, but by telling me to stay away from this boy, I took it to mean he thought I *might* do something wrong. In reality, Dad likely was worried more about the boy might do rather than my actions, although I did long to have him kiss me. What did I know about kissing? Nothing.

My dad was worried that Pete might try to harm me, but it wasn't him. It was someone else.

Like most incidents, it happened with someone I knew. That is all I am going to say about that, but there is much to say about what happened. He and his wife lived right off the square in a section overlooking the town, and like so many others I visited; they invited me to drop by while I was riding around their neighborhood on my bike.

I was in the kitchen watching the lady bake cookies for her grandchildren who were to come by later. Her husband was sitting in his chair in the living room, facing away from the kitchen door. I had been in their home many times, so neither of them was a stranger to me. Unexpectedly, he yelled for me to come where he was, so I did what he asked.

"Come here a minute. I want to show you something." Thinking nothing about it, I skipped from the kitchen over to his chair, and he wanted to show me something all right. There he sat, sunken in his recliner, with his pants unzipped and his penis sticking out.

"You want to touch it?" he whispered. I was stunned. I glanced at the kitchen entrance and back at him. What if his wife came into the room? Would she think I had asked him to show me his "thing?" I usually found a way to blame myself when bad things happened.

"No! Put it back up," I said as I turned away. I had never seen a penis and did not want to see his. In an instance, he grabbed my wrists and tried to force my hands toward it, but I pulled back with all my force, saying "NO" loud enough his wife could have heard. Trying to wriggle out of his hold but not strong enough to do so, I thought quickly. With all my might, I kicked him. When he let me go and grabbed his leg, I doubled my fist and socked him in the face. As fast as I could get away, I was out the door. What had just happened to me? I felt dirty and sick and wanted to throw up.

Immediately, I made my way to Aunt Mag and told her the story. She was enraged and tried to console me. "You need to tell your dad, and he can decide what to do." By the time I found Dad, standing outside the store peeling an apple and watching the men whittle, I was trembling.

"Dad, I need to talk to you," I said out of the corner of my mouth. Rather than go inside the store where one of the clerks might hear us, I led him down the street, recounted every detail, and waited for him to respond.

Instead of charging across the square and up the hill to his house just as any normal father would, Dad thought for a minute and said, "He didn't make you do anything did he?" *What was that supposed to mean?*

"No, I didn't touch him," I said, wondering why that was his first question. *Did he think the man raped me? Would that have made a difference?*

He thought for a minute and then said, "Well, the best thing to do is to stay away from him. He has always been odd." Dad said.

Odd? A man who shows a young girl his private parts is odd? Men like him preyed on kids and were called "dirty old men." I knew to avoid them, but no one warned me about this one.

His wife may never have known about this incident, but I am reasonably confident that she was aware that he had a history of being a "dirty old man." I was just as sure this wasn't his first time to expose himself to some innocent child. Maybe the last one was afraid of him and did touch his private parts. She might not have had the courage to run out the door or down the street. How many had he violated?

"You mean you aren't going to do something?" I asked, shocked that he would not defend me.

"What do you think I should do? I could go up there and kill him, but do you want everyone talking about this or me go to prison?"

Ever protective of the family name, this would be yet another secret.

Maybe this episode didn't have a traumatic effect on me, but if it didn't, why would I dwell on that day for many months and even years to come? The feel of his hands gripping my wrists and forcing them toward him is as vivid now as it was back then.

Why did he think he could do this to me, especially with his wife in the next room? Did he not fear Bill Wilson or worse yet, Cloteel? I thought all bad things happened to me because I was adopted.

Dad didn't have to tell me to stay away from this man because I was never going anywhere near him again. I told no one else about this pervert, even though I should have warned my friends. For some reason, I was too embarrassed and felt as if I had caused this to happen.

I doubt that my dad told Mother or she would have gone after him with a gun. At least, I like to think she would have. When I saw the man on the street, I ran in the opposite direction.

Dad was closing up the store years later, and I was helping him with the lock when out of the blue he said, "By the way, Johnny Sanders died."

I didn't blink, "Well, I hope the old son-of-a-bitch is in hell."

I was in my forties before the old man finally died.

Maybe Dad regretted not settling this matter many years ago, but on the other hand, I should have known he wouldn't. Keeping up appearances was important to my family, but his protection of me should have outweighed his pride. It was shortly after this that I began to twist and twirl my hair.

CHAPTER NINETEEN

MY DAD AND I BONDED at the store; my mother and I bonded on shopping trips. There were no malls in the 60's and only a few good department stores. Even though I could have taken any item from our inventory, Mother did not shop in our store. She preferred upscale department stores and children's shops in cities where she would lose herself in the bows and lace while I wandered through the shoes and play clothes. I never liked frills, and I still don't; however, she never gave up trying to turn me into a girlie girl.

Girls weren't allowed to wear pants to school except in the winter, and they had to go under a dress. In high school, they weren't allowed at all. When the pantsuit became the fashion statement, I had found my style.

Even though dresses were confining when I wanted to slide or swing or run through the woods, those pretty outfits elevated me to celebrity status among my peers. I should have been ashamed because these girls had very little in the way of clothing and certainly not many items that were "store bought," but the attention those dresses and skirts brought me superseded my humility.

I enjoyed the focus on what I wore rather than who I was. Elementary playmates complimented my clothing, and when we stood side by side, I knew they saw the contrast. One part of me was ashamed of feeling so proud of what I wore, while the other part knew my appearance gave me a certain amount of prestige. If a child said, "I wish I had shoes like those," my instinct was to take them off and watch her walk away in them, but I knew better because Mother would have been mad. I owned nice things, but I also gave away many when I could. The cycle was to own it, give away, to make friends. That didn't work, but I would be a long time realizing this misconception.

The desire to have expensive clothing stayed with me, but the number of items in my wardrobe decreased when I had to buy my own.

Even though Mother only bought top of the line, she wasn't as uppity as her sister Jewell. "It is better to buy quality than quantity," Mother reminded me when we shopped. To an extent, that became a problem for me when I wrongly assumed I was identified by what I owned rather than who I was.

Because Dad often went to the horse races at Churchill Downs in Louisville, Mother and I enjoyed frequent shopping trips while he was at the track. Mother wore high heels, a suit, and gloves to shop on Fourth Street in downtown Louisville, so I tried mimic her and learned some clever tricks from watching her maneuver Dad.

Mother was sly. She would pack clothes for two days; we would end up staying four if he were winning, so she had to buy more. He gave her money and off we went to Stewarts or one of the other notable department stores.

Eating lunch at Stewarts taught me a formal side of dining. The finger sandwiches, with the crust removed, were not something I ate at home. "Mother, why do they cut the crust off?"

"It makes them fancy." At times like this, I liked being a lady.

When she was no longer able to shop, I brought her a new outfit when I came home. By then the clothes were for comfort rather than style. In my formative years, she craved nice things and owned many, including a mink coat I found in the back of her closet years after it was taboo to wear one. Her need for more and more clothing came from growing up without many. I knew that about my mother and her sister Jewell, and it seemed that no matter how many dresses or pairs of shoes she had in her closet, she was never satisfied. Her self-worth came from what she wore but it was really in who she was, and I wished I had told her that before she died and learned that lesson for myself long before I did.

My dad was a contradiction when it came to money. Although he took pride in the way our home looked and how put together Mother and I were, he thought she could do this on a thin budget. Therefore, she created clever ways of prying money from him. Not that she couldn't write a check for what she bought, but she didn't want him asking questions. However, I never heard her complain or question him about the money he lost at the track, and we always knew when he did because of his bad temperament.

Many of our clothes came from Aunt Jewell's store where Mother made payments without alerting Dad. Hiding many items on the top of my closet and bringing them out a few at a time so my dad wouldn't notice became a game. How long could we do this until Dad would make a comment? "This old thing? Why I've had this for ages. You just never noticed," Mother said when he caught her. He bought it every time-so we thought.

Dad had no concept of the price of items outside his store. He never shopped except for inventory, which was not expensive, so every time he asked her how much something cost, she said, "I only paid $24.99." If she didn't go over that amount, he would not complain. Considering gas was only thirty cents, $24.99 was a lot of money to the general public.

I hate to admit it, but in my early days I was materialist and wanted to impress others with the price of items, often tossing out numbers when someone complimented me. "I had to give $19.99 for this blouse." Anyone could buy a good blouse in the 60's for $5.99, but not my mother.

Later in life, I wouldn't announce the price of items, but I still thought I had to "buy" my way.

One year, twelve of us went somewhere special at Christmas, and I sneaked and paid the bill. When they were ready to pay individually, the waiter said, "It's been taken care of." Why did I need to pay for friendship? The fact that I could be loved for being myself never occurred to me.

What I do know is that I must not have been overly obnoxious because Carol, Roberta, and Judy have stayed my friends since the cradle and now if I go too far, they call me out on my behavior. Sometimes it works, but other times I forget.

CHAPTER TWENTY

BY SEVENTH GRADE, I finally consoled myself that nothing had changed. My brother was not as needy of her, and my mother was more attentive to me. As a matter of fact, I was so contented that weeks passed without my lying awake, thinking about my birth mother and why she gave me up. Moving away from the mental wrestling match, I resolved to put that fight to rest. "I don't care who she is or where she is," I told myself when thoughts of my birth mother hung over me like a vapor. That wasn't the truth, but I thought as long as I kept telling myself this, I would believe it.

My brother began to have terrible nightmares when he was around five, so my dad slept with him many nights until James outgrew them. Logistically, I needed to move across the hall to a half bed at bedtime so they could have my bed. I didn't want to give up my bedroom, and often thought about why they didn't move Mother to that half bed and Dad and James sleep in their bed.

Many nights Dad and James went to bed early, and Mother and I sat up watching scary movies, which was quite ironic since he couldn't sleep because of the horror going on in his young mind, and I was thriving on the terrifying black and white scenes on the TV.

I loved those private times with Mother because I always felt special. "Don't tell your daddy we sat up so late!" she said as if we had a secret. He was only a few feet away in another room, but he might as well have been across town. I am addicted to horror movies even today.

By this time, I was emerging as a musical talent, singing for local festivals at school, at church on Sunday mornings, and at 4-H Talent Shows. Art and piano also interested me, and I continued to play trumpet in the band. My parents bought me a gold trumpet when I showed a commitment. I still have that trumpet. My mother wished I had chosen a different instrument because she thought playing trumpet would make my lips larger.

My artistic ability also flourished in the seventh grade, but I would not stick with that talent. Once again when I took an interest in something, my mother made sure I had an abundance of supplies. Schools did not furnish crayons and construction paper back then, so we all brought our own. My friends will remind me that while they had a regular box of crayons, mine had three or four levels of colors, including pastels, and even a trimmer on the side of the box. To top off my fortune, I had a bag of colored pencils. No one had colored pencils. My drawings looked more dimensional than they would have otherwise because of those pastel colors blended with primary ones.

I can still see my artwork hanging on the wall in my seventh-grade classroom with marks at the bottom where classmates voted mine the best. It wasn't necessarily the best; it was unique. "I stopped drawing in the seventh grade because of those damn colored pencils," Carol laughed many years later. "My pictures never got any votes, and I was ashamed to vote for my own." That wasn't the best practice for encouraging art.

Playing the piano proved difficult, even though my parents bought me a used upright as soon as I started taking lessons and pushed me to practice. For fifty cents a lesson, I could leave my classroom and walk to a tiny annex connected to the big building. That was my motivation.

The piano teacher was a classmate's grandmother and, like my own, could be cranky. If I hit a wrong note, she bristled. We butted heads on the type of music I wanted to play and the music she insisted I learn. At the end of each school year, she hosted a recital at her home. I dreaded that day.

Recitals bored me, mainly because I was forced to play classical pieces and even worse listen to other student banging out pieces too difficult for them. There might have been a couple of older guys whose playing did not hurt my ears, but that was it. I could tell most parents were just as bored as I was and wondered about the money they had spent on these lessons.

Miss Lasca and I had made a deal; she would allow me to play a Rock'n Roll number if the classical one proved to be above average. That meant I had to practice and play two pieces compared to the one my friends were playing. While they were sitting at the baby grand in her living room, trying to remain poised as if they were playing at Carnegie Hall, I was embracing the "Rock'n Roll Waltz."

Miss Lasca's love for music and singing offered kids an opportunity to participate in events outside of school. When the "Five O'Clock Hop," a popular live TV show in Nashville and a spinoff of "American Bandstand," solicited young people from small communities to be on the show on Saturday mornings, she arranged for some of her students to dance. She scheduled a bus, found parents to chaperon, and collected money for meals. Most of these young people had never been out of the state.

Although we could all dance well or she wouldn't have selected us, I must have had a little more showmanship due to my hours in front of

A Girl Named Connie

"American Bandstand" mimicking the best of the dancers. For whatever the reason, Lasca placed me with a guy who could rock'n roll with the best, and then positioned us center stage. Center stage was where I thrived.

My mother bought me a new wool skirt, neat vest, and long sleeved blouse for the occasion, and my saddle oxfords were perfect. Fanny had fixed my hair the day before and Mother applied a little makeup before we left home.

When the lights came on so did we. "Let's Go To The Hop" was the opening song, and we forgot we weren't at a sock hop back home until we looked into the camera. Dancing was a part of my life until I went to college and discovered it was a sin.

Singing was a gift, and I became well known for it. Being in front of an audience transported me to a happy place where strangers applauded and tossed out compliments like candy.

"Your voice is a natural," admirers often said. It was not something I had to learn. I might have lacked self-esteem at home but never on a stage.

When I was no older than twelve or thirteen, I sang in churches throughout the community. My principal invited me to sing at a revival at his country church after he forgave me for the hair incident. Roberta and Carol often sang duets, so the three of us made the rounds singing at revivals. When I was in high school, political candidates invited me to sing at rallies. I was in a different world than my friends through these opportunities, and each gave me the confidence I longed to have but never seemed to get from my parents.

My parents were always supportive of my singing and if Fanny didn't drive me, Mother would. That was only one of my many outlets.

All through elementary school, I belonged to the 4-H Club. My interest wasn't in learning to sew or raise crops or give "how to" demonstrations at competitions. My interest was in the talent shows. Winning blue ribbons for singing meant more to me than winning one for a garment I might have sewn; yet to be in 4-H, I had to participate in projects the same as other members did.

Boys made lamps and gave demonstrations on crops and topics of interest, but girls were expected to learn to sew. I didn't want to sew, but if I wanted to participate, I had no choice.

Our instructor taught us the basics and within a few afternoon sessions, we made an apron. I would never wear an apron, but in the 50's ladies always had a drawer full of them, and my mother would appreciate wearing it.

Then she instructed us to make a simple garment, which I could not and did not want to do. Carol and Roberta owned sewing machines by the time they were in the seventh grade and learned to sew through these 4-H lessons, but I hated every step of the process because it stumped me. What was I going to do? During all those times our leader showed us what to do and how to cut out from a pattern and how to thread a needle and all that went with sewing, I wished I were wiring a lamp. When I told my mother my dilemma, I thought she would show some sympathy, but when I said, "We have to make a dress, and I don't want to make a dress. I'm not going to do it, and Ms. Pascall will be mad."

Her response was, "Oh, yes you are going to make a dress just like everyone else. We'll go to the store tomorrow and get the material, and we'll make this dress!" She meant business.

The next afternoon I dreaded picking out material, but Mother had already been to the store, chosen a pattern, and was ready to cut out the outfit by the time I arrived. This was one time I wished we didn't have a store. At least the dress was a two-piece, which was better than a dress, and the pattern was a simple top and a pleated skirt. Mother sat at the treadle sewing machine, an antique one with a pedal that she seldom used but, at least, knew how. "What do you want me to do?" I asked dreading the answer.

"You just sit right there and watch me, and I will explain to you how to make this." Never thinking this might be cheating and frankly, not caring at that point, I pulled up a chair to watch. Bored and weary, I continued for three afternoons to monitor this procedure, because she insisted. As the outfit came together, I was amazed how cute it was. She dutifully explained each step, but I listened absentmindedly as she progressed. I asked one question. "Why do you have to turn something inside out to sew it but then turn it right side out and it looks good." My mother just laughed. "Don't worry; you'll get it." I didn't want to get it. As a matter of fact, I did not sew one stitch of that dress that I took to the 4-H meeting and passed off as my own.

Each district entered its winners in the Kentucky State Fair 4-H competition. "MY" outfit won a blue ribbon and overall best outfit, which qualified it for the Kentucky State Fair. My mother was elated, but I was mortified. How could I with a clear conscience compete with girls who had made their own?

Once again among rows and rows of garments at the state fair likely crafted by others my age, lay my outfit, but it wasn't mine and I knew it. Guilt overwhelmed me, but my mother was so proud as she walked the aisles, looking at the entries in my age group. I was keeping my fingers crossed that it would not win anything at that level, and I could put sewing behind me. This was a time when everyone didn't get a participation ribbon; only a few were given.

Then to my dismay at the end of the state fair when it was time to retrieve my garment, on top of it lay a blue ribbon. Oh no, I had won a blue ribbon! I should say my mother won a blue ribbon, which made her so very proud of our project. There was no OUR. My mother made the dress and won the ribbon, but I could never tell anyone the truth, not even my friends. Even though she tried to justify making the outfit by saying I helped, I knew better and was ashamed that I had knocked out those who had not cheated.

Embarrassed that I won, I sensed that my 4-H leader probably knew that I had not made that garment. I hated sewing, knew nothing about it, and never wanted to learn, so I had allowed my mother to make that dress. Telling the truth at that point would have embarrassed the leader and my mother, so I kept it to myself.

I am not saying that I never skirted the truth, but this incident created so much guilt, I had a hard time continuing to participate in 4-H. If not for the many talent contests sponsored by the club, I would have quit. I didn't know how to react to my mother's indifference or why she was not embarrassed. From that experience forward, my mother had no input in my school projects because I never told her about them.

No matter what the issue, being deceptive is the same as lying, and my goal from that time on was to try to tell the truth. I say "try' because sometimes telling the truth led to more trouble than the trouble I would have been in. Human nature intrudes on wisdom.

When I reached high school Home Economics Class, which the majority of the girls chose as an elective, I signed up knowing I was not as domestic my classmates were and would dread most of the curriculum. Even though I served as song leader for the FHA Club for four years, I was not an exceptional Future Homemaker of America.

Part of the curriculum was a nine-week sewing class. This time, however, I pleaded with my teacher to give me an alternative assignment. I was not going to endure the agony of making a dress if I could escape it.

A Girl Named Connie

"I can teach you to sew, so don't back off yet," she said. My teacher and I started making this dress. She showed me what to do and I did it, but not to suit her. After taking the dress apart four or five times, she finally agreed that I could not sew. "Is there something else I can do instead of sewing?" She had a binder of project suggestions, and one of them was to make a lamp from scratch and wire it. Finally, I was going to wire a lamp, but more importantly, I was to make it from scratch.

Perhaps the 4-H curriculum did not vary too far from that of home economics after all. Each lesson was to prepare us girls to be successful homemakers. Knowing how to sew must have been considered a key to being a good wife and mother, but I never put the two together.

I bought a thousand pop sickle sticks, designed a double-globed lamp and glued each stick with Elmer's glue. When I plugged the final project into an outlet, it came on with a blast of light, and I was grateful it wasn't a dress.

Carol and Roberta both went on to become excellent seamstresses, and I learned to take any lamp apart and wire it. This teacher was ahead of her time. Long before the term "individual instruction" became popular, she knew to find something meaningful for me to do that suited my interest. She also wanted to keep me involved in the FHA because I would go on to become a regional song leader, which was a feather in our club's hat. I think I still have my white "officer's" dress.

Incidentally, I was no better with the nine weeks of cooking, but at least, I saw the value of learning. I might never need to sew, but I would need to eat.

CHAPTER TWENTY-ONE

OUR TOWN WAS SO CALM and so stuck in the past that we had no red light: only a light blinking on and off, day and night. There was no need for a red light because not enough cars came through to hold up traffic.

Saturday night and Sunday afternoon, a few cars lined one side of the square with couples who came to town to visit each other or to bring their kids to the movie and wait for them. Men stood around their cars or leaned on the hoods while wives rolled down their windows and chatted across the way. Ladies would not have stood on the street after dark the way men did. Often the only sign of life was the spark from the end of a cigarette.

My parents never sat with couples on the square. They had no set of friends and didn't appear to want any. My friends talked about their parents playing Rook (a card game) twice a week at someone's home while the kids played board games, and I envied them for being part of family fun. I couldn't picture my parents sitting at the dinner table playing cards and laughing at something funny. I longed for them to be more social but they were not.

A Girl Named Connie

Mother did belong to the local Homemaker's Club and went to meetings once a month, but that was it. When she talked on the phone, it was to one of her family members. Unlike my friends' mothers, she never hosted an Avon party, a Stanley party, or a Home Interiors party.

In a small town like mine, holidays were celebrated with quite a bit of fanfare. One of the most wonderful times was Christmas. No one was in a bad mood. This was the time of year when my family was the happiest and the most united. Dad's business boomed, so he was always jovial. Mother shopped for gifts so she was happy. For a child as sensitive as I was to their dispositions and their tempers, I could rest a little more at ease that the month of December would be a joyful one.

Farmers sold their crops this time of the year and paid Dad what they owed. He sorted through the IOU box and destroyed their debts by ripping up the note card in front of them. Then the men and their wives, with money to spend, were loyal to Dad and bought most of their gifts from him. That was the cycle among farmers and business owners in Edmonton.

Santa always brought me a doll even though I never played with it. Mother was determined I was going to have one like all the other little girls, so to please her, I acted as if I loved the doll, but I didn't. My desperate mother tried so hard, but I simply could not pretend I was a mama or play in a playhouse or amuse myself the way my girlfriends did. I had rather have a ball and a glove and a bike.

Dad's gift to Mother was money, and she bought him a tie or socks or something practical. We opened our presents; Mother cooked a traditional Christmas breakfast, and by late afternoon, we were on our way to Aunt Hazel's house to celebrate with her and her children. We didn't exchange gifts, but Mother always slipped something to Aunt Hazel. Christmas at her house was lovely chaos even if they didn't have the luxuries my family had.

Wearing a brand new dress to Aunt Hazel's was essential because all of us dressed up for Christmas, including her children and grandchildren. Among the crowd gathered at Aunt Hazels were her children and grandchildren, but not any other nieces and nephews except James and me. We never gathered with my uncles or Aunt Jewell. When I asked about that fact, Mother would simply say, "They go to their wives families." Therefore, the family I was closest to all my life was Aunt Hazel's.

Why we didn't gather with Dad's family still puzzles me. I presumed Dad had no desire to sit down with Aunt Kathleen, but he and Aunt Mag were close. Did anyone invite Mammaw to a Christmas dinner? It never seemed to concern anyone but me. Leaving her out of this joyous time seemed cruel. Did she feel abandoned on Christmas Day or glad she didn't have to see any family?

Of course, we visited Mammaw and gave her a present, but she never gave us gifts. The only gifts we received were under our own tree. What were Aunt Mag's family and Aunt Kathleen's family doing at Christmas, and why didn't we celebrate together at least for a meal?

As for Christmas in Edmonton, I often stared out my bedroom window when we lived in the apartment at the decorations on light poles that lit up the square. Business owners decorated their windows with brightly colored bulbs or Christmas trees, which created a winter wonderland spirit for shoppers. Every business that is, except Wilson's Dry Goods.

My dad's store was the only dark spot on the otherwise bright square, and he had a reason. Not that he was a humbug but because he didn't want anyone to get hurt climbing over the bolts of material that lined the window in order to reach the platform to decorate. If my mother had tried, he would have been yelling at her not to fall or be careful or directing her every step. He was too large to do it, so it remained undecorated until I was old enough to beg him to let me try and he finally did, but that happened one year only.

Other business people, as well as those who drove through town to look at the lights, probably thought he was a scrooge, but he was just odd about things like this. It didn't bother him one bit to be the only business owner whose window was undecorated. However, his contribution to the spirit of the season was providing free gift-wrapping to customers, and as soon as I could do the job, it became mine. He loved Christmas because that was the money making season of the year, but he also had a little spirit beneath his crusty image.

Every year until he sold the store, I dressed up and came home on Christmas Eve to work alongside my father. The pleasure of seeing customers each year that I had known since I was a child, and the pride my dad felt to reintroduce his daughter was a gift in itself. "You remember Connie don't you?" he asked customers. I held my breath that no one would remind me that *my daddy wasn't my daddy.*

"Sure, but we haven't seen you in years." I heard that dozens of times throughout the day. My job continued to be wrapping gifts.

At the end of that day, I sought my friends for a glass of wine and a Christmas Eve party where we told tall tales, year after year.

Even though most people in our area cut their own cedar trees and put them up a week before Santa came, the idea of my dad in his long-sleeved white shirt in the woods with a saw was comical. There were always kids willing to cut a tree for a dollar or two and bring to our apartment. When we moved to the subdivision, my mother bought an artificial aluminum silver tree with lights that changed colors. Dad didn't like it, but it looked beautiful in our picture window. I wish I had that tree.

Christmas at school was electrifying, too. For some kids, this was the only Christmas they knew. We drew names and put gifts under the tree in our classroom. Older boys in upper grades cut cedar trees from the woods behind the school and made wooden bases for each, nailed them to the bottom of the trees and set them in the classrooms. How thrilling it was to see that huge cedar tree carried through the door. The smell lingered until after Christmas vacation.

Usually, gifts for classmates were inexpensive trinkets such as cheap bottles of perfume or dime store bracelets, and it was not unusual to buy a boy a pocketknife. My mother shopped for my exchange gift and some kids said, "Whose name did you get, Connie?" I didn't care who drew my name; I cared more about what I gave. Receiving gifts embarrassed me because I didn't think I deserved to receive. I was meant to give.

When stacks of gifts surrounded our teacher, among them would be handkerchiefs, glass dishes, and boxes of chocolate covered cherries, we joyfully watched her open them and swooned over each one as if it were the best.

The first year I taught, my sixth graders showered me with gifts just the way we had done ours back in the 50's. One gift I particularly remember came from a boy whom I considered being the least likely person to give his teacher a gift, but I learned never to make assumptions at Christmas.

This gift wasn't wrapped. He held it in his hand, and when I had opened all the others, he slipped it to me. "This is beautiful, Tony, and I will keep it forever." He smiled and looked away. Later a few of the kids whispered, "I bet he stole it." He had a little bit of a reputation for taking things, but I didn't really think he did. I did, however, assume that when his mother searched for her favorite broach, she was going to be surprised.

Before going home for two weeks off, our teacher gave us a brown paper bag with an apple, orange, stick candy, and maybe a pencil inside. We students left happy to end half a school year and prayed for snow to delay our return for at least a few days.

If any substantial amount of snow fell in the winter, the school was canceled and most businesses closed. My dad never closed for any reason, and sometimes I went with him just to have something to do.

The winter months meant selling dozens of snow boots. These were rubber slip-on or four-buckle boots that came up to the calf of the leg. Farmers wore them year round to go to the barn and feed cattle or to milk, but those who didn't live on farms mainly needed them for playing in the snow or clearing off driveways. Right now there are closets in Metcalfe County with boots bought at Wilson's Dry Goods.

During my final years at Edmonton Elementary, I was almost moving away from thoughts of my birth mother. No one had mentioned my adoption or slung nasty insults. Our principal forgave our transgressions; we walked through eighth-grade graduation in our lovely white dresses and marched toward high school with enthusiasm and a little apprehension. After all, we had seen high school students at the drugstore after school and eavesdropped on their conversations. We had watched them at the movie, girls giggling and tossing popcorn at the boys in the row in front of them. I was never sure I could master the giggle. Life was fun until it wasn't.

PART II

CHAPTER TWENTY-TWO

MY FRESHMAN CLASS-the "Class of 1964" consisted of over a hundred students from three area elementary schools. Even though I had made a place for myself among my elementary classmates over the past eight years, the new students didn't know me personally, even though they might have known about me. Sometimes I thought the entire county whispered behind my back.

During the summer, I worried about what these new students might know or not know about my life, and if they would treat me accordingly. Would I be a target for another Lisa? There is always a Lisa in a group of people, and I didn't want to start my high school days having to face one.

While new clothes, boys, hairstyles and the latest Ricky Nelson hits filled Carol and Roberta's thoughts before starting to high school, I stewed over how to avoid controversy. Teenagers are often mean-spirited and, by now, I was paranoid. The invisible Connie dreaded the first day of high school, even though the visible Connie was ready.

I was sure that I was the only adopted child in my class and undoubtedly, the only adopted student in the entire high school; the Baker kids were much younger. Consequently, I was on the lookout for antagonists who might think it their duty to inform me of what I already knew. It didn't take long for one to appear, but not in the form of a student.

The first episode occurred in my freshman science class. Our assignment was to create a family tree. This was a simple assignment and one I could do, but evidently my "kind" teacher thought this might cause me embarrassment. As I was leaving the classroom, she called me to her desk and whispered over a stack of papers, "You don't have to do this project."

I immediately knew what she meant and could think of no other response other than "OK." I walked out wondering if all my teachers discussed how to deal with my "secret." I was furious.

First, I questioned what she knew and who had told her? Then I thought about what I was going to tell classmates when or if they discovered that I didn't have to do the same assignment? What would the others think when I didn't submit one? Those who might not know my story would likely question why I was being given special treatment. After all, I had a family tree. I knew my mother's side and my father's side. Why would she assume that I would try to track some other family for my tree? The best favor a person can do for an adopted child is give him/her equal treatment.

Unlike many other times, I did tell my mother about this incident. Maybe I wanted her to come to my defense and finally break the silence. Indigently I said, "Do you know what that Ms. Charter told me today?" Then I relayed the story, expecting a degree of infuriation to follow.

She never looked up from the cake batter she was stirring. "Well, just do whatever she asks." No explanation or fury. Most mothers would have ripped that teacher from one end to the other, but my mother had nothing more to

A Girl Named Connie

say. Most mothers would have called the teacher and expressed how singled out her daughter felt. Not my mother; she kept stirring her batter.

As instructed, I didn't do the family tree; I think I did a report instead. My friends handed in their projects and never mentioned mine. The bulletin board displayed the "trees," and no one asked about the one that was missing. I didn't want to be singled out or treated differently, but I was. It was at this point I concluded that my entire class knew I was adopted. I didn't want to be known as the "adopted" kid.

My first year brought no more incidents like this one. Academically, I would not only excel in biology, but also in physical education. Every freshman was required to take a physical education class because President Kennedy had mandated it for schools, so I was happy for this chance to do what I liked best. We had girl classes and boy classes and wore ugly uniforms. In PE we tumbled, exercised, and learned a variety of games from volleyball to basketball. I was good in all areas. Not a ninth grade girl and not too many boys could challenge my athletic skills. Some academic areas might cause me headaches in school, but this wasn't one of them.

We were required to display our tumbling skills during halftime of a high school basketball game. It didn't matter if a girl was large or tall or a boy was short and robust; everyone had to tumble over obstacles, which resulted in either a round of applause or uncomfortable sniggers from a huge crowd. I couldn't wait to perform, but my friends dreaded it because they could not roll or dive without deathly fear. I reveled in the praise and applause. No doubt I was the best gymnast on the floor, and that night was also one of the few times my mother was in the high school gym to watch me do anything. My friends were never jealous of my athletic ability because they were much too feminine to want to be. They tumbled like a girl; I tumbled like a boy.

Looking back, I know how strong a competitor I could have been if I had been born ten years later. In addition to my singing, I was known as the girl who could hold her own against any boy. By the time I was interested in dating, however, I began to curb my competitiveness and many of my boyish ways to become what my mother always wanted-a girlie girl. I learned that being feminine and being athletic could work together quite well but not as long as I was living in my mother's home.

The second incident happened my sophomore year on a set of stairs going from the lower level of the classroom section to the upper level. This new high school was a split-level structure. At the time I was dating a guy that was quite popular with other girls-particularly one girl who obviously didn't like me very much. I knew it, but didn't realize the intensity of her feelings. Without warning, she verbally assaulted me in front of classmates on the concrete steps leading upstairs to my home economics class.

I was two steps in front of her and could hear her mumbling behind my back. Whenever I was near her, she had this "mumbling" going on. Even though I couldn't comprehend what she was saying, I turned around to face her with a look that said, "Bring it on!" She went berserk, and the next thing she knew, I had thrown a punch that landed her at the bottom of the steps. This time, I did not run.

One of the teachers escorted me to the counselor's office while another helped the girl off the floor. Because this action was so out of character for me, the counselor knew I had been provoked. I didn't want to tell him the account, but I had no choice. The principal would have suspended me, and then what would I tell my parents?

Sitting in front of his desk, I relayed the story that concluded with her saying, "I know where you came from and I know who your mother is. 'That's when I hit her.' "

"You go back to class, and I will handle this."

In the meantime, his "taking care of it" included calling my mother. When I got home, she was watching one of her soap operas. "I heard you had some trouble at school today."

"Yes, but it was no big deal and it's fine." I had let her off the hook again. Neither of us said anything else, and even though the school buzzed with the fight, no one mentioned it to me. As far as my classmates were concerned, I was justified in socking her in the face. I'm not sure how she explained her appearance to her parents, but there were no repercussions for me. Although she left me alone, I constantly watched my back.

Career development was a major part of my freshman year. We had to take a test (provided by one of the branches of the Armed Forces) that would show our top five areas of aptitude. My top one was nursing, so I decided that a career in that field would suit me well. Dad found that idea objectionable because he did not trust doctors, nurses or hospitals, a fact quite ironic since he owned a drugstore.

Even though my father considered himself quite knowledgeable when it came to medicine, he had an intense fear of hospitals and viewed them as a place to go to die. "They'll kill you in a hospital," I had heard him say more than once. There was no reasoning with my dad.

I remember his disdain for doctors and hospitals because of an incident that happened with me. During this year was the first time I had been so sick that I thought I was going to die. I woke up one morning in extreme pain, so mother rushed me to the local doctor's office. "You've got to get her to the hospital right now," he said. "Her appendix is near rupturing."

I was not going without my dad, who had gone to Nashville to buy supplies. I didn't want him to be mad at Mother for taking me to the hospital, and she didn't insist probably for the same reason.

"I'm waiting for Dad. I can't go without Dad." My doctor looked disapprovingly over his glasses, but Mother took me back home where I spent the rest of the day curled up in a chair in misery. If this had turned out to be a false alarm, Dad would have been furious, but if I had died, he would have never forgiven Mother.

Finally, he came home from his trip and I tried to suppress the pain.

"Why don't we see how you are in the morning?" When I exploded into tears, he swept me up, dashed to the car, and left for the emergency room twenty-five miles away. I had surgery (my appendix removed) that night with my dad pacing the floor in the waiting room.

The next morning, I expected to see my parents, but instead, my preacher was sitting in the chair next to my bed. Astonished to see him, I yelled so loudly my mother heard me from the hallway. "What in the hell are you doing here?" I was still coming out of the anesthesia.

Mother threw open that door. "Connie, what did you just say?" She turned to the preacher. "I have never heard her talk like that." He laughed. Honestly, I thought I was dying, and he had been called to pray over me. Dad had put the fear in me that a hospital could kill a person, so I thought I must be dying.

Then I realized that I knew nothing about my medical history and how important that information might be. When the nurse asked questions about family health, my dad responded with his and my mother's medical history. What good was that going to do? The value of knowing my medical history had never occurred to them or me.

CHAPTER TWENTY-THREE

By APRIL OF THAT YEAR, I started dating and driving, in that order. My boyfriends came to the door, met my parents, opened the car door, and then walked me back to my front door by eleven that night.

We girls dated once a week and a boy never came to a girl's house to visit. Nightly, my dad assumed his position in his favorite chair in the living room, relaxing in his underwear and long-sleeved shirt, so I would have been mortified to bring a boy home. I grew up in a morally strict environment when it came to boy/girl relationships. The latter part of the 60's would bring the sex, love and rock'n roll revolution, but I missed it. *Beach Blanket Bingo* with Annette and Frankie was more my generation.

My mother made a point of knowing details about the boys I dated. Coming from a respectable home was a priority. When I told her I had a date for Saturday night, Mother immediately said, "I don't know his family. Where do they live?" or she would say, "He comes from a nice family."

Ironically, she never considered our family imperfections or the possibility that a young man's mother might be telling him to avoid Connie Wilson because she was adopted. "You don't know where she came from." That might not have occurred to my mother, but it did to me. In a small town, who your parents are and what they do is your life's résumé.

I turned sixteen in April of my sophomore year and begged my dad for a car. None of my friends thought about having cars, but I was obsessed with the idea. Dad had no intention of buying one, but I continued to plead and laid out all the reasons I needed transportation until he found a Plymouth for $450 and announced we were going to "look at it."

It was green and white and built like a tank and certainly not as ascetically beautiful as the ones I had admired in the Ford dealership show window. He balked at the price, but I didn't give up hope. Since he was an expert in haggling, he thought he could talk the man down to $400. He was wrong. "It is worth four-fifty, and that is what I want."

"I'm not paying that," he said beginning to walk away.

Tearfully, I looked up at him. Weakened by those tears, Dad wilted. "Ok, we'll take it." I hugged and kissed my dad and thanked him profusely right there in front of the owner. My dad never quite knew how to react to affection. Since my father found some bit of prestige in vehicles, buying one for me likely gave him a sense of pride that his daughter would have a car. Few girls my age did.

Now that I had wheels, more adventures would follow, but first I had to get my license. I knew how to drive because on Sunday afternoons, Dad took me on back roads and put me under the wheel of his car. To get a driver's license, I first had to take a written test, and to do that required a birth certificate. This was going to prove interesting.

A Girl Named Connie

"I'm going to take my written test Monday, and I'll need my birth certificate," I announced over dinner one night. I assumed it was kept in his lock box at the bank and wanted to give Dad time to get it. Finally, I was going to see this document. Waiting for a response, Dad just nodded.

On his way to work, Dad dropped me off at the testing location, but I had no birth certificate. Just as I was about to ask him, Dad handed me a notarized letter from an office in Frankfort (our capitol) stating my identity. This wasn't a birth certificate, but I took it and got out of the car.

My friends might have said, "This isn't a birth certificate. What is this piece of paper supposed to mean?" I knew what it meant, so I said nothing, and evidently the guy who gave me the test already expected this document, so he did not question it. Throughout my life, Dad had "fixed" things concerning my identity.

Being overly confident in my ability to pass the written part of the driver's test without studying for it backfired. I sat at a long table alone and read the questions. This was harder than I thought it would be. Thinking these would be common sense questions, I had not studied the manual, so I guessed at the answers, wishing I had not been so overly confident. Consequently, I failed the written part of the test. Totally humiliated, I had to confess first to my dad and then go back to school and tell my friends. That was not easy, but it was a good lesson.

The next week I passed the test. Then the following month I took the driving part and passed. I was the first among my group of friends to get my license. However, I have never forgotten the day I had to admit I failed. What I didn't know was that this gave my friends the incentive to study hard because if Connie, who had been driving at least a year, could fail, so could they.

I might have failed the test the first time, but I was the only girl in my class to have a car waiting for her when she did pass it!

CHAPTER TWENTY-FOUR

MUCH TO MY MOTHER'S APPROVAL, I began focusing on make-up, high heels, and hairstyles about the same time I started dating and driving. I was one of the few natural blondes in school. Fanny Fields, a renowned hairdresser, entered many competitions throughout the state where she won prestigious awards. When Fanny asked me to be her hair model, I was honored because she had never used a high school student. That meant I would go to shows with her, meet many new people, and none of them would know anything about me.

This time before having anything done to my hair, I asked my mother for permission. "She'll be bleaching my hair," I explained. Reluctantly, Mother gave in but never told my dad. Did she think he wouldn't notice?

Fanny practiced on me after hours at her shop. Sometimes I would stay until 10 PM because she had no concept of time. My dad didn't think anything about my hours there because Fanny and I were always practicing for singing events.

"Fanny, I have to get home." One of the stipulations to my doing this was that I would not let my homework slip. I eased the car into the driveway, hoping Dad wouldn't hear.

One night thing didn't work out too well. I don't know what she tried on me, but my hair turned pink. Fanny wasn't worried. "Oh well, tomorrow after school I will get to the right color." She knew she could correct her mistake. When I got home, Mother was still up and nearly fainted when she saw me. "Connie, what happened to your hair?"

"It's no big deal. Fanny said she would get it back to blonde tomorrow after school." She didn't get upset, but my dad sure did.

The next morning at breakfast he stared at me, "What is going on with your hair?"

"Fanny has just made a little mistake in the color, and she is going to work on it after school today."

He laid down his fork and looked at me. "If you think you're going to school with pink hair you are wrong. You go back out to the beauty shop this morning and get your hair straightened out and then get to school."

I called Fanny. "Come on out and I'll take care of it," she said and opened the shop early. Once again, I had annoyed my dad, but this time, it wasn't my fault. What kind of an impression would I have made with pink hair?

That weekend, Carol, Roberta, Judy and I went to a neighboring town to a swimming pool. We didn't have a public pool in Edmonton, and we were looking for cute boys and dark tans and what better place to find them than a pool.

We stood on the edge of this public pool and dived in the water like Ester Williams. We came up at the same time and edged to the side of the pool, but unlike those three, my hair had undergone a chemical transformation. "You're hair is green!" Carol gasped.

"No, it isn't." I didn't believe her.

"Yes it is; look at it."

I went into the shower room, and there it was; wet, green hair. I sure wasn't going to get a date that way, so I threw a towel over my head and sat in a pool chair, pondering how this could have happened. Later, I realized that chlorine and bleached hair did not mix.

I didn't go home when we left; I went straight to Fanny's. My dad would have killed me if I had gone from pink to green in public. Fanny knew right away that I had been in contact with chlorine. Once my hair was back to normal, I went home, and Dad was none the wiser.

Fanny won several contests using me as a model, and Mother kept a picture of me with my bleached blonde hair styled in a beehive hairdo taken at one of the shows. For years, it hung prominently over the TV. I wonder what happened to that picture.

CHAPTER TWENTY-FIVE

FOR NO PARTICULAR REASON, I named my car "Pearl" after Mom Bybee. My fetish for cars began with this monster Plymouth but has not ended.

In addition to keeping her clean, I never parked my car near what might be a careless or reckless driver in the school parking lot for fear of a driver banging a door against the side or spinning gravel and nicking my car. However, no matter how protective I was, I couldn't stop what happened one afternoon in town.

Just as I was backing out of a parking space, someone from behind plowed into the back of me, jolting my face into the steering wheel. Immediately, I swung open the car door only to see the other driver swerve around me and zoom off. Not knowing what to do, I froze until I saw Mother dashing across the street as fast as her high heels could take her.

From a few feet away, she had witnessed this hit-and-run and flew into superhuman mode. "Get in," she yelled and pointed me to the back seat.

A Girl Named Connie

Before I could shut my door, she took off in the direction of the run-a-way car, wheeled around every corner as Judy, who was with me, held securely to the dash. When the criminal was in sight, Mother floored the accelerator, caught up with him, and pulled around his car the way a state trooper would do, cutting him off. He barely stopped within inches of Judy's door.

What was she going to do now?

It wouldn't take long to find out. She jumped out of my car, rushed back to his window and pecked on the glass with her knuckles.

"Get out," she ordered.

He obeyed. *What will she do next?* In front of her stood a rather young man who, by now, wished he had been more careful.

"What do you think you are doing?" *Oh, please God, don't let him hit her.*

He made some excuse I couldn't hear, but I could hear her clearly. "I'll tell you what you are going to do right now. You're going to turn this car around, and I'm going to follow you back to the police station."

Was he really going to do what she said?

Once we escorted him back to town and to the police station, she drove my car to the store to show Dad the damages. The man didn't have insurance, but paid for fixing my car, week by week. Once again, my mother protected my interest, and the man made sure that he paid Dad every penny on time.

I learned something about my mother that day: she could be "hell on wheels."

My car also gave me the ability to get a job, but not one Dad found suitable. I decided that I wanted to be a carhop at Jerry's Restaurant in

Glasgow, but Dad put his foot down. "It is too risky for a girl to do that job. No telling what kind of people you'd have to deal with."

The manager hired me, but not for the job I wanted, but one that Dad approved. I became a waitress inside the restaurant.

I had never waited tables, but I caught on and was good at it. Some of Dad's customers couldn't believe I would work at such a menial job (so they thought). Why would my parents allow me to wait tables, clean them off, and sweep nasty floors? That was not something they thought Dad's "princess" would be allowed to do; they had the wrong idea about my dad's work ethic, which also became mine.

If restaurant work were good enough for Aunt Hazel and her girls, why wouldn't it be good enough for me? Like my dad, I had never been a snob when it came to "classes of people." I can't say that about my mother.

Those with whom I worked were not doing so for spending money; they were paying bills. It didn't take me long to realize that being a good waitress required something a college education could not provide. People skills. I had learned how to deal with the public at my dad's store, but nothing prepared me for working in a restaurant.

I didn't mind the work, but most of all I liked being in a different atmosphere. The waitresses, the cook, the carhops, and the dishwashers became my friends. Although most of them were working to support a family, some were college students paying their way through school. No one was more important than anyone else, and I liked that feeling. Sometimes I knew I was given special treatment in Edmonton because of my parents, but in this setting, I was equal to the others. No one knew Bill Wilson.

Like most restaurants, a group of men had coffee each morning before going to work. Some were retired. I usually served these men and came to know them well. One of them said to me one day, "You need to go on to school and make something out of yourself. I can tell you're smart." He had no idea I was headed to college in the fall and was not going to have to worry about how to pay for it. "I plan to do that," I said in reply. They were all full of advice.

However, working long hours during the summer cut down on my social life. My friends came by to see me on their way to the drive-in or a skating rink, and part of me wanted to be with them. Not that they didn't work, but they didn't work at night like I did.

I wasn't going to quit my job because I thought that would have disappointed the manager and Dad, but I was wrong about my dad. One day he said, "Don't you think you need a little free time your last year of school before you go off to college?" I told the manager the next day that I would work until he could replace me.

That experience was worth a semester in college.

I have worked all of my life. Being secure financially at home did not mean I had an excess of money. There was never a time I had five dollars in my wallet; I had what I needed on an "as needed" basis. I asked for a dollar here and there but never had the cash to spend at random. No one my age did except boys who cut tobacco or raised and sold cattle.

Working, to my dad, was a sign of integrity and worthiness. He never thought I was too good for any job as long as it did not put me at risk.

CHAPTER TWENTY-SIX

RISK WAS TO BE PART of my life when away from home and not under the eye of my father. No matter how perfect I tried to be, I could not resist putting myself right on the edge of life. These "risks" were doing things that might leave me crippled or dead. Never wanting to be less than the bravest in the group, I often did things I knew were dangerous but did not want to appear afraid.

"Come on, Connie, let's drag race on the Old Glasgow Road," one of my guy friends might say. Off I would go! I never considered wrecking, running off the road, or possible oncoming traffic. My friends would not ride with me, but watched in fear from the side of the highway.

"Connie, let's go over to the state barn (where gravel piles were the height of small buildings) and climb the rock piles." We could have been buried if this pile of rocks had fallen like an avalanche, but the only damage was scarred hands and dust-covered clothing, both hard to hide from Mother.

"Connie, let's ride our bikes down the town hill and see how fast we can go without peddling." Off I went with no concern that I could have been hit by a car or truck on this busy highway.

A Girl Named Connie

Then I began to say to them, "Come on, let's loosen this parking meter and take it to a parking spot (where couples smooched) and stick it in the ground." That was an adventure that could have led to an arrest for stealing public property. I never thought of that.

I might say, "Let's get some cigarettes and try smoking." Our parents smoked, so Carol, Roberta, Judy and I sneaked cigarettes out of the house and learned to smoke, too. What is worse, we learned to enjoy smoking. Most of them stopped, but I would struggle with this addiction for years.

Why couldn't I have been content to live like most of the other teens in my class? They weren't trying to endanger themselves.

The anger and frustration in me pushed me toward activities that endanger myself. My anger was never toward people; at least not directly. Perhaps I was self-destructive. Perhaps I was trying to see how far I could go without failure or injury. The attempts at self-depreciating activities came outside the home rather than inside. At home I was quiet and compromising.

As a matter of fact, to Bill Wilson, I was as steady as a rock, but to Cloteel Wilson, I was too careless sometimes, didn't always make good choices and had to be "taken down a notch or two" even when I thought I was too big to be hit. To my friends, I was the one who bridged the gap between ladylike and deviant behavior. My pattern of flirting with danger became somewhat curtailed with age, but when I was young something in my nature made me seek the tightrope.

If my friends, who included a couple of guys, went sleigh riding in the darkness of the night on a car hood, I pressed them to swerve around trees and jump snow banks. Only the guys would ride with me. The fact we had no control of this manmade snowmobile invigorated me just as driving over bumpy gravels roads, topping hills a little too fast and bringing my stomach to my throat did.

If my friends and I went out on Halloween night, which we always did, I wasn't content to soap windows or string toilet paper across doors or steal a pumpkin from a teacher's doorstep. I wanted more mischief. So when Carol's future husband Guy Perkins and his friend Lee showed up in town in Lee's dad's truck, I didn't hesitate when Lee said, "I know where we can get some pumpkins. If y'all want to go, hop on."

We bumped along back roads until we neared a farmer's patch. I had no clue where we were but felt safe with these two guys. Not that I was worried about safety, but I did want to live!

"Are we gonna be shot?" I asked Lee. I had heard stories about farmers shooting at intruders. I also didn't want to have to explain to my dad what happened to me if I ended up in the hospital.

"Naw, I know this man and he won't shoot us."

I envisioned buckshot in our rears.

Lee stopped the truck in the middle of the road and gave us instructions. "When we get near the patch, I'm going to turn off the lights and you all jump off and scatter through the fields and throw as many as you can on the back."

With nothing but a slight hint of the moon from an otherwise dark sky, he backed up to the edge of the patch and we jumped off.

The pumpkins were wet and heavy, so we chose the smaller ones and soon loaded a few dozen. I had enough sense to know the danger we were in, but Halloween was a forgiving holiday. Farmers expected kids to raid their patches. That's how I justified stealing this man's harvest.

The back of the truck was so high off the ground that when we jumped off, our knees collapsed in the mud. Getting back on required a foot lift and a push. Lee was in the driver's seat watching for vehicles when he quickly turned on the engine and yelled, "Everybody get on!" He had seen something.

A Girl Named Connie

We girls scrambled to help each other, stepping across and in fresh pumpkins.

"My foot is stuck," Judy yelled just as Lee shoved the truck in drive and we felt it easing away. She had stepped into a pumpkin that clung to her shoe. "STOP," we screamed, so he slowed down enough for us to get her and her pumpkin foot on to the back. Lee was more afraid of getting caught than the rest of us because he was driving his dad's truck. His punishment might have been worse than the buckshot fired in the night.

When we heard gunshots, we didn't know if they went into the air or were aimed at us. Feuding men had killed one another over land, and we were edging in on illegal activities. Maybe this farmer did not know it was Halloween.

Lee gunned the engine and showered us in mud. Before long we were on our way back to town.

After we were safe, we made plans for these pumpkins, and it involved out-of-town boys who had showed up on our "turf." We were going to run them back to their hills and hollers and across the county line.

We hid below the level of the bed of the truck, and when we passed one of their cars, someone would yell, "BOMB" and one of us would toss a pumpkin over the side. I'm sure the weight of the pumpkin hitting their car was like a gunshot, which is why they turned around and chased us. Before long we were engaged in a full-fledged pumpkin battle on a side road just out of town.

Severe injuries could have put us in the hospital, but we were lucky that we ran out of pumpkins and fled the scene. In their arsenal were eggs, pumpkins, and firecrackers. What a mess and what fun. The other girls were so scared they never raised their heads over the truck bed. However, they could retell this incident along with those of us who did the damage.

"Where have you been?" Mother asked when I got home looking as if I had wallowed in mud and smelling like rotten pumpkins. I could do one of two things: tell her the truth or make up a story. I told her the truth. I should say I told part of the truth. To my surprise, she didn't lecture me or make me feel guilty. I had a feeling my mother had had a little bit of a spark in her during her teenage days, which made her much more tolerant of my escapades than Dad. He always worried that I would get hurt or embarrass myself (or the family).

Both could have happened, but being the daughter of Bill Wilson gave me some leeway. Others in the community didn't seem to judge me as harshly as some other kids might have been, which caused me to take more chances than I should have. Respectability was important to Bill Wilson. Sometimes I wonder if I were deliberately trying to sabotage it.

Why would I want to do that? I knew how much worse off I could have been in the home of someone else, but that also didn't stop me from wondering what my "other" life might have been. At the most inappropriate times I dwelled on my real mother. During class, my mind would drift to thoughts of where she was and what she was doing. When I was driving around town with nothing in particular to do, I considered various reasons why she gave me away and what I might say to her if I met her. The truth was I was mad at my birth mother and hoped she missed me. I wanted her to see what a good life I had and envy me for having it.

CHAPTER TWENTY-SEVEN

MOST OF MY LIFE I have suffered from anxiety, yet I plunged into situations that created more of it. Losing at anything was a sign of weakness, so I could not lose. In thinking about this trait that has followed me throughout my life, I must have thought I was a loser by being born out of wedlock and was determined not be a loser the rest of my life. If losing was a possibility, I hesitated putting myself in that position.

When one of the most important competitions arose within the first few weeks of high school, I didn't want to lose so I almost didn't try for it. If I didn't try out, I wouldn't lose. However, I wanted to be a high school cheerleader so badly, I had to take the chance. I would be facing students I didn't know and who didn't know me. Because there were only five on a squad, three girls from my class and two from the sophomore class were to be "elected" by popular vote among the many trying for those spots. I had not done anything to win their loyalty the way I had done in elementary school, so I was certain to lose.

Never did I consider that I might have some merit on my own without giving something to somebody first. "You go out there and do your best," Mother told me before I left for school. She gave me one of her nerve pills to calm me down.

I will never know if I was good enough to be elected or whether the sponsor, who was also part of my church, wanted me to be on the squad, but I won, along with Carol and Roberta. Judy was not yet in high school, but she would later be elected, too.

Although I would have rather been playing ball (this was many years before sanctioned teams), social status and popularity were connected to being a cheerleader, and I liked being popular. If I were popular, that meant I was liked. I needed to be liked.

During the summer after my junior year, our sponsor sent us cheerleaders to a cheer camp at a college in Tennessee. I had never been that far away from home without a chaperon and certainly had never stayed on a college campus or in a college dorm room.

Our cheers were simple and backward compared to others squads, and we were embarrassed. We had much to learn about cheering and about life outside our rural area. That experience was also our first with a panty raid.

I had heard of them but had no idea what they were. Honestly, I thought boys stormed the dorm and stole panties. So when we heard there was to be such an event, we hid our panties. I stuffed mine under the mattress. When we later heard a commotion outside the dorm and saw a gang of boys chanting to the girls who were hanging gleefully from their windows, I knew my panties weren't in danger. Instead of stealing them, guys were darting around the yard catching them as they flew out the windows. We didn't throw any of our underwear out the windows! We were as green as the grass the boys stood on.

A Girl Named Connie

The best part of the camp was after hours when we socialized with other cheerleaders and our "floor" leader, who was a college girl. She and I immediately bonded. I had a habit of finding one person not part of our group and befriending her, so this was typical behavior for me. She was stylish, graceful, and what I wanted to be when I was a young woman. For a while, we kept in contact, but then we didn't.

During all of these experiences, my parents were indifferent but not disinterested. There is a difference. Unlike many young people today who confide and share their daily events with their parents, I would never have considered doing that. Upon my return Mother probably said, "How was camp?" I likely said, "Fine." That was the way life was in my house. "Fine" as my go-to answer.

The less time I spent at home, the happier I was. The atmosphere of the house was dull for a teenage girl with her dad in his chair, her mother on the couch, and her brother on the floor watching TV. Quiet times were lonely times. As much as possible, I tried to avoid being at home. I was constantly on the go, looking for something to fill the void and the silence.

Many nights I drove to Judy's house to get her, and we would drive out to Carol and Roberta's, and then the four of us would end up at our favorite hangout (and one for every other teen in town) Gene's Freeze. Genie Wyatt and his wife Geneva opened Gene's Freeze about a mile out of town and ended up giving teenagers a place to gather.

They didn't seem to mind that we had little money. Sometimes after closing, they allowed us to play cards in one of the booths. We watched their three small children grow up and have children and grandchildren of their own. Generations of kids went to the Freeze at least twice a week and many teens took their dates there either before or after a movie. It is still a thriving business.

The four of us rode around town, hoping to find other kids to be with, but always ended up at the Freeze. When they added a skating rink to the property, we four skated at least once a week, usually on Saturday or Sunday afternoon. One of the popular skating "moments" was called "crack the whip." A line of guys held hands and whipped around the rink. The one of the end could have and often was slung against walls and nearly out doors. The goal was to hold on, but doing so was almost impossible. I wanted to be the one on the end just one time, but this wasn't for girls. I knew I could do better than some of these men did.

Later, we also gathered at what we fondly called "Depp's Dump." It wasn't a dump but a gas station, a grocery store, a restaurant, and a family dwelling combination. As soon as we discovered the new jukebox, we cleared enough space to dance, someone put in a quarter, and we shook the building with rock'n roll moves from the twist, the swim, the mashed potato, and the stroll. Ball players, cheerleaders, band members, spectators and anyone else who came along danced the night away after ballgames. Because I was such a good dancer, I never lacked for partners. Dancing, like singing, came naturally for me.

Before I could drive, Dad often waited outside Depp's for me. Bill Wilson, still in his dress shirt and tie, sitting on a stool at the counter, drinking coffee with other fathers would have been out of character. Just once I longed to see him relaxed and comfortable, but that only happened at home in his underwear.

CHAPTER TWENTY-EIGHT

As a family, we sat at the dinner table and ate together almost every night until my dad clashed so badly with my brother that James ventured away from the table and to a tray in front of the TV. It didn't seem to bother anyone that he wasn't eating with us. Often Dad treated strangers better than he did family. That is the way I saw it.

Many nights as we would be eating dinner, someone would knock on the front door. Dad would leave the table and go outside where he and a man I usually did not know engaged in a conversation. I would see Dad pull out his wallet and hand the man something.

"Who is that?" I remember asking my mother on one of those evenings.

"Somebody needing a loan," she would say. Dad, as I would learn when I was much older, was sometimes referred to as the Bank of Wilson. When a fellow didn't want to go to the local bank for a small loan, usually because he didn't want anyone to know he needed money, my dad would loan him money and charge interest. The Bank of Wilson gave my dad power.

Sometimes unsavory characters would show up, asking Dad to "go a bond" for a relative who had been locked up. Dad knew everyone in the county, so he would "go a bond" for most of these men because the crime was often being drunk in the wrong place. Those who borrowed from Dad knew not to cross him. He was almost like the Godfather without the criminal aspect.

I also learned much later that Dad was a political "go to" person. A local resident once said, "After David Dunn lost the election, he told me that if Bill Wilson had endorsed him, he would have won."Dad didn't stand in the courthouse yard waving signs or giving speeches for candidates, but he had "pull." Obviously, he had much pull because he was able to get whatever piece of paper I needed out of Frankfort (a birth certificate) to avoid my knowing I was adopted.

As for my brother, I felt sorry for him because of the way Dad criticized and corrected him, and was sometimes so demanding the child totally shut down. The problem was that they were very much alike. Dad tried to make him do what he thought he should do, but James was not as malleable as I was, and this annoyed Dad. From James's viewpoint, I was probably the favorite child, but I never felt as secure as he thought I did. I was the obedient child, which Dad appreciated.

In my brother's defense, my dad bullied him; he couldn't eat the right way, drink the right way, or speak the way Dad wanted him to do. While Dad criticized him, Mother defended him. I was an observer of this battle of wills all my brother's life, yet he lived with them, off and on, until they both died. He couldn't break away from the hold my mother had on him and the support my dad provided.

On the one hand, I wanted my brother to try harder to please Dad, which I had done all of my life. I knew the buttons not to push while James pushed them all. On the other hand, I wanted him to stand up for himself and do something with his life and be an adult. Instead, my brother antagonized my Dad knowing Mother would save him.

In the family picture, I might have been the only truly rational person. Sometimes I was even glad not to be blood-related. Even though James tried to work with Dad, the two could not sustain a working relationship. The difference in my actions and James's, however, were vast. I wanted to please because I wanted to be accepted; he didn't have to please because he knew they were not going to abandon him.

I was very eager to insert myself in my dad's life to make sure he couldn't live without me. What a ridiculous thought, but at the time I was concerned with making sure I was important to my dad.

Every night as long as I can remember not long after supper, my dad drove back over to town to "shake" his door handle to see if it was still locked and often I would tag along. *What if we get there and the glass is broken and someone has stolen our stuff?*

This door was nothing more than a glass panel with an ancient wooden frame around it; and with one swift kick, anyone could have broken in. I never understood this routine because a crook only had to watch when he came to shake the door to know when to rob him, but it was his routine and I did not question it.

Sometimes he would stay about an hour, sitting with other men on the benches and listening to stories. I never heard him tell one of his own. Once in awhile he took James, but this was just about the limit to their going anywhere together or of my dad's socializing.

The times I tagged along allowed me to have my dad to myself. If Mother or James were around, I felt in the shadow of them although I'm sure that was not reality. Dad gave me a sense of importance, and every opportunity that presented itself was a learning one for me. He would point out buildings and tell me about what was once there when he was a boy. I learned about the town from my dad, and felt his sense of pride in being born there. My mother, not being a native of Edmonton, did not have the same attachment.

Dad and I shared many experiences, but I never expected him to show up at a ballgame, a 4-H event, or anything at school. The only time my teachers saw Bill Wilson was if or when they went to the store.

As secure as he appeared to be, I later thought about my dad's lack of involvement in the community. He never served on any boards or was part of the city council, yet he was well known throughout the county.

He never showed any interest in belonging to the Lion's Club or the Rotary Club. Certainly he was not interested in the Rod & Gun Club. My dad was a loner but was seldom alone. I feared my brother would not learn to be any different.

CHAPTER TWENTY-NINE

I FELL IN LOVE in high school (Metcalfe County High School) and thought I might marry this wonderful boy, but off he went to college and left me behind. Honestly, I didn't have the first thought about getting married until I was with my girlfriends who were writing "Mrs. So and So" across their notebooks or naming their children according to the latest trendy names they had heard in the movies they watched on Saturday at the Strand. "Annette" and "Debbie" were favorites. I thought I might need to name mine, but I couldn't come up with any suitable ones.

I certainly didn't have the last name to put with the first names of my pretend children since my long-time love and I were no more. My girlfriends found great comfort in naming their future babies. I wasn't sure I wanted any.

Looking back, all of us girls claimed to be in love at least once in high school. Just as most of my classmates did, I went steady and wore my boyfriend's senior ring, wrapped in angora thread, on my finger, or put it on a chain and wore it around my neck. Before going steady, a boy taking me home from a ballgame or sitting with me in the gym before school was the beginning of a "relationship."

One of the most romantic signs of a budding relationship was when a boy gave a girl something of his to "hold" while he was playing basketball or football. I can remember vividly keeping my boyfriend's watch while he played ball. I tucked it under the sleeve of my cheerleading sweater and every time I clapped my hands or jumped, that heavy watch smacked me.

Suffering a broken heart is "romantic," so I suffered a long time when mine was broken. I listened to sad songs on the radio and looked across the classroom or gym to see if he were looking at me. When he sat with someone else, I thought I would die.

Young people get some bit of reward in wallowing in lost love, and I was no different. Then when the boy started dating a different girl, all of my friends "hated" her while I cried tears of rejection. No matter where life takes us, we always remember our high school "loves." As far as my "loves," we are all close friends today.

I didn't seriously date again until I was in college. I had rather been with my friends during my senior year.

When we were together, we had so much fun that in our later years we thought we should still have that much fun and never stopped trying to capture it.

One of those unforgettable times happened on a spring night my senior year. "Let's paint the Class of "64" on the water tower," someone suggested. No other class had attempted this feat, and there was a reason for that. It was dangerous. We were going to set a trend that many classes would follow, but we had no idea we would be breaking the law.

A Girl Named Connie

The tower was located on Water Tank Hill directly off the square, visible for miles in every direction. There were five of us in all with only one boy in the group. He was the same person with whom I had danced at the "Five O'clock Hop."

I don't remember where we got our supplies, but we ended up with red paint and some stiff paint brushes. Donnie insisted on being the first one up the ladder, so I followed with a can of paint and a brush in one hand, holding onto the rung of the metal steps with the other. Another of our friends followed me with a second brush. We were slowly moving, one behind the other, up this tower in the late night seclusion of the town's eye. This tower was much taller than I calculated when looking at it from the ground, and the higher I climbed, the farther away Roberta and Carol appeared. "We'll wait right down here for you," they said. Neither was as daring as I.

While Roberta was crying because she thought we were going to fall to our deaths and Carol was trying to console her, the three of us slowly moved ahead.

Half way up the ladder Donnie froze. He locked up, frozen like a stick. He couldn't even move his eyes or lips. For a minute I didn't know what was wrong. Why had he stopped? Then I realized he was in the middle of a panic attack.

"You have got to go up, or you've got to come down," I ordered because this was no time to lose control. I had felt panic and knew it could lead to a feeling of fainting. If he passed out, what would happen to Karen and me?

If he had let go of the railing, we would have fallen behind him like dominoes. If he couldn't go up, how were we going to get around him? What if I have a panic attack, too? *Keep calm, keep calm.*

Within seconds, as if his voice might cause him to lose his grip, he whispered, "Go around me."

"How are we going around you?" I yelled as if to say *"What's wrong with you. Get up those steps."*

"I can't move. You have to go around me." He stood to one side giving us just enough room to edge around, but it was a tight squeeze. Then he backed down the steps and stood with Roberta and Carol. We never let him forget this moment! (He later volunteered to serve in Vietnam.)

Up we went until we reached the top. "Man, this is great!" I said admiring the view very few had ever seen. Then we opened the paint cans.

"I can't reach high enough," Karen said as she stretched as high as she could to begin the first word. If we were going to do this, we wanted to town to see. Soon we realized that neither of us was tall enough, so we strategized.

"Can you stand on this railing?" I asked her. I knew she was as daring as I, but the thin railing that circled the tank was not meant for anything except protection for the water department crew. Standing on it could have been a death-defying moment, but we didn't think about how fragile the rail was until much later.

"I'll give it a try," she said, and before long she was standing on that thin railing, leaning toward the belly of the tank.

Dripping red paint in the night, she printed the word "Senior" and I painted "Class of "64" under it. When we finished, I looked down and saw the town night watchman staring up at us. Not thinking about the trouble I might be in with the law, I said, "Hi, Mr. Williams; it's just us," reassuring him that nothing was going on.

"Who are you?" he yelled back. His tone made me a little nervous.

"Connie Wilson." How dumb was I? The fact we were defacing public property never occurred to me.

"COME DOWN!" he ordered with his neck craned so far he could have fallen backward.

A Girl Named Connie

"We're on our way!" I didn't realize he was mad. He didn't look mad. However, his voice should have been a clue.

"Do you all know how dangerous that was?" he said when we were on the ground facing him.

While he was talking, I was admiring our work. Finally, he told us to get out of there and never do anything like this again. Since I had supplied him with a name to go with my face, I should have known he would go back to the station and call my dad.

When I got home, Dad was waiting. I could see his shadow through the picture window. This was a bad sign. I walked in the door and he said from the darkness of the room, "Where have you been?"

"Oh, a bunch of us have been riding around like we always do." That wasn't a lie exactly.

"Are you sure that's all you've being doing?"

"What do you mean?" I had a pretty good idea what he meant but thought playing dumb might be a good start for what was coming.

"Well, I got a phone call from Mr. Williams, who said that you said "Hi" to him while you were standing on top of the water tower."

I was going to try to make him see the humor in our deed. "Dad, you're going to love what we did. Wait 'til you see it in the morning."

"Do you know you could have gotten killed?"

"No, not really. We were very careful." I didn't know what else to say.

"Don't ever do anything like that again." He was not laughing.

"OK, we won't." That wouldn't be entirely the truth, but I would try for him not to know anything else I did. Mother had been listening from the other room because when I passed to go to bed she said, "Now, get some sleep."

The next day when the entire town, so I assumed, was looking up at the tower, Dad smiled with a little pride for the courage of his daughter.

However, we never told anyone else about doing this, and the parents of the others involved never knew until much later.

Soon students spread the word about what they had seen on their way through town that morning. Seniors were thrilled to be the first class with "Seniors Class of '64" on the tower. The editor of our local newspaper, *The Edmonton Herald*, wrote a front-page feature story on the painting of the tower. He couldn't mention names because no one except the night watchman and my dad knew.

Of course, the townspeople loved the spirit of it all, and each year for a long time after we graduated, other classes followed suit until those "class of" mottos went from one side to the other. It is a shame the city finally painted over them and now the tower doesn't exist at all. Other classes might have followed, but we always knew we were the first, and I always knew that I made it to the top.

A Girl Named Connie

Carol Perkins

Mother and Dad looking very stylish. In the picture with Dad, I remember thinking that I didn't want my picture made anymore, so I moved to the background.

I was around eight-years-old when this was taken.

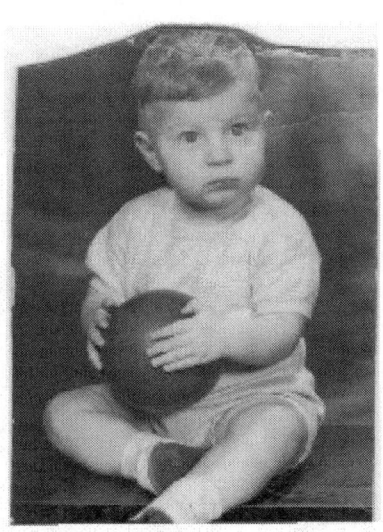

My baby brother

A Girl Named Connie

Dad was in his thirties and Mother in her late twenties when they brought me to Edmonton. I was six weeks old.

My dad's mother, Pampy Wilson, terrified most of the community with her abrupt tone, but she was loving and kind to me. I carried my purse everywhere I went.

Carol Perkins

My cousin was my teacher, and she had no problem paddling me. I am in the "E" sweater. Carol is third from the right on the top row with the dark hair and bangs. Roberta is on the bottom row fourth from the right.

Made when I was around twelve. This would be during the year I learned the truth about myself.

My eighth grade graduation picture.

High school graduation picture

A Girl Named Connie

My high school basketball team, the Metcalfe County Hornets, won our district tourney. This was taken after the trophy presentation.

Homecoming candidate my sophmore year. Escorted by Jerry Irvin

I was part of homecoming court when I was in the second grade. Escorted by Jimmy Shives.

Wilson's Dry Goods in its later years.

Cloteel Wilson, Bill Wilson, Dorothy Franklin, Aunt Mag Isenburg and Frances Pemberton

Even after I left home to teach in Louisville, I came home every Christmas Eve to work alongside Dad in the store.

Mother and Dad celebrate their 60th wedding anniversary.

Mother and Dad behind the counter at the store.

Mother and Aunt Hazel at my aunt's house in Smith Grove, Kentucky.

At Aunt Hazel's birthday party when she turned 93.

Aunt Hazel's daughters
Top row left to right: Betty, Jewel Frances (Fran), Wanda
Front row: Phyllis and Pat

Carol Perkins

On one of our cruises with my "hometown" girls.

Judy, Connie, Carol and Roberta. The last picture the four of us had made together.

Celebrating a birthday!

Peggy Hourigan

Brenda, Connie and Sharon

CHAPTER THIRTY

THE SCIENCE TEACHER who excused me from the family tree assignment was also my Beta Club sponsor and took me under her advisory wings when it came to singing. She could have been a judge on American Idol.

She wasn't an overly enthusiastic lover of science, but she was beyond passionate when it came to talent; and the Beta Club, much like the National Honor Society in other states, held an annual Beta Convention in Louisville each year.

We stayed, along with thousands of other students, in a hotel downtown near Fourth Street. Our sponsors were so competitive that not winning the talent show would have crushed them. Each year they chose a theme and then students interpreted it by singing, dancing, or being in a skit. The ending was always patriotic with a soldier returning from battle, which tugged at the heart of the judges. By the time we were seniors, we had won so many times that the National Beta Journal featured our club in one of their editions. I sang "Blues in the Night" my senior year.

After we had won the talent show our last year, four of us girls who were sharing a room decided to celebrate, and the only way we knew to do this was with champagne. We weren't drinkers, but we knew that fancy people celebrated with champagne. We heard a rumor that some of the guys were going to a liquor store down the street from the hotel, so we put in our order.

Three bottles of champagne appeared within thirty minutes, and we locked ourselves behind closed doors and drank one bottle that night and the other two the next day. One bottle among three girls would not normally faze a person who was used to drinking, but we weren't. We knew the consequences but thought we were invincible.

Because we were not drinkers, it did not take long to feel a buzz. Students were free that next day to walk around the city, so no one missed us when we spent most of the day in the room. No one, that is, until my sponsor came looking for me because I was singing at the awards banquet that night. From among all students at the convention, I had been selected for that honor. My mother drove up for the dinner to hear me sing. She was going to surprise me. It could have been the worst surprise of her life.

By early afternoon, my sponsor was nervous because she hadn't seen me all day and wanted to make sure I was ready for the night. I heard banging on the door but never considered it might be her.

Not only was I not ready for the night, I was drunk NOT ready for the night. "What have you all been drinking?" she yelled when she came into our room and with one look knew I was tipsy.

Within seconds, she threw me into the shower and yelled, "You better get yourself straightened up. Your mother is here." The principal could have expelled me for this, but Mother would have killed me.

A Girl Named Connie

Not only did I feel like hell, but I also looked the same. By the time the dinner arrived, I had shaken off much of my hangover and told Fanny, who was playing for me, to keep going no matter what I was singing. I wasn't sure I could remember the words to "I think that I shall never see, a poem as lovely as a tree...."

After I finished the song in better form than I might have, one of the dignitaries approached me and said, "Your song was lovely, but I think you got the third verse mixed up with the second verse." I smiled, but what I wanted to say was I was lucky to get any of it right.

"I know I messed up but I kept on going," I said. As if that made a difference.

He replied, "I admire that in you. A lot of young people might have stopped, but you didn't." He wouldn't have admired me if he had known I was suffering from my first hangover.

Carol, Roberta and I did no more drinking in high school. The fourth girl did not drink at all; she was the lookout. That one drinking binge taught us a lesson. Soon this antic would be forgotten and we were grateful our sponsor did not report us to the principal or our parents. She didn't need to make life any more miserable than the worry about what my mother might have done. Then something much worse than we had done happened, but it didn't just happen to us. It happened to our nation.

In November of 1963, the fall of my senior year, John F. Kennedy was assassinated, and I watched as Americans grieved as deeply as if a relative had died. I was in class when I heard the crackly sound of the intercom pop on. At first, I thought the principal might be spying on the class.

Then came the voice of Walter Cronkite. With no preface from the principal, Mr. Cronkite revealed that someone had shot our president. Gasps went up from my classmates as we listened for details. Our teacher was stunned. On September 11, 2001, I would be in a classroom as a teacher when the Twin Towers were hit and had much the same feeling as I did when the news came to us students about President Kennedy.

Within a very short time, the words we didn't expect to hear came once again. Once at home and watching the recap of that moment, I would take note of Mr. Cronkite's demeanor as he took off his glasses and wiped his eyes. Our president was dead and nothing would be normal for a long time in America.

Of all world events that have unfolded during my lifetime, nothing touched me quite like this tragedy. Kennedy was a hero to us young people and Johnson was not. We were going to be left with this "foster" father of America. I didn't want him and I'm not sure who did. However, he was sworn in as we watched from our TV's in the quietness of our homes, and we were now in the hands of a different personality and a man who would keep us involved in the Vietnam War that killed many young men.

It was during this time that I began to think about my country. Registering to vote was almost equal to getting my driver's license. I was a liberal when I didn't know what a liberal was, which was a direct contradiction to some of the conservative choices I made in the future.

I also thought about my desire to be a nurse and how I might use this career in the military, serving my country. I could be an Army nurse. There was one nursing school above all others in Kentucky as far as rank and to be admitted to that program as akin to being admitted to West Point, in my opinion. Being accepted, of course, depended having good grades but primarily on passing the entrance exam. Once again, as I had done with my driver's permit test, I thought I knew enough to pass the test without studying. I thought my classes in biology and general science would serve me well.

A Girl Named Connie

Coming from a small school has its social advantages, but not necessarily its academic ones. I had taken what the school offered as far as science classes, but a semester of chemistry, one year of biology, and general science did not prepare me for the rigors of this test.

I traveled to Louisville and to the college campus where administrators gave the test. I sat at a table surrounded by young women from all over the state, and many from large high schools where cheerleading was second to academics, I felt out of my league. As I read the questions, my hopes sank. I knew only about half of the answers and guessed at the rest. Guessing wasn't going to get me into this school.

When I left the rest of the girls, I knew I would not see them again. *If someone would let me try. If I could just be given a chance; just a semester I could show them I can do this!* It was on my way down the long road to Edmonton that I decided that I would have to find another career. If I could not be an RN, I would not be a nurse at all.

What was I going to tell my parents? My friends? As usual, I said nothing until I had to and then I honestly announced, "I didn't pass

CHAPTER THIRTY-ONE

JUST AS HAD ALWAYS been my nature, I didn't wallow in my failure, but focused on going to college and doing something else. At the time my high school days were ending, I wasn't sure what that "something else" was going to be. Because I didn't pass that test, I worried that I might not be a good student in college. What if I flunked out? What would my parents think? What genes might keep me from learning well enough to get a degree? I doubted my ability for a long time. I had to turn my future over to God.

Having taught a Sunday school class for teenagers since I was barely one myself, my devotion to the church was strong. I never missed a Bible school session during the summer not only at my church, but also at other town churches. All of us kids were expected to go from one Bible School to another one. I don't know who expected it, but we thought we were supposed to attend, and our parents took us.

A certain confidence and a sense of acceptance when I was teaching Sunday school and singing in the choir assured me that my church was the one place where I found personal peace and acceptance. I might not know my true identity, but God did. Only He knew the personal sadness and loneliness I had felt for so many years, and every night I prayed, *"Help me let it go."*

Lesson after lesson about loving oneself and pleasing God led me to a sudden wave of happiness one night at a revival, and I felt an immediate urgency to serve God in a more profound way. I was caught up in the moment. Many young people get caught up in revival moments.

A professor at a religious based college not far from Edmonton held a revival in the spring of my senior year and for some reason singled me out one night as the crowd was leaving. "Have you ever been to Campbellsville College?" he asked.

I had been on the campus with our band, but I had never toured it. He spoke with me about the possibility of my attending college there. "I think it would be a good fit for you." Why he thought I would fit in there might have had something to do with what my preacher had told him about my service to the church. I later realized that churches often steer their members to colleges of the same faith. That was the workings of the system. He didn't know me well enough to make a judgment about where I might fit, but my head swelled from his attention.

I thought about what he had suggested and was impressed that he had singled me out. He was paying special attention to me, so that equated to my being special. I craved attention and recognition. By the last night of the revival, I felt God was leading me up the road about thirty miles to this college. If God were calling me there, I didn't need to know anything but that. I wanted to think God was leading me when actually I was leading myself.

During the alter call, I asked to speak to the packed house. I hate to admit that I knew what I was going to say would make me the center of attention that night, but I did. I looked at the congregation and avoided my mother's eyes.

"I want to confess tonight that I feel God has spoken to me, and He wants me to be a missionary." While this might have been a good thing in some families, my mother was mortified. Never had I mentioned anything to her or my dad about doing missionary work. I was going to be a nurse and when that didn't work out for me, I was going to be something else. A missionary had never been a consideration.

I remember my mother's face; she almost choked. "If I can arrange it, I will attend Campbellsville College where I can prepare for this work." The congregation gathered to congratulate me on such a noble decision, as I knew they would. Reveling in their attention, I had lost sight of my mother until I spotted her standing at the back of the church against a doorframe with a look of dismay I had seen many times. It was a look of "Have you lost your mind?"

On the ride home, she did not speak. With each mile of silence behind me, I knew it would not last. She would not be silent very long. When we got home, she was visibly upset. "When did you make THIS decision?" she asked with my dad sitting in his chair confused about why my mother was so mad.

"A few nights ago."

"Do you have any idea what a missionary does? How she lives?" I felt her anger.

I didn't know one thing about being a missionary except it sounded like a self-sacrificing thing to do. I also didn't think about the many other ways of serving God without going to a foreign country with no modern conveniences or indoor plumbing. Not only did I not know the duties of a missionary, I had never met one. Imagine my surprise when I learned that not all mission work requires going overseas. Being a missionary was my road to sainthood.

"Not really, but I think God is speaking to me." She did not believe that God was speaking to me.

A Girl Named Connie

Dad didn't say a word, but I knew Mother would tell him every detail. He let her handle this just as he did most things. This time, however, she wouldn't cuss, rant or go into a fit of anger that she could do so well; this time she probably thought that if God were inspiring me, she didn't want to mess with Him. Seeing her disappointment, however, was unsettling.

My parents had expected that I would attend one of the universities, along with my friends, but I was dead set on this small college if they would finance it. After all, God was calling me, so how could they refuse God? For the first time, I was asking for more money than they would have had to pay if I had gone where Carol and Roberta were going, but I wanted no distractions by sororities and parties and the evils in the world. How naïve was I?

My decision to do mission work was not only a shock to my parents, but also to my friends. "Have you really been called to be a missionary?" Carol asked. Honestly, they thought I had lost my mind; this was not the girl with whom they had been to school for twelve years. This was not the dancer and the singer and the person who led the pack when danger arose like a warrior in "Chariots of Fire." Although they didn't say so, they thought some invisible force must have possessed me. They couldn't see me foregoing my standard of living for a life of poverty. That's all we knew about mission work.

In a few months, we would be graduating, and I would be leaving Carol and Roberta for the first time in eighteen years. Judy would have one more year in high school before joining them at Eastern Kentucky University. I was on track to go to Campbellsville.

As the last month of school approached, my classmates were looking to the future. Some of the boys planned to join the Army. Guy chose the Navy. Several of the girls planned to marry guys from the class ahead of us, set up housekeeping and have children by the time they were twenty. A few enrolled in beauty colleges and became noted stylists. Many planned to be teachers and others something in the medical field. Many of the guys turned home to their fathers' farms where they remained. Our interests were as varied as our personalities.

My high school days were the best ones of my life. I would not know how wonderful those days were until they were gone, or how much I would miss my friends until I was without them. Even though I was different, they never made me feel that way. Outsiders took on that role.

The day after graduation my mother presented me a jewelry box. Inside was a gorgeous Kentucky cluster diamond ring. I had always admired my father's Kentucky cluster, which he wore every day, and it was the only thing I wanted from him when the time came. I had made this well known to both my parents. This was not my dad's ring.

They intended, I realized, to give my dad's ring to my brother. It was rightfully his, so I wore my consolation prize. This was my graduation gift.

During the summer before college Carol, Roberta, Judy and I were offered jobs as aids for a new program called Head Start, intended to give incoming first graders a jumpstart. It was not limited to any particular income or educational level, so every kid in the county attended.

Being an aid for a group of five and six-year-olds and working, side by side, with a seasoned teacher was the worst job I ever had. First of all, I knew nothing about children and didn't want to learn. Having a motherly instinct was missing from my genetic make up. They didn't bond with me and I didn't care. Children, like horses, know when a person fears them, and I feared kids because they were unpredictable and needy. I managed to hide my true feelings in order to get through the day and earn a paycheck. I had spent eighteen years acting one way and feeling another, so doing this came easily. I had been a fake in so many aspects of my life that faking my caring for these kids was not difficult.

Head Start was at the same elementary school where I had gone only four years before. The white-sided buildings were at least fifty years old by then and in much need of repair. The same wooden tables and chairs lined the walls where I had sat twelve years before. The smell of small sweaty bodies from those years lingered. Covering up that smell was impossible.

The four of us worked for different teachers and saw each other at recess, during lunch, and nap time, which was in the "big building" gym. What we had thought would be a fun job, turned out to be the hardest work I have ever done. Not physically, but mentally and emotionally.

Basically, my task was to assist the students in "my" room with individual skills. When Sally could not pick out a B from a D, I wanted to shout, "Can't you see the difference?" I know that sounds insensitive, but I had no patience and never developed any with small children. A therapist might be able to tell me why.

The teachers turned recess over to the four of us. I can understand why. They were exhausted and needed a break. We were to monitor the playground and keep kids from hurting each other or themselves. That did not include keeping us from being kicked, head butted, scratched, or sassed. Judy, among the four of us, had the most patience, and these kids loved her. "Sit by me," they would request of her at lunch. I was afraid one of them would *want* to sit by me.

"Push me higher," they would yell as she pretended to use all her strength to toss them through the air. One time a kid asked me to push her higher, and when I did, she flew out of the swing. I thought I had killed her, but she brushed herself off while I pulled the gravel out of her arms. She kept her mouth shut, and the teacher never knew.

The worst incident happened on the merry-go-round. One little girl was a whiner. "I don't want to slide; I don't want to play with them." I have never liked a whiner.

Although her complaining annoyed me, Judy was going to conquer her. "Come with me and we'll ride the merry-go-round. You can sit on my lap." Judy was much too happy and I could not begin to fake that much happiness.

That satisfied the girl for three or four spins and then she started crying. Judy yelled at me from the ride, and when she had my attention, she mouthed the words, "Catch her." Not calculating that when a child is thrown from a moving object to a stationary object, it will land somewhere else, little Sally hit the ground a few feet away from me. Wriggling in the dirt and gravel, she finally lifted her head and proceeded to have the worst outburst of hysteria I have ever witnessed.

I dashed to her while Judy dragged her foot in the dust to stop the ride. We knew for sure we would both be fired, but by giving Sally such attention, she rallied in her injuries and wore them proudly. The teacher assumed she had fallen. No, she had been thrown without the least consideration of the laws of physics. If parents had known about lawsuits the way they do now, Judy and I would have been sued.

Naptime was my favorite time of day. Each child was supposed to bring a blanket, but naturally all of them didn't, so teachers spread towels out on the hard gym floor to make mats for them. We aids were to lie down beside those who wouldn't be quiet and try to get them to shut their eyes.

"If they will just be quiet and shut their eyes, they will go to sleep," my teacher said. She was wrong! Some of those fellows never closed one eye, but I fell asleep every day. I was so tired I could not keep my eyes open, and the hardness of the gym floor did not keep me from wishing I could stay the

A Girl Named Connie

rest of the day in the fetal position. Often, a kid had to wake me up to go back to class.

Finally, this six weeks' program ended and reaffirmed what I had always known: I would never teach small children, and I would never be a parent.

After that program, I planned to concentrate on college preparations, but then another opportunity came along that could have changed the direction of my life.

I was being recognized more often for my singing ability. So much so that a very prominent attorney in town, Tom Emberton (who would later run for governor) asked me to visit with him and his wife, Julia. They wanted to talk to me about something. I had no clue what to expect but assumed it had something to do with my college ambition. We went to the same church.

However, they wanted to discuss something entirely different.

When we met at their lovely home, Mrs. Emberton told me about her brother Jan Cruthfield, a songwriter in Nashville and with whom she had discussed my possible singing career. I was stunned. I never thought about having a singing career.

*Crutchfield is credited with establishing MCA Music Publishing as a major publishing house, and signing and working with writers such as Dave Loggins, Don Schlitz, Gary Burr, Rob Crosby and Mark Nesler. During his 25-year career at MCA, Crutchfield left to serve as Executive Vice President/General Manager of Capitol Records for four years. He then returned to MCA Music Publishing for a three-year period as president of its Nashville division.[2] Crutchfield has served as National Trustee for The National Academy of Recording Arts and Sciences (NARAS), and has served on the board of directors of the Nashville chapter of NARAS, the Country Music Association, and the Gospel Music Association.

I knew her brother was famous in the music industry, but I never considered being able to work with him or even meet him. I was elated that she was taking so much interest in me. She not only arranged a meeting with him, but they volunteered to take me to Nashville.

After telling Mother and Dad about this potential meeting in Nashville, they suggested that I work up a few songs with Fanny and ask her to accompany me, which I did.

When we arrived on Music Row, I knew I was in the big leagues. I might not have known much about music, but I did know a little about presentation. So when Mr. Cruthfield, a very kind gentleman, asked me if I would like to sing for him, I took on the persona of a star by combining moves of Brenda Lee and Patsy Cine. He made a demo and the experience of being in a sound studio with the possibility of being a famous singer was beyond my grasp. How would I describe this to my mother and dad? The equipment, the padded walls, and the acoustics changed the quality of my voice to a sound I almost didn't recognize. This was one of those moments a person always remembers, even if the outcome isn't necessarily positive.

"You have a very good voice, Connie," he said, "but you need more experience. I suggest you sing wherever you can find an audience, work on your range and your voice control, and in a few years, we'll try this again." He was not brushing me off; he was sincere.

Before arriving I had imagined a contract lying in front of me with a promise that I was going to be the next star, but I was not delusional. I wasn't in the right league yet; but I was going to take his advice and every chance I had to sing and improve, I would take it and eventually return to Music Row. An opportunity landed in my lap.

Fanny played at various restaurants in the area. She was a showman. One of these was at a swanky place in Bowling Green called the Manhattan Towers. On our way home from Nashville, Fanny said, "If you might like to go with me to the Towers and maybe sing a few songs, I think I can arrange it."

Having heard Mr. Cruthfield's suggestion, Fanny was going to help me gain experience. My parents were hesitant about the late hours because she usually played until midnight, but they were proud that I might be headed for stardom.

The next time she was to play, I went with her so we could talk to the manager and, hopefully, audition. "I'll give you a chance to sing few songs, but I don't know if this will work or not because I've never had a singer before," he said after I sang a couple of Patsy Cline hits.

I had sung mainly in churches and for school events and a few political rallies, but never in a restaurant or a bar.

The piano sat on a small stage with a dance floor in front, surrounded by tables covered with white tablecloths. In front of this piano was a microphone stand. When I began to sing, I assumed customers would politely listen, but instead what I heard were the clanging of silverware, chairs scraping across the floor, laughter, and constant talking just above a whisper. Even though they applauded after each song, this was just a courteous reaction.

After three numbers, I sat beside Fanny in a folding chair while she finished her set. Not having a captive audience troubled me and naturally hurt my feelings; but most of all, I was embarrassed. I was glad my parents had stayed at home.

"You did just fine. Those people were listening, but they just weren't looking at you," Fanny said. "They came to have dinner, and you are just a bonus. Don't let it get you down."

I went back on the following Friday night with a brighter outlook. *Tonight they will listen.* Once again I sang my selections and once again, the patrons were rude. I might as well have been singing from the parking lot.

Just as I was about to wind down, a very distinguished looking man stumbled up to the stage and requested a song. "I will be glad to sing it if I know it."

He wanted me to sing "Misty."

"I'm so sorry, but I don't know the words." He cut loose with a string of curse words directed at me that caused Fanny to stop playing. It enabled the entire room to hear him making an even bigger fool of himself. He called me a "stupid bitch" and "untalented" and a host of other derogatory names. The owner finally moved him away from the stage and I found my way to the bathroom. If this was what singing in public was like, I was finished. Before this experience, I thought I could sing well. Now I wasn't sure. It was one thing to sing for people who knew me, but quite another to sing for strangers.

If this practice was what I needed to be a star, I was not interested. My short-lived singing career ended at the Manhatten Towers in 1964. The sacrifices required to be a singer would have included performing in unsavory places. I had seen very few drunks, had never been cursed except by my mother when she was mad, and certainly had never performed in front of inattentive adults who poured wine like water into their glasses. I was young and naïve about the world outside of Metcalfe County.

If I had been a little older, I might have dealt with the environment more maturely, but I was just a teenager and still obsessed with a fear of failure. I feared that if I continued pursuing a music career, I would likely fail. So rather than take that chance, I made excuses for not trying, even though I might have been successful if I had not taken myself out of the game.

I graduated from high school and throughout my college days continued to sing but sometime after that, I stopped. I can't blame it on losing my voice because I didn't. Eventually, I lost my desire to sing. Maybe I was afraid it would let me down as it had done those nights in front of strangers. "Get rid

A Girl Named Connie

of it and it can't abandon you." This was my one true talent, and I abandoned it. Then it abandoned me.

CHAPTER THIRTY-TWO

BY SEPTEMBER, I was ready for college, and my parents moved my possessions, including a new wardrobe, into my dorm. On the outside, this building resembled a homeless shelter with cracked molding around the windows and broken concrete steps. I could feel my mother's disapproval, but hoped she didn't share it.

I located my assigned room, and when I opened the door, I met my roommate for the first time. She wore a long black dress and was sitting passively in a rocking chair, looking out the only window. "I think we are supposed to be roommates," I said as a way to introduce myself.

"I don't want a roommate." She kept rocking and staring outside.

"Well, I guess I don't either."

I backed out of the room and searched for the "dorm mother" with my mother at my heels. "But we don't have an empty room," the dorm mother insisted. Mother waited for me to say something.

A Girl Named Connie

Luckily one of the senior counselors overheard this conversation and offered to let me room with her that first year. Dorm counselors were usually given private rooms as part of their stipend.

Chelsea saved me. Several years later I would be a bridesmaid in her wedding. As for the rocking chair girl, I never saw her on campus, so I assumed she didn't last. She was the first of many strange people I would encounter outside the bubble of my small Kentucky town.

When my mother saw the dorm and especially my room, she twisted and turned with nerves and once outside, lit a cigarette. "You weren't raised like this, and you are not staying in this dump."

Plaster hung from the ceiling and paint chips lay on the floor. After a lengthy debate about the horrible conditions of this dorm and how I wasn't brought up to stay in such filth, she relented. "Mother, just give this a chance. I need to do this. Dorms all look rundown."

"Well, if you see you can't stand it, you come home and go to Western." I promised I would. She didn't realize that freshmen were traditionally housed in the oldest dorms. She did not understand the ways of a college because she had never been inside a dorm room or on a college campus other than to drive by one.

Within a week or so I settled into my schedule and began to meet a few people but was a little depressed and lonely. While back home my social life was never at a standstill, college life was slow paced. I had not expected to be underwhelmed. After a few weeks of classes, I asked a fellow student, "When will there be a dance?" I assumed there would be a campus dance for new students to mix and mingle.

"Are you kidding? No dances are allowed here." She was shocked that I would think such a sinful act was possible on this campus. That was the first time I realized how strict this school was going to be. I was a Baptist, but my church did not frown on dancing or I would have known about it.

During my first year, I became very involved in several campus Bible groups. After all, I had chosen this college to serve God. Other students called these kids "The God Squad."

I sang at Vespers (Bible studies) and became very reverent (which fit my overall plan to serve God) and made friends with like minds. As a matter of fact, three of us began our mission work almost immediately. I sang, another played the piano, and the only guy preached. All we needed was a tent!

On weekends we traveled to small communities in Eastern Kentucky. According to administrators and ministers in the area, those were towns that needed to hear the word, so we three volunteered before anyone else had a chance. We couldn't wait!

While in the mountains, we stayed in homes of coal miners. My mother would have been shocked at some of the conditions if she had known. She would have also been disappointed that all the new clothes, with matching accessories, were hanging in my closet back at my dorm. This was not the place to show advantages if I wanted to be a messenger.

I had never been in the Eastern part of the state or seen a coal miner except on television. In one home, a man that I assumed was the father came in that first night and I thought he was African American. He greeted us kindly and disappeared into another room. In a few minutes, this same man reappeared, but this time, he was white. I couldn't believe this was the same person.

I said, "Are you the man who just came through this room?"

"Yes, I'm the same man." He knew what I was thinking.

"I thought you were a black man."

A Girl Named Connie

He laughed. "I guess you could say I was!" No wonder so many died from black lung.

These small town churches embraced us and fulfilled my desire to spread the word, which God had called me to do, but I went a little overboard and became what most would call a religious zealot. I couldn't talk to anyone, including my parents and my friends, without getting on my stump about sin, salvation, the end of time, and hell. I dressed simply and wore little make-up. My adventurous spirit was sitting on empty. No wonder by the end of my freshman year most of my high school friends avoided me during Thanksgiving and Christmas vacations.

My social life no longer involved immature antics and spontaneous activities with friends. The college students to whom I migrated were lackluster; and a part of me missed the days of painting the water tower or driving around town with my car full of teenagers.

All classes were geared toward the Bible, no matter what a student chose as a major, so I submerged myself in religious fervor as I prepared for a degree in biology. I knew exactly how the new Connie was supposed to act based observing others who were part of the religious sect on campus. Once again, I put on an act and was good at it. I wasn't Connie at all. Even my parents feared I was being brainwashed.

In addition to my religious obligations, I wanted to play sports. The two did not mesh on this campus, but the need to play was like a magnet. Finally, I was in a setting where women could play sports. I had never played on a team so I didn't know if I had the talent, but I was not lacking in desire.

Between my all-consuming hours of devotion and weekend missionary work, I found time to play pick up games of basketball, volleyball, and tennis and soon was recruited by coaches. Making all of these teams was one of the highlights of my life.

The time required for these activities limited my mission trips (which did not please my traveling partners) and at first I felt I could do both adequately, but I couldn't.

I surprised myself with my tennis ability because I had never held a racket. Edmonton had no tennis courts and no one I knew played. Gradually, I was noticed on campus for sports more than missionary work.

At the end of that year, I placed second in the OVC (Ohio Valley Conference) in tennis. During this time, I also made two new friends on the basketball team who were not like my God Squad friends. These girls liked to party and drink, which were both grounds for expulsion. At that time, I was much too religious to drink, but my new friends were free spirits. I was torn between my loyalty to God and my desire to be with my teammates living on the fringe of trouble. I had forgotten what it was like to laugh and hang out with people who didn't think the world was ending. However, in befriending the new girls, my first friends on campus were not happy with me and later I would learn that the professors were not either.

One of the girls in my dorm kept liquor in her room; so when I heard there was going to be a raid, I searched for her. Keep in mind this was around 1965 at a Baptist college.

When I couldn't find Lucy to warn her, I went to her room, found the liquor, and started to pour it out the window. Within minutes, she burst through the door yelling, "What in the hell are you doing?" I was hanging out the window with a bottle turned toward the ground. I don't know if she saw the whiskey streaming out or someone told her, but she was not happy.

"Get over here and help me," I said. "They're coming."

"Who's coming?"

"The Dean of Women and who knows who else is on the way."

A Girl Named Connie

By the time they arrived, we had poured out four or five bottles of whiskey and I stashed the empty bottles in a paper bag, slipped outside and threw them into a dumpster. I did not fear being stopped because no one would suspect me of drinking. Meanwhile, my friend escaped expulsion and was forever indebted.

I had never known a person like Lucy. She was tall, strong, and rough around the edges, yet she was funny and loyal. How she ended up in this college I never knew. Maybe it was a punishment. Lucy was from a wealthy family, but no one would have ever suspected. She certainly was not lavish.

By then I was spending less and less time with the God Squad and more and more with the members of my basketball team. The God Squad accused me of turning my back on them. It took me two years, but I realized that those with whom I was associating were very narrow-minded and judgmental and I had become one of them. The turning point of disassociation came when several of them staged an "intervention."

"Connie, I don't think you realize exactly the kind of people you are with now. They drink and break curfew and some of these girls are gay." How did they know they were gay? Was this an assumption they applied to all female athletes? Labels.

My drinking friends were not acceptable, and I should stay away from them. That was their summation. I wanted to lash out, but instead, I stood and calmly said, "Jesus ate with the Publicans and sinners. If you stay in your little group, how are you going to reach the rest of the world?" I was now preaching to the preachers.

From that point on, they snubbed me. I was an outcast and didn't know how to handle it. This was my first social rejection. It would not be the last.

There were no more invitations to minister to the families in Eastern Kentucky; and without notice, I was no longer a member of the God Squad.

Finally, after months of soul searching and praying for guidance, I concluded that He was happy with me as I was and there were many avenues to spread God's love. I did not totally regret my decision to attend Campbellsville because of participating in sports. However, my mission work ended. I had come to this school for a chance to do good work and to be a girl without a label. Both became impossible.

In the meantime, those who were considered the elite of the campus religious world shunned me. Even though I was ignored, I continued to attend Vespers. I had not turned my back on Jesus; I had turned my back on them. They became invisible to me just as Lisa had years ago.

Once a week these student Bible studies were held in an auditorium, and for three years I seldom missed a meeting. However, by the time I was a senior, I had become so fed up with their prejudices and their condemnation of others whose lifestyles and cultures were different that I couldn't tolerate their hypocrisy. Where the power to do this came from, I'm not sure, but I made my way to the stage and asked to speak.

I took the microphone from a skeptical professor leading the Vespers that night and in front of both adults and students spoke these words: "If all the people in heaven are like you, I don't want to go." I surveyed the group for a few minutes, wanting to give them details of how I felt, but I turned away and walked out. That was my last Vesper service. I was soon to be a junior.

While I was having my meltdown on campus, Mammaw was in the hospital. My mother called, "Connie, Mammaw is having her leg removed tomorrow." I had no idea she was in such a shape, even though diabetes had invaded her body years ago.

A Girl Named Connie

"I'm leaving now so I can be there with you all in the morning."

The next morning I left my house early for the hospital, so I could be with her. "Don't worry. Everything is going to be ok, and we will take care of you," I said as I held her hand. I had never heard those words from anybody.

That seemed to comfort her. Once again, she said, "I've been so hungry to see you; I'm glad you are here." I fought back tears. Losing her leg would be a tremendous blow to such an independent, proud woman. As they were wheeling her out of surgery hours later, she was awake and yelling for my mother. "Help me, Cloteel" could be heard all over the hospital.

Mammaw lived another year, but instead of being the loud, boisterous character she once was, she was now broken. Her children could not take care of her, so she went to live in a rest home in Edmonton.

Early one Sunday morning when I happened to be home, the nursing home called to tell my dad that she had passed away. Dad had no skills to handle grief. For all his bravado, he was a fragile man.

By now, I hated this school. Sports kept me there because I was established on the team and had won many awards. The "religious" leaders of this school wanted everyone to be the same and noticed that I had once dwelled in the world of the godly and then entered the world they thought was godless.

Several times I was called before the Dean when a student's behavior did not suit him, and he thought I might have some "insight" as to what was going on. Translation: the Dean knew my friendship with a rather rowdy group and thought I might tell. It was a very small campus.

I never told of their drinking, smoking, or sneaking out to go to town after curfew. Even though I would have enjoyed doing so, I didn't want to risk being kicked out. I was also vaguely aware of the underground life some of these students were leading sexually. This was 1967, and lesbians and gays were still in the closet. Campus rumors ran rampant and this Bible-beating college was out to get them.

My last two years were pure hell on this holy campus because I became a target of rumors and gossip. Someone was out to get me.

A couple of girls started a rumor that I was gay. The best way to ruin a boy or girl on this campus was to start that kind of rumor. They were gay themselves and lived in this underground world where they thought no one knew. I assumed they targeted me because I played sports and many of the girls on teams were gay. I have never chosen friends based on who or what they were. I had never been prejudiced or homophobic. I had not known gay people before coming to this school.

I let this play out without attacking them but never turned my back on them either. I prayed the rumors would die. One of those girls was on my tennis team, which added another level of jealousy. By the time I was a junior, my coach had left, and a new lady took over who made her dislike of me obvious. I could only assume that my teammate had spread her rumors to the new coach. One day the coach challenged me. "You think you are good, but I can whip you all over this court." She weighed at least three hundred pounds.

"I'll tell you what. I can beat you and her," I said, pointing my racket toward my teammate. I took them on and beat both of them. Two against one. That made the coach despise me more, but her bad behavior didn't stop on the tennis court.

At basketball games, this coach harassed me while I was playing, yelling at me, giving instructions, and overall trying to intimidate me. I told the coach to take me out. I walked to the edge of the bleachers and looked at this woman and said, "If you don't stop yelling at me I will NOT play one game of tennis

A Girl Named Connie

for you this year." She shut up. Her job depended on players like me, and she knew it.

She was as much of a bully as Lisa had been back in the sixth grade. She was just like the girl who yelled at me on the stairs. I might have taken that attack back then, but no more.

Then my senior year, another episode could have caused me to be expelled. One of my friends invited another student and me to go to her grandmother's overnight one weekend. When we got there, there was only one bed for the three of us, so like many young girls in my youth always did at slumber parties; we piled into bed and tried to sleep. However, this wasn't Edmonton, and these weren't my lifelong friends. When we went back to school, all hell broke loose again about Connie Wilson.

The Dean called me to his office, but this time, I was the subject.

"Connie, do you have something to tell me about what happened when you went to visit Sue's grandmother?" How did he know I had been to visit her grandmother?

"What are you talking about?"

"I was told a story about something that occurred." He cleared his throat.

"Well, tell me the story, and I'll tell you if it did." I had no idea what was to follow but I knew it wasn't good.

"It has been reported that you and Sue (not her name) engaged in an inappropriate act while spending the night at her grandmother's. Is that true?"

"Who told you that?"

"That isn't important."

"Yes, it is important, and I know who told you. What I don't know is why."

"We cannot tolerate that kind of behavior on this campus."

"I can promise you that I have done nothing with Sue or with Trudy and why Trudy told you that I can't imagine." I was shocked that this man was asking me such personal questions. I nearly laughed at the idea that my first experience with being around gay people was at his school.

He was oblivious, and I wanted to laugh at his naivety. What was he going to do-round up all the suspected lesbians and send them home? Any good Baptist would have done the same to protect the innocent from being led astray. Today he would be sued, and I might have been the one to do it.

"If this is true, you could be expelled, so why don't you think about this for awhile." Expulsion looked through the window.

Unable to contain myself, I leaned toward him, eye to eye just like my dad had taught me to do.

"I'll tell you what. You look at my balance sheet, and you look at Trudy's. I don't owe you one penny, but you know that she does. My dad has paid you every semester. He didn't want me to come here anyway, so I'll be happy to leave. Now, you think about this for awhile."

I knew money meant more to leaders than whether or not I was gay. I stood in front of his desk and looked directly at him. Dad would have been proud. I was proud of myself. Twice in a short period, I had stood up for myself.

"I'll talk to the other girls and then let you know what I decide." Without another word, I walked out and slammed the door. Never had my character or my reputation been in jeopardy. What if my parents heard about all of this?

Sue (my roommate at the time) told him the same story I did, so he called me back in for another conversation. "I am going to believe the two of you; and Connie, I do not want you to transfer. What I do want is for you and Sue not to room together next year."

A Girl Named Connie

I exploded. "No, I refuse. If we don't room together the entire campus will know that you forbid it, and that makes us look guilty. We have done nothing wrong." By then the entire campus had heard that I was gay anyway.

How does one fight a lie? I was now the campus sinner.

Sue and I roomed together; she got married when we graduated, and I was her bridesmaid. Trudy and a few others were determined to destroy Connie Wilson, and they almost succeeded. I had encountered a few vicious girls in my life, and three of them were at Campbellsville.

Once again, I did not tell my parents any of this. First, I would have been embarrassed. Second, my dad would have gone after that Dean with my mother in front of him. I fought my way through the collapse of my spiritual life, the spiraling of my grades to barely passing, the insult to my character and then graduated with nothing but loathing for those who played any part in these circumstances. My parents were proud as I walked across the stage for my diploma but I felt only relief to be leaving this institution before being institutionalized.

CHAPTER THIRTY-THREE

I ENDURED RUMORS that I was gay while continuing my dating life. The Dean never asked me about my boyfriends! He never asked about the men in my life. Even though finding the right man never worked out for me, I dated several guys on campus, but could not find the deep love my dad had described, although with one of them, I tried.

I was engaged twice. The first guy was unlike anyone I had ever met. He was a pilot, who in his own plane flew over the area to impress me. He was so persistent that after a six-month period of dating, he proposed. Because his parents were well off, I knew I would live a prosperous life as my parents had done and wanted for me. The thought of being married to a pilot from New York impressed me, but I had not felt the tingle I knew could be there with real love.

One day when I was alone in my dorm and thought about what marrying him would mean, I panicked. He never intended to stay in Kentucky and naturally would expect me to move to New York. I wasn't interested in going

A Girl Named Connie

to New York. I didn't even know anything about New York or his life there. In my analysis, I also knew that I was not in love with this man. The only solution was to break this relationship off. I felt a great relief, but he was not happy. Maybe he did love me, but I never felt that from him. I wanted to feel the way I had felt in high school.

The first engagement was very short lived and happened my first year, but with the second I had the dress, the church, and a notebook of plans every happy bride creates. I met this man at Walnut Street Baptist Church in Louisville after I moved there to teach two years after I graduated.

He was generous, kind and certainly a gentleman. The two times he came to Edmonton my mother observed that his appearance was a little less than stylish. "Does he own more than one pair of pants?" she asked. That was important to Mother. She did not want me to marry a poor boy with whom I would struggle.

My dad never seemed too thrilled with him, either. He might not have wanted to lose me, but I think he didn't want to lose me to this particular man. He saw something that I didn't see. Maybe I did see it but I thought I could fix him. We did have a lot in common. He loved the outdoors, and so did I. He was funny and made me laugh. In reality, he didn't need "fixing" at all; I was the problem.

Frankly, if I had loved him he would have been a good husband, but I realized that I was not in love with him. I had been desperately trying to find someone for my mother's sake. More and more often I was marching down an aisle in yet another church as a bridesmaid. My mother longed for me to be the bride. She didn't say this, but I felt it.

I was not a happy bride-to-be. "Mother, I may never get married. I am independent, make good money, and don't need someone to take care of me. I will be fine." I confessed this to her when I told her about my desire to call off the wedding, and she was very direct. "You don't have to get married, especially if you don't love him or anyone else." She gave me permission to live a single life. By this time, I was in my twenties.

My dad pulled me aside the next day. "Sister, I don't care if you live with a man or a woman. I just want you to be happy." Now that I had their permission to live as a single woman, I felt the pressure lifted of forcing myself into a relationship with yet another man.

Relationships were never easy for me. I could make them, but couldn't sustain them. My best friends were the only relationships I have maintained all of my life.

I graduated with a teaching degree and a job waiting for me back in Edmonton. I based my decision on the fact my parents wanted me to come home. "You can live here and save your money." Once again, I owed them for my college education and for my good life, so that is what I did.

I was a PE and biology major but taught sixth grade because that was the position open. It didn't matter that my major was not in elementary education; I was given a spelling book and told this was my subject to teach. The principal would never know that that had been my worst subject. Thankful for the job, I quickly learned how to teach students to spell even though I could never spell well myself. In the past, I had relied on my mother to spell difficult words for me.

I decided that I wanted to begin a tumbling team, so I asked the principal for support.

"Where would you practice?"

I suggested a large room located above the announcer box at the football field, which was not too far from our classroom. That was the same football field where I had cheered.

A Girl Named Connie

The principal bought mats, and I began recruiting elementary boys and girls. One young man asked to be on the team. I said, "Ok, what can you already do?" He jumped up in the air and with no hands, did a back flip. I was so excited that I said, "You're hired." He was self-taught.

About three times a week we practiced after school. Many of these kids were very talented and could have been gymnasts if they had had opportunities once I left. I was so confident in their ability that I decided they should perform for the community but not during a basketball game as I had once done, but rather in a performance of their own.

We invited the entire community, and the high school gym was filled with parents, grandparents and community supporters. The crowd gave them a standing ovation, and none of them ever forgot their Bonnie and Clyde routine. Even today when I see those former students, who are now grandparents, they talk about how much fun they had when I was their teacher and coach. If my students excelled, I excelled.

Living at home put me back in the shadow of my past plus limited my chances of doing what I passionately wanted to do: teach biology and coach. I explained to my parents that I needed to be in a larger place to be able to do what I wanted. That is why I moved to Louisville.

Before I could leave, I had to have a job secured, so I called the Jefferson County Board of Education to request an application. After mailing it back, I waited. No word. I waited another week or two and still no word. "You might want to call them," Dad suggested. "Let them know how interested you are." Finally, one school called for an interview, which I thought went well, but I didn't hear from them and the end of summer was growing closer.

I had decided that no one in Jefferson County was going to call a country girl to come up there to teach. What did I have to offer? Just as I was thinking I would be spending another year or more back home, my dad made a bold suggestion. "Why don't you call Wendell Butler?" Mr. Butler, at the time, was Superintendent of Kentucky Schools; but more importantly, he was from my county. Dad could have done this for me, but I was now an adult and needed to do for myself.

As soon as I told Mr. Butler who I was, he was more than willing to help me. "What school do you want to teach at?" he asked. I didn't care as long as I had a job. He suggested that I work in the county system rather than the city because of the consolidation in progress. I would have taken any job at that point.

The next day the principal of Southern High School offered me a job. I learned that it is very true that who you know will often help more than what you know. However, what you know will keep you on the job and I stayed many years.

Today young people can move across the country for jobs, but in the 60's we were limited in our knowledge of the vast land beyond our own doors. I chose to live in Louisville because I had been so often and knew how to drive in that city. Otherwise, I might have gone elsewhere.

CHAPTER THIRTY-FOUR

WITH A LITTLE MONEY that I had saved while living at home, I was able to rent a furnished apartment and pay my bills until my first paycheck came from the Jefferson County Board of Education. Once I left home, I paid my way. No more depending on my parents for the things I took for granted: food, clothing, and shelter. The twenty dollars my dad gave me each time after a visit kept me in gas and food. In the 60's, that amount could provide a week of meals.

However, if Mother had seen the place I lived, she would have been mortified. On a beginning teacher's salary, I was not able to afford "upscale." There was no plush left in my wall-to-wall carpeting. I owned a bean bag chair, a couch, tiny TV, and rented a bed from one of those furniture rentals. My silver spoon life was now one of paper plates and plastic forks.

At Southern High School, I soon bonded with students who found my country accent amusing until I grew on them, and I made close friends with co-workers. My social life flourished with school activities, collegiate basketball, football games, and associating with colleagues.

On my first day at Southern High School, I met the lady who would be my co-worker. We were both newly hired. Standing about 5'10" with long blonde hair, she had a daunting presence with her long fingernails, which she used to express herself. She was an "East End" lady, and I was a girl from a town with one caution light. "East End" meant the rich side of town. Because her husband sold golf equipment and clothing for golfers, she always wore cute little golf skirts and tops. Physical education teachers were permitted to dress casually in order to work out with students. Even today, some coaches wear their shorts and polo shirts all day at school. Before long, I was wearing cute little skirts and tops at discount prices. I wanted to be her.

She had taught five years in a Catholic school; so she was ahead of me in organizational skills, especially in PE classes. After all, teaching spelling wasn't exactly a stepping stone to high school PE classes.

She set me on a path I continued to follow throughout my career. One thing I had to see for myself was when she told me to tell kids to find "their spot" on the floor.

I said, "There are no spots on the floor for them to find."

"Trust me, they will find a spot and go to it each day."

I was stunned when I made the announcement and the kids lined up on their "spot" and stuck to it all year. She had many tricks of the trade up her sleeve, and I learned all of them I could.

Dealing with high school students was challenging, but I soon saw there wasn't much difference in their behavior and that of sixth graders.

Almost immediately, I immersed myself in after-school programs and Lavada helped me not to become overwhelmed. When the school needed a girls' track coach, I volunteered. I ran track in college, so I felt confident I could handle this task.

A Girl Named Connie

This track team was pitiful; but on our first meet, which involved four teams, we placed third. The students, however, were elated with third place and jumped up and down when announced.

"What is wrong with you all? We are not going to get third place ever again." My competitive nature kicked in and off we went. If they weren't first, then neither was I.

Every day I worked them hard. The girl that ran the mile would go to the side, throw up, and come right back onto the practice track. Crossing the finish line was a must. Four of the girls had six-foot legs and ran the two twenty like racehorses gliding around the track at Churchill Downs. I put these four together and formed the four-forty relay, and we also did the 880. I also knew I had the best hurdler in the county. She knew she was good, but I don't think she knew how good. Her stride was perfect; she was fast and confident.

What was different about my team was that I not only paid attention to the runners, but also to my field people: the long jumpers, the discus throwers, the shot putters, and the high jumpers. They were the stars, but I was the director and producer. My thumbprint was all over this team.

We started winning, and the girls liked that feeling. Third was no longer an option. My motto was "No Guts; No Glory." This was long before I had heard anyone else use the slogan. No doubt I had one of the hardest working track teams in Louisville. For that, I was admired. I needed to be admired.

After four years, they were ready for yet another state meet. Many were now seniors and this was an especially conflicting time with the end of year activities and competitions. Unfortunately, the state track competition was scheduled on the same day as high school graduation, and this could have been devastating for my seniors.

"We have to have a meeting with all parents," I told my team.

One evening all the parents showed up in the cafeteria. "I know how hard you have worked to get your child to the twelfth grade, and I would not stand in the way of you being able to watch them walk across that stage on graduation night." They were quiet.

"The meet is at one o'clock in Lexington. Graduation is 8 PM in Louisville at the fairgrounds. You have to decide what to do."

Knowing the answer, I was not at all surprised when they stood and applauded their decision to compete. I almost cried. I was not a crier.

To get to this point, we had won district, region, and county. Winning the county qualified us for state competition. We placed third overall in the state. Third place at state was a more than acceptable and I was proud of that.

Because we had to travel by car, once we received our awards, kids dashed to vehicles and off we went toward Louisville. As we drew near the city, girls changed clothes in the backseat of cars. Off with the track suits and on with their dresses and caps and gowns. Cars lined up in front of Freedom Hall (the arena at the fairgrounds), and they jumped out fully dressed and in time to get in line for the ceremony. The adrenaline was flowing.

To be able to have so many state winners and participants and all of them also be able to walk their graduation line was a miracle. Among those were Pam Smith, state high jumper for two years; Babs Laha, state discus thrower for four years; and Peggy Stephens, Debbie Sinclair, Cindy Cunningham and Terri Watts, state 440 team champs. Susie Delozier was my award winning hurdler.

Although no one at home knew anything about my track team or the awards we were winning, my reputation became well known in Louisville schools. I was now important in the sports arena.

A Girl Named Connie

Three sisters at this school who had attended our track meets asked me to form a gymnastics team. I didn't feel very qualified to coach gymnastics on a competitive level. After months of begging, I caved. "Ok, we'll try."

In preparation, I attended every gymnastic clinic or coaching camp in the area. We did balance beams, uneven bars, vaulting, and free exercise, which was the entire gamut of gymnastics. I discovered that some of my track girls were also great gymnasts. Unknown to me at the time, many students at Southern had been taking private gymnastic lessons, so they also came on board. From three until six each day, I coached track. From seven until nine, I coached gymnastics. Needless to say, I had no social life during this nine-year period.

One of my track girls offered to help me keep stats for the gymnastic team and must have noticed that I usually grabbed a hamburger between the two practices, so she invited me to her home for a meal. "Mom always cooks," she said.

That was the start of many meals with Charleen and her children. I now had an "adopted" family in Louisville. This family, however, did not know about my "real" adoption and would not have cared. Living away from Edmonton was so therapeutic; not one soul knew or cared about Connie Allen Wilson. I wasn't the center of gossip or speculation.

Charleen would later save me from being homeless.

Her daughter Peggy, my statistician, later played college tennis, which landed her in the University of Louisville Hall of Fame. She was a member of the Louisville Orchestra and is now a gold medal winner in National Racquetball. She graduated from UL, went to UK to medical school, and is now the CEO of a state psychiatric hospital. I am always proud of my former students, but she was more like a niece. She is one of my best "city" friends.

CHAPTER THIRTY-FIVE

CAROL HAD MARRIED Guy by 1967 and was teaching English at Metcalfe County High School. She would have two children by the time she was twenty-five. Roberta was teaching art in Lexington and had a daughter and a son. Judy lived in Edmonton most of her life, losing her first husband after a few years of marriage. Then she met another guy and when they married she moved with him to a town not far away.

Carol, Roberta, and Judy were together often but I seldom saw them the first decade after graduation. I was the one who had moved away from them.

They had what my mother wanted me to have, so it was easier to stay away. I didn't want a husband, meals to cook, laundry to do, and children to rear. From an early age, I knew I was never going to be able to take care of anyone other than myself emotionally. In the city, I was living a very happy single life; but in the country, single life was a sign of imperfection.

"You ain't married yet?" a customer in the store might ask.

"No, not yet." I said but thinking behind my smile, *Not ever, you stupid idiot for asking such a personal question. What is this, the dark ages?*

A Girl Named Connie

Another might ask without knowing I wasn't married, "How many kids you got now?"

I was nearing thirty, so I should have had some kids by now according to those whose lives revolved around marriage, children, Sunday dinners, and work. I could tell by their reaction when I said I wasn't married that they thought something must be wrong with me. Maybe something was.

Too bad I didn't keep a log of the number of times well-meaning acquaintances tried to fix me up. It would have provided interesting conversations in the future. Everybody knew "a nice guy" who was a cousin or a cousin of a cousin. They knew a "perfect" match for me, but what they didn't know was I was not ready to settle for just anyone. As my dad once said, "You will know when you can't stop thinking about him." I had never reached that point.

I never allowed myself to be "fixed up." In the city, no one made me feel awkward because I wasn't married. Some of my friends were married, but many were not. However, in the country, the majority of women were married by age twenty-one.

I began to refer to going to Edmonton as going to the "country" and my friends as my country friends. That was my way of distinguishing my hometown friends from my new ones. I became a city girl.

During the nine years I taught at Southern, I moved often, trying to improve my living conditions. My second move was to yet another "furnished" apartment that was a step up from the last one, but not a life-changing step. The place was larger, but I soon knew the neighborhood was not where my dad would have wanted me to live. At night loud music kept me awake, along with raised voices. To protect myself, I put furniture in front of the only door and then pots and pans on the furniture, so I could hear if anyone tried to break in. During this time somebody robbed me twice. I soon moved.

Since leaving home and making my way, I was forced to live very differently than I had in my days in Edmonton. Back then I never thought about money or the lack of it; if I needed something I got it. Even though I never asked for too much, the fact that the money was in the bank to cover my needs was comforting. I admit that I missed that secure life. I didn't like living poor. Having no new clothes or wondering if I was going to be able to go out to eat on the weekends with my friends was new to me. The princess was now the chambermaid.

For the nine years I was at Southern High School; I was happy with my job, but in 1978, my professional life changed. Teachers wanted more money and better benefits. We had not had a pay increase in many years, so Jefferson County teachers went on strike, which made national news. Teachers were supposed to be much too dedicated to strike.

My faculty voted me as our school's team leader, which entailed giving motivational speeches to the faculty and informational ones to those outside of school, laying out our requests. My job was to encourage my fellow teachers to keep out of the classroom, and not cross picket lines and to make sure our requests were heard. I reveled in this leadership. Teachers were listening to me and responding and being swayed by me. I was once again invaluable.

A little bragging on Connie Wilson and I would move mountains to please a person or an entire school system. I later felt like more of a stooge.

We took to the streets holding our protest signs while single digit temperatures made us miserable. Anyone hoping to get inside the building had to go through us first. "Scabs" were hired to take our places. These were teachers without jobs and were to replace us in our absence. However, they were not going past the picket line. This continued for weeks, and I was front and center.

Our teacher's union mediated with the school board every day for long chilling weeks and finally reached an agreement. Teachers returned to classrooms, and the wedge between administrators and teachers widened.

For me, one of my main issues was the inequality between women coaches and male coaches. Female coaches were not paid; male coaches were. After this strike, women were paid but not at the same rate as men. At least, this was a start. Inequality concerned me. Perhaps that came from never feeling equal to my peers.

The first of the summer, only weeks after the end of that grueling school year, I received an official letter from my principal stating that I had been "surplused" from my school. This meant that I was considered a "surplus" teacher rather than the tenured one that I was. Therefore, according to the letter, I would be moved.

Considering all I had done for the students of that school, working long hours without pay, and how I had sacrificed my time for the faculty, heading up the strike, I thought I was indispensable, but no one is. None of this mattered to this principal. He was going to prove a point, which was, "If you cross me, I will get you." Like most principals, he was following orders, but I was disappointed he didn't have the backbone to defend me.

After that letter, I was so angry that I came back to Edmonton and stayed three weeks until I cooled off and thought about how to handle this. My first instinct was to storm his office and tell him what a piece of crap he was, but I didn't have the nerve. I could fight for others, but not for myself.

I told Mother and Dad what had happened. Dad listened. "Does this mean you will lose your job?" my mother asked.

"No, but I will be moved from that school."

Dad said, "It is okay to burn your bridges but don't try to walk back across them when you do. People have a way of getting even." He was right. I concluded that I was to blame for allowing my pride to speak rather than my common sense. Like other teachers, I should have remained neutral and carried my sign but not been in charge of the march. Keeping my mouth shut was a lesson I never learned.

By the time I returned to Louisville, gossipers were at work. Friends called to warn me that they had heard from the gossip mill that I had been talking badly about the principal and what I said had gotten back to him. Did that matter? What was the big deal? However, I hated gossip, so to nip the stories "in the bud" I went directly to his office, unannounced, and with no visible anger, I said, "I assure you that I have not been degrading you or discussing my situation with outsiders. You make the decisions, and I have to live with them. I am, however, upset that you would cast me off so easily."

"Well, I wouldn't blame you if you had said things about me," he said. He knew he had wronged me, but his job was more important than our professional relationship. He had to live with his decision.

"I didn't say a word." I put out my hand as Bill Wilson would have done and he shook it. He might not have known, but I never quite came to terms with being let go.

He had no loyalty to me and no qualm sending me off to another school if anyone would hire me, or letting me float off to an unemployment line. This was my first time to hit the wall of politics. I was not offered my old job back as I hoped I would be. People like me were a threat.

To my surprise, the principal of Thomas Jefferson High School, one of the worst locations in the city, heard about my plight and quickly offered me a job running a program called Push Excel. I would not be a classroom teacher, but would be assisting underprivileged children from the worst part of town in their classrooms studies. Working with needy kids or rich kids mattered not to me. I just wanted a job.

These students were not without hope. They loved learning but what they lacked was a decent environment. It wasn't long before I was going beyond my job description. On Saturday, I organized a football program for these kids because they needed to be playing something rather than hanging out on the street. I was the only white girl on the field, which made for many laughable moments among these high school students and their parents.

Working with these black students took me back to my days on the back porch of Miss Bessie's restaurant where I sat with Beulah and her family and ate lunch. Even during the time when busing became such a hot topic and produced dangerous situations in my city, I couldn't grasp the big deal among adults of going to school with black students.

I also didn't understand the need for busing when with enough money all schools could have equaled those in the East End of the city. Why would a kid need to ride a bus for an hour when his community school was next door? That never made good sense.

My mother worried about my safety. The evening news coming out of Louisville often focused on the busing situation.

"I watched every night hoping not to see you on the air." I knew she was worried and sometimes so was I. Guns, threats, protests, rocks, eggs, police officers in danger-these were the times I faced and endured for several years.

While I was in the midst of racial tension in the school where I was teaching, the KKK was watching my dad because of his association with a black man. Often Max would accompany Dad to card games or to make trips for merchandise or simply ride around, so the clan must have thought Dad was too friendly with him. Some of those poker games were in the black neighborhoods in adjoining counties. Max was Dad's ticket into the games and his safety net getting out with no trouble.

It is a good thing no one approached my dad about this because he would have blown a fuse. Dad's lack of prejudice did not sit well with hooded white men, but they would not have tangled with Bill Wilson for long.

After two years at Thomas Jefferson High School, I applied for a job at Southern Middle School. The next year Thomas Jefferson was closed.

After moving from one apartment to another, trying to better myself, I bought a small home in Indiana not far from Louisville where houses were less expensive. Living just across the river, however, made me feel less of a Kentuckian, and I didn't like that. However, I lived there three years.

My parents never saw where I lived. Not that they didn't want to see it, but it wasn't a priority. When my dad came to Louisville to the track, I often met him there. We saw each other, but they didn't come across the river for a visit.

Even though I had never taught middle school and was still not qualified to teach sixth grade, I was grandfathered into the program. Southern Middle was one of those schools that received many students who had been bused from the most unsavory parts of the city, so once again I knew this would be a challenge. Unlike the students at Thomas Jefferson, the ones I was facing were at-risk, rowdy and ill-prepared.

However, growing up in the country and dealing with the boys from the hills and hollers prepared me to tackle hoodlums. I had never wrestled a rattlesnake, but I knew the best defense was to assess its next move. I did a lot of assessing my first year.

I approached these students with a strict attitude and stayed that way until they started learning. My type of "strict" was not with words, but with looks. My father had been a good example of control without words. Seldom did I raise my voice to a student and never thought about hitting one of them although that strategy would have been a natural one for me, considering how often I was smacked growing up.

Inside, I ran my own after school detention, keeping the students for at least thirty extra minutes for an infraction, and I included parents in each problematic situation.

The parents or guardians were very supportive in spite of what I had been led to believe. Just because students live in run-down neighborhoods doesn't mean their parents don't care about their education. Many times they care more. These kids reminded me of what kind of home I might have lived in if not for Bill and Cloteel Wilson.

Once again I dived into extra activities. A young teacher named Peggy, a guy named Don, and I worked with the Academic Team that participated in the Governor's Cup competition in the spring. We also did a program called "Odyssey of the Mind," which consisted of involving students in engineering projects. Don was the idea man and Peggy and I followed his lead. I worked with such a good team of teachers that by Christmas we had our students under our thumbs. The more we worked together, the more I appreciated Peggy's youth and enthusiasm.

At this school, we taught in teams. Six of us were so good together that we developed a book on how to integrate math across the curriculum (we had planned to do books on each subject area) and presented our ideas at conventions as far away as California. We set up booths and sold our books. I was the science "expert." Feeling a part of a group without buying my way in was a change in my life. Could I really fit in without bartering?

Once again, I did not share my activities with my parents. I saw no need. In retrospect, maybe they would have enjoyed knowing about my life, and I should have been more forthcoming, but since they didn't ask, I assumed they didn't care. The feeling of being "written off" consumed me when it came to my parents, but in looking back, I think I did that to them. If I didn't see them, I wouldn't have thoughts about what they were not.

Unlike when I was in school, these kids didn't even know each other's names, so I was going to "fix" that problem. They came from different areas of Louisville, so my task was to mesh them together. I could only do this through play, so I created times for playing. Often I would take my sixth-grade team out to a big field in the back of the school and let them play just to give the other teachers a break. Even though I still contended that my head start job was the worst one I ever had, monitoring the kids at play back then came in handy. Kids have many common denominators, and one of them is having fun. They loved Miss Wilson.

Some played kickball, others football and would have played basketball but they had no goals. I walked around the area with them and showed them games I had played growing up such as Red Rover and Tug of War. They would go home, most of the time, to an empty house or be in charge of younger siblings, so this was as much fun as they might have all week. I loved watching kids play.

CHAPTER THIRTY-SIX

IN ANALYZING MY TEACHING experiences and my need to stand out among my peers, my insecurities were transparent. Never feeling totally equal to anyone, I had to go beyond the expected. Students loved Miss Wilson. Students wanted to take my classes. Students gave me Christmas gifts and yelled at me across the gym during ball games. I attended their activities. Never wanting children didn't keep me from wanting the love young people could give. Even today they make me feel special when they introduce me to their children.

During this time I had gone back to school and gotten a master's degree and Rank I, which placed me in a position to be an assistant principal or principal. Frances Jones, the principal at the middle school, took me out of the classroom for a year to be her assistant and jack of all trades. It was during this time that I decided I did not want to leave the classroom. Even though the pay would have been much greater, I was not the administrative type. However, that did not mean I wasn't growing tired of paper work and after school meetings and insufficient pay.

After nine years, my teacher team and I began to tire and need a change. One had been offered a job as an assistant principal, so she took it. Peggy Hourigan went to a middle school on the other side of the city, Don Wiggenton moved to Oklahoma, Carol Skinner became an assistant principal, Vickie Mahan stayed there and continued to teach English, Lynn Bridwell went back to school and became a librarian, and Roberta Brown quit teaching to write novels. Doris Mann left to work in another system. All I wanted at that time was to teach science and biology to high school students and to coach tennis, so I applied for a position at Butler High School, one of the most traditional in the district, and was hired. We went our separate ways professionally, but met once a week for dinner and maintained our "team."

Back home my brother had graduated from high school and gone to college for one semester but discovered that was not for him. I didn't know what his aspirations were or his talents. If he had been young during the age of computers, he might have gone that way. What I did know was that the older he became, the more exasperated Dad was with him, and the more my mother made excuses for his lack of direction. I was home enough to evaluate the life they led in my absence, and it was not a pleasant one. A few times when I tried to intervene on his behalf, I was quickly put in my place.

"You aren't here, so you really don't know the situation," my dad would say. He was right. What was the situation? The three of them could not function without each other. Even when my brother married, they remained connected.

He married a lovely girl, and they had a house in Edmonton. Gradually, they were spending more time at Mother's than they were at their own home, especially when their son was born. My mother turned her attention to her new daughter-in-law with the same exuberance as she had been with me when it came to clothing. I was not jealous; I was happy Mother had someone to focus on when I left, but there were times when I could have used their help. He was blood and I was not. That is how I felt, and when I thought of the help they gave him and the help I needed, I told myself that he was theirs so naturally they would give him more financial and emotional support. Time and distance healed my moments of envy.

When my brother and his wife divorced, I was disappointed because I really liked her and she was good for him. His ex-wife and my nephew moved to Glasgow, leaving my parents broken-hearted. By the time the child was twelve, he asked to move back to Edmonton to live with Granny and Pa. The court listened to his plea, and they gained full custody of him. Now there were three generations under one roof.

CHAPTER THIRTY-SEVEN

DURING THE SUMMER, before I began teaching at Butler, I pondered about going in a different direction. I had grown discouraged with teaching, tired from the after school activities and never having extra money beyond paying my bills.

Worn down by long hours and my meager salary, I was intrigued by a possible opportunity outside the classroom. Even with all my degrees, I was still not making the money that someone in the corporate world was. Looking for a change, I fell right into an opportunity. Perhaps I should say I waded into this opportunity without any boots.

I first met Emily at the St. James Art Fair, an annual event in Louisville. She was with a group of ladies, and so was I. Some of her friends also knew some of mine, so we all ended up spending the day walking around the area together.

A few weeks later Emily invited me to dinner with a group of her friends. I listened to them tell about their jobs and I thought about my future.

A Girl Named Connie

"Why don't you come to work with us?" she said.

These ladies took home much more money than I did and the work was less mentally challenging. Presently, my extra hours were donated and never a night did I get home before the evening news.

They talked about shortages of employees and overtime pay, so I thought about applying.

"I bet I can get you a job," Emily said. I had never worked in a factory, so considering such a change was intimidating. My parents did not send me to college to work in a factory.

Just as contradictory as my waiting tables in a Jerry's restaurant and then wearing designer clothes to school was my considering standing on an assembly line. Money meant more to me, at this time, than a job title. No one would know me and say, "What is Connie Wilson doing working in this place?"

What if I couldn't do the work? What if I didn't like the job? Would I be able to go back to teaching? Did I want to forego my retirement to start a new one? I had the summer to decide my plans but instead, I made a quick decision.

In June I applied for a job at this company. The ladies were very persuasive. I didn't hear from the company, but I did hear from Emily. "I have had an offer for a promotion if I move to North Carolina. It is going to be much more money, and I can get you a job." I believed her.

North Carolina? I had never lived that far away from home. The more she talked, the more intrigued I became. Being included sways me.

I pondered as to what to do, but within a few weeks she made a bold suggestion: "Why don't we sell our homes and buy one together and move?"

Totally caught up in the possibilities of living in another state and working at a new job, a deviation from the routine that had become less and less financially rewarding, I considered her offer.

I wasn't particularly interested in selling my home, but what she said made sense. There was no need for me to make a house payment and not live in it. I could always buy another house with the equity in our new home if I decided I wanted to move back.

In the meantime, I discussed this proposal with my parents. Since leaving home, I had sometimes felt left out of their lives. I continued to need my family.

Dad asked, "Why are you going to sell your house?" In his view of life, owning a home meant security and stability. As I told him, I could hear the doubt in my voice. I knew this wasn't a smart move.

"Don't count teaching out," my dad warned. I sensed he didn't approve. However, I was caught up in the moment.

They never said anything derogatory about Emily, but I knew Mother found her a little "rough around the edges." This woman and I did not have much in common, but I wouldn't realize just how different we were until I moved with her.

I went to my principal (whom I had known for years) and told him my plan. "I'm going to quit teaching," I said abruptly. Mr. T, as we referred to him, refused to allow me to do this.

"No, you can take a leave of absence, and when you decide to come back, you will have a job. I will write a letter to the board of education asking for a leave of absence for you. You won't be happy outside of teaching." Would he do that for me? That was an act of kindness I would soon appreciate.

A Girl Named Connie

Within a few weeks, Emily and I made several trips house hunting in North Carolina and looking for a home was fun. She took care of details. It was nice not to be in charge for a change, but also a little unsettling. I had never been out of control of my life.

Finally, we bought a house together. Then as we were getting ready to sign the documents, she dropped a bomb that would later explode. "If I put the house in my name, the company will move us free of charge," she said.

At the time, I accepted what she said as the truth, but later I thought of questions I should have asked. *Why would the company need the house to be in your name? Wouldn't they move you if you were moving in with a relative. Moving is moving. Would they not move you if you were renting an apartment and had a roommate?*

My trusting nature led me to do what she suggested. A moving company loaded my belongings, including the furniture I had collected throughout the years, and her belongings into a moving van and off we went to a small town in North Carolina. I made a life altering decision based on an empty promise of a job, but I had no one to blame but myself.

"Emily, when am I going to hear about a job?" I asked repeatedly. Days and days went by as I sat in that new house, knowing no one. Finally, when no job came through for me, I had to look for work elsewhere. She ignored my questions and often snapped at me for asking.

Soon I was activity director for a nursing home where I made ten dollars an hour, a far cry from my teaching salary but it was something to do while I was waiting for my corporate interview and "fabulous" job. I enjoyed working with these older people. It took me back to the porches in Edmonton.

Day by day, I dreaded going home. The feeling of being homesick within my home seized me, and I went from a size twelve to a size six. My appetite disappeared and my will to get up in the morning waned. Depression overshadowed any joy I felt working at the nursing home.

I went to North Carolina in June and escaped November eleventh of the same year. I say escape because that is what happened. Emily watched my health fail and when I told her I wanted to go back home she said, "Wait until you get better." She worked long hours, which was my only relief, but I was lonely. She began to make friends at work and bring them to the house for parties. They were not my kind of people: they partied too hard for me.

However, I never blamed anyone else for my poor judgment. I was so homesick and miserable that I finally called my mother.

"Things are not going well, and I am sick," I said to her. "I'm not sure I'm going to make it."

In a loud voice, she said, "What are you talking about you aren't going to make it?" and she handed the phone to my dad.

"Dad, I have made a huge mistake in moving here and I have lost my house investment, and I don't have any money, and I'm sick."

I waited for his voice. "Don't you worry about anything. Don't worry about the house. One morning you get up, get in the car and come home." He didn't pause to think about what to tell me. When we hung up, I cried. How could I have ever looked at him as anything but my father?

He called every morning at seven o'clock for a week and told me to come home. I wasn't sure I was able to drive. I wasn't sure I could face the fact that I had sold my home and invested with a person I didn't even know-a person I thought I could trust. She had my money, and I had nothing.

One morning after she left for work, I packed all my clothes and whatever else I could get in my sports car and left with nothing but a credit card. I felt like a child who had been imprisoned by a kidnapper and kept inside for years; I didn't know if I had the wherewithal to get out of there. No matter how distressed I was, I found the strength to drive off without even leaving a note. When she came home, I was gone.

After being away from her and regaining my confidence and my health, which took months, I called her. "I'm coming to get my bedroom suite." We set a time, and I solicited the help of the college girl whose liquor I had poured out the window. Lucy now owned a line of semi-trucks and was doing well. She was also fearless, and I needed someone fearless to assure me I could do this. Emily brought out the vulnerable little girl in me who did not want confrontations. I didn't think I could match her loud, overbearing personality, so I took Lucy with me because she was not afraid of anyone.

We loaded the bedroom suite with her glaring at us and then we left. She likely wanted to make sure I didn't take anything else although I should have taken all that was mine. What we had bought together was now hers, including the house.

There was nothing but my word to prove I had invested in this house, and she was not going to concede that she owed me anything. Lucy was more than willing to load whatever I pointed to, but I didn't want trouble. Emily might have called the police, and I had no proof of anything.

A year or so later, she did call and assure me she would pay me my half of the house, but I have never seen a penny. I miss the many small and sentimental objects I had left behind. I never knew what happened to her or them.

Once back in Louisville, I went back to Southern Middle School to talk to Mr. T. I will be forever grateful for his wisdom.

"Connie, I don't have anything here, but let me see what I can find." Trying to get a job in November would be nearly impossible, but he phoned a friend who was a principal at another middle school. "There is an opening at Johnson Middle School if you want it."

Of course, I wanted it. "When do I start?"

"Tomorrow."

In the meantime, I had to think about where I was going to live, but I didn't have any funds except a credit card and didn't want to knock on the doors of my friends, admitting I had made a huge mistake. If I had to live in my car for a few days, I would survive. Fortunately, that didn't happen. Something led me to a basketball game at Southern High School on that first night back in town and to Charleen.

I immediately saw her as she motioned for me to sit on the bleachers with her. "Are you back for good?" she asked, giving me a hug.

She had never thought moving was a good idea.

"Yes, I am here forever!" I gave her highlights of my stay in North Carolina as we kept one eye on the game. Her daughter was playing.

"When did you get back?"

"Today."

"Where are you staying?" When I explained my situation, she rescued me.

"I have an empty bedroom, so you come with me and stay as long as you need." What she never knew until I told her later was that I would have been homeless if she hadn't invited me to live with her. Of course, I could have asked for money from my parents, but I couldn't begin to think about taking anything from them. Dad had asked if I needed anything, but I acted as if I could "get by." They would have been mortified that I was so broke I had no place to live. With them, I minimized serious issues as if I had everything under control. This was one time I was far from it.

I stayed with Charleen for five or six months; long enough to save a deposit for an apartment. She embraced me like a sister and saved me from sleeping in my car.

A Girl Named Connie

It took a while to emerge from a bout of depression and vowed never to allow anyone to control my life or my business and personal situations again.

Johnson Middle School was in the absolute worst part of the city. The first day I parked in the main parking area; and the secretary, seeing where I had parked, warned, "You better move your car to the teacher's lot, or you won't have any hubcaps when you come out!"

This neighborhood was accustomed to weekly shootings, and often gang clashes played out in the classroom. I was the third teacher this group had had in only three months. Before giving them a chance to try to make me another notch on their belts, I announced the first day, "I know you have run off three other teachers, but I am here to tell you that I am going nowhere. I have no money and right now, no place to live, so I have to have this job. You can't run me off so don't even try." Silence fell over this unruly group of kids. Chances are many of them lived with relatives and had no home of their own.

I never put on a show with students. What I am foremost is honest and a survivor. I let them know my life had not been easy either. As far as the silver spoon I once had, they would never know *that* Miss Wilson. The privileged life I once led was gone the minute I left Edmonton for good. Not that my parents tossed me aside, but I could not ask them for anything else. I don't think I was any more unusual in that thought than my friends were. Once a person left home, she/he was on his own in my way of thinking.

Being tough with these kids was a necessity because that is how they related to authority until they relaxed a little. One day a kid came in late, and I scolded him about it. "Where have you been? You know you can't be late?"

"I've been to juvie."

"Why have you been to juvie?"

"I stole my aunt's car." I had never met kids like these, but soon I would have them in my heart.

The principal came to the door one day and called me outside. Automatically, I assumed I had done something wrong. He said, "I never thought I'd see these kids under control. Congratulations."

This was one group who didn't play. There was nowhere safe outside. I kept them in the room for another reason; I didn't want to take a chance one might run off.

Through their insistence, I resumed my weekly dinners with my team from Southern Middle. I had been gone only a few months, but it felt like a lifetime. Peggy, one of the young teachers on my previous sixth-grade team, invited me to Sunday dinner with her large family consisting of her parents, her three sisters and their husbands and children. I agreed to go and from that Sunday forward, I was invited to every Sunday dinner. I had never been part of such a happy group of people except at Aunt Hazel's.

Peggy's three sisters, all married with families, included me in UL tailgating parties, swim parties at their homes, birthday parties, and later on, I even went on camping trips and vacations. They chose a state park each year and every member of the family, including Peggy's parents, went unless they were incapacitated!

Before long, Peggy was also vacationing with my lifelong friends from Edmonton, something we had begun to do by the time we were in our thirties and continue today.

Even though Peggy's family included me in their activities, I couldn't shake that third wheel feeling. Once again I needed to fit in, so I started my old pattern of making sure I paid my way into their hearts. To the picnics, I brought a Honey Baked Ham; not just a ham. For the dozens of birthdays, I always bought over the top gifts. Christmas was the same. I couldn't afford these gifts, but I had established a pattern and couldn't find a way to stop.

"You don't need to buy gifts like those. You don't need to buy any gifts," my friend would declare, but that was how I felt worthy.

What I didn't know was how uncomfortable I made them feel with my expensive gifts. They could have afforded Ipads and Xbox's but were not extravagant. They saved money; I spent mine. I flashed brand names and gadgets but didn't have anything but an overused credit card to keep me solvent. I thought if the gifts were nice enough, I would be more welcomed.

Within a year of returning from North Carolina and paying rent to Charleen when I finally could, I started looking for another home. Having been a homeowner, I saw the value in owning rather than renting, but I had no down payment. I contemplated asking Dad for a $5,000 loan, but I had never asked for one cent since I graduated from college.

"I really want this house," I told the realtor, "but I don't have a down payment. I will need to find the money and can pay it back within six months, but right now I don't have any savings. I don't guess the owner would work with me would he?" I will never know why, but this lady loaned me the $5,000 down payment, and I paid her back within six months. My new home was a small two bedroom in a good location, and I lived there for several years. I was now closer to Peggy's family in distance as well as forming an emotional tie.

My friendship with Peggy grew. After watching me go through the process of buying a home, she began to talk about getting her own place. She had been living with her parents. For a year, she rented an apartment.

We spent so much time together that I suggested that she move into my house. "We can split the bills, and you will have more space."

She was hesitant at first, and later I learned that her greatest concern was a lack of privacy in my small house.

Shortly after she moved in, I found her in the basement many nights, piddling around or reading. This was a utility basement with nothing but a washer/dryer and storage. "Why do you go down to the basement every night?" I asked. I thought she might have regretted moving in the way I regretted my move to North Carolina.

"I just have to have some time to myself." It was then that we decided to pool our money and buy a larger house. This time, however, my name would be on the deed as well as hers.

Peggy soon learned that I also needed my quiet time. One particular night while she was talking on the phone and giggling the way she usually did, my nerves must have been "on end." "Do you laugh at everything?" I said in a tone I wished to take back as soon as it came out. Peggy had an infectious laugh that was too much like giggling for me. I had never giggled in my life.

She didn't reply, but I knew I hurt her feelings, and I could have kicked myself. For several days, she stopped laughing.

When I asked her why she wasn't laughing, she said, "You told me you didn't like it."

"Don't listen to me!" I apologized and soon she was laughing again.

I miss that laugh.

Our new home was a two-story brick in the southern part of old Louisville. The upstairs had three large bedrooms and a bath. The main floor had a dedicated dining room, small kitchen and a huge living area with a fireplace. Like all old homes, repairs soon took on a life of their own, but I knew how to do many of them myself. Also, I had some good neighbors with skills beyond mine that pitched in to help.

I laid a patio, planted shrubs and later we added a swimming pool. A magnolia grew next to my driveway. Over the years, I would screen in the back porch and try to redo the massive basement, but work is never completed in a historic home. I am still living there today.

With Peggy's influence, I was soon saving money and feeling more secure about my finances as well as my personal happiness. I didn't worry that she would abandon me or leave me. She was not the type to hurt anyone.

Butler High School was my next move, and the place from which I would retire. My principal, Kenneth Frick, was a straight-to-the-point type of guy, and I knew immediately we would work well together. One of his jobs was to observe all new employees at that school and at the time, I was teaching biology and he choose the last period of the day to observe me. The last period of a "bad" day.

By the end of sixth period, I had "had it." A very long science desk with a black slate top, filled with beakers, papers, pencils, test papers I needed to grade, sat in front of me. To get the kids attention, I went from one side of the desk to the other and swiped very item off the desk and onto the floor. This stunned the students. At the same time, Mr. Frick walked into the room, looked at me and smiled, "Miss Wilson, are you having a good day?"

That was the type of man he was, and after he left that day, the students paid close attention to every word I said.

This would be such a change from my other schools because it was a traditional high school. Students were expected to behave in a certain manner and would be sent home if they didn't. I taught science and biology to exceptional students and going to work each day without worrying about one of my students being a victim of a drive-by shooting was a joy. At Butler, I coached tennis for five years and focused strongly on academics.

When an assistance principal's job became available in the county several years later, I applied for it so I could enhance my pending retirement. However, I did not get the job, which was one of the most disappointing moments in my professional life. There was no doubt of my ability, but I had not the "in" nor the "pull" to move beyond the classroom. This was another rejection.

A pattern formed in my life's quests. If I could control my circumstances, I was usually very successful. If I did not have control, I usually failed. I had no control over whether or not I would be hired for a better job, but I did have control over how to handle it.

So, I went to work and tried not to think about the job. What I would be missing was only money. Money is never "only" money.

CHAPTER THIRTY-EIGHT

Since I had moved away from home, thoughts of my adoption did not plague me as it once had. My city friends knew only what I told them, except for Peggy, who said, "You need to focus on the present and not think of the past." That was easy to say, but every time I went to Edmonton or saw my childhood friends, I slipped back to the Connie I was and not the Connie I had become.

I can't explain what prompted me to open up a conversation about my life and my so-called adoption among my traveling friends, but one night eight of us sat around a table in a rented condo in Florida on yet another trip when I said, "I have something I want to talk about." I was the quiet one in the group; the listener, so something serious was about to happen, and they were baffled

"You all know I am adopted but what I want to know is what you have heard about me. Don't anyone at this table say you don't know anything because I have a feeling you do."

I looked at each of them and almost regretted bringing up the subject. I didn't want to risk alienating them, but I also needed to get this out in the open. Times had changed, and adoption wasn't a life sentence anymore like it had been for me. Now I wanted information, but couldn't bring myself to ask my family. I thought I would see what these ladies knew and then tell them what I had learned.

Evidently, I had once been the hot topic in the entire county and even in other counties as well.

One account is still thought to be true in the area, and the girl on the steps who landed on her behind at school was alluding to it when she said, "I know who your mother is."

One of the ladies began. "By all accounts, a single woman (one of the ladies gave names but I won't) had been having an ongoing affair with an older married man and had gotten pregnant. She went to Louisville to deliver the baby, but it died. The family privately buried the baby in the family plot, but there was no baby in the plot. According to the story that instead of keeping the baby, the family pretended it died and even created a grave. They gave the baby up for adoption. You are supposed to be that baby."

"Believe me, I am not that baby."

"I don't know if this is true, but those who lived in and around these people vow it is. I hear what you are saying, but I can take you to that grave."

"I don't know who was passed off as being in that grave, but I don't think that is my story."

"You were supposedly taken by Bill and Cloteel."

"When did we start talking about this?" Judy asked Carol later when they sat on the balcony listening to the ocean beat against the sand.

"Tonight," she replied. "Something must have caused her to bring it up."

Another account was very similar except with different players. "This one involves a woman whose husband was in the war, and while he was gone, she had a fling with a married man. Because her husband would obviously know the difference, she had the baby in Louisville and gave it to your mom and dad," another of the women said. Both ladies provided me with names of my so-called mothers.

I laughed, "It appears that many people were trying to help out the Wilson's."

Another narrative perplexed me a little because it could have had some merit since I didn't know anything about my father.

I never saw this girl or her picture and she passed away when she was in her thirties, but according to those who knew her, I was the spitting image of a young woman who was only slightly younger than I and had graduated in a nearby county. Carol had seen her photo and thought the picture was of me.

For hours, we talked about my life and what they knew or had heard, and Carol took notes so I would remember. Even then I wanted to learn all I could about what others knew. Even then Carol and Judy said nothing.

I might have believed in any of the stories earlier in my life and actually might have sought the grave that I was supposed to have been in, but by then I knew my real story. In the early 80's, this truth came to me in the form of a phone call late one night.

CHAPTER THIRTY-NINE

"I HAVE SOMETHING TO TELL YOU," my cousin Brenda said loudly enough for anyone else in the room to hear. I waited. We (she and her husband) had a fight and in the middle of our spat, and he told me that he knew something I didn't know." I waited. Thoughts of another time when I had heard those words came back to me.

"He said that you weren't my cousin; you were my half sister!" I wasn't sure I had heard what she said, so when I didn't respond; she repeated it louder. "You and I are half-sisters. My mother is your mother, too! Can you believe it? All this time, we thought we were cousins, and then I find out we are half sisters!"

I couldn't speak. Words hung in my throat. This news was like receiving a phone call from a family member giving bad news, and the person goes into shock, drops the phone and collapses. What the devil was happening?

Through all the years of investigating and suffering with bouts of desperation and anxiety as I chased endless, disappointing clues, I now learn that my biological mother is not a stranger, but was a woman I had seen at least one a week all of my childhood! My birth mother was Aunt Hazel's oldest daughter, Fran? That meant Aunt Hazel was my grandmother. Cloteel Wilson was my great-aunt. How could all of this be true?

I paused and responded calmly, "How does he know this?" He could have the wrong information. What if he had made this up? Why would she believe him?

It didn't seem to matter how he knew or how long he had harbored this information. "I guess someone must have told him." Her life had been full of turmoil and hard times, that this moment was not earth shattering to her. It shook the ground under me ferociously.

She brushed off what I considered to be vital. If he were right, who else knew? Did the Smith family know and keep this from us? I felt sick.

"We have to tell the whole family that we know. This news is the best ever!" *What is happening right now? This person is my half-sister? I belong to the woman I thought was my aunt? I should be happy enough to burst, but I want to yell at someone. They made me suffer thinking my mother was a tramp when she was related to me? What I would have given to have known my real mother was not a stranger. How did I end up with Cloteel Wilson?*

"Brenda, we have to take this slowly." I was still reeling from this news, and she wanted a party? Until I sorted out this information and found a way to substantiate it, there would be no family gathering.

To say I was stunned would not be strong enough to capture what this news meant. If it were true, my birth mother was not a tramp, a hooker, or a woman from another part of the world. She was Fran Smith. What I didn't understand was how I ended up with Cloteel and Bill Wilson. I needed the entire story and there was only one person who could answer my questions; but before I went to her, I had to keep Brenda and her sister Sharon from spreading the word. The last thing I wanted was for my adopted parents to know about the phone call.

As a first step, Peggy suggested I invite Brenda and Sharon to my home where we spent an afternoon discussing what each knew. They, in reality, knew very little. They knew nothing about their mother's life before she married their dad, which meant they had no details about my birth or my father. By putting the timeline together, Fran must have married their dad about a year after I was born because Brenda was only two years older than I was.

"We can't go to the family with this yet. My parents have no idea that I even know I am adopted, so I can't just burst in with this news. I have to think about how to handle this." Brenda, however, did not want to wait. Sharon was more patient.

There was one person who could assure me Brenda was right.

Within a few days, I called Aunt Hazel in Smiths Grove. I would never have asked my mother. "I have to talk to you, and I can't do this by phone," I announced. She didn't ask questions.

"Well, come on down here." I took off a day from school and drove down during the time when I thought no one else would be at home. This was in 1982, and her children were all married.

"She is one of us." I had missed another clue. Aunt Hazel now lived in a large farmhouse style home in the city of Smiths Grove rather than on the farm where she had brought up her family. She and Uncle George had divorced and he had a new family. That was a relief for Aunt Hazel except that when he was old and sick, she took him back to take care of him.

She always had a pot of coffee, so she poured me a cup, and we took it to the living room. She sat in her easy chair, and I sat on an ottoman in front of her and we pretended to be company. I wasted no time. "Brenda called me a week ago and told me that Fran was my mother. Is that right?" Aunt Hazel did not flinch. She did not hesitate. Taking a risk of alienating her sister by telling me, she said, "That is right." As simple as that I had finally learned that her daughter was my mother. I felt my blood pressure rise.

"I need some answers. Will you tell me who I am? Who is my father? What happened?" She unraveled the story as if it had happened yesterday and with very little emotion.

"Fran went to a party in Glasgow with a group of other teenagers, and there was drinking. What happened to her would be like what we would call a date rape. Fran was backward in a way; she hadn't been to many parties or dated. Then when she found out she was pregnant; George (her father) laid down the law that she was not bringing that baby into this house. So, I was upset and didn't know what to do. I couldn't put her out so I told Cloteel, and before long, she called and asked me if she and Bill could raise you. She didn't think she could have children so this seemed like the best solution."

I couldn't help but wonder what input Fran had in this decision, but I presumed no one asked her. Aunt Hazel continued, "She was only seventeen, and this was 1945, so things were different back then and he didn't want a scandal, so this seemed like the best thing to do. That way you could still be part of us and Fran could go on with her life."

All those times when the families were together, I never understood why Fran was distant. Unlike her sisters, she had nothing to say to me and often would venture to another room. Now I understood why.

"Cloteel said they would take Fran to Louisville, and when the baby came they would bring Fran back home and take the baby with them. I couldn't believe they were willing to move to Louisville because of the store, and then when they said they would stay the entire time Fran was in the home,

I was so relieved that she wouldn't be alone." I would later learn that I was born in Susan Speed Davis Home for Unwed Mothers.

"Who is my father?" I asked.

"I don't remember his name. Just some boy at the party."

I could not and did not believe that Aunt Hazel had forgotten the boy's name. A mother would know the name of a guy whom she thought raped her daughter. She was likely sparing me from some further truth. Perhaps there had not been a date rape at all. Maybe they were both drinking, and she consented. I would never know the truth about my conception, and I assumed he never knew about me. If he had known, maybe he would have whisked Fran away and married her.

"In all the time I have been coming here," I said, "why would Fran not talk to me? For heaven's sake, I was her daughter, but she never acted like she wanted anything to do with me."

"I don't think she could stand it," Aunt Hazel replied. *Yet the rest of you didn't seem to be bothered. How could you let this happen?*

"So, I stood over the casket of the woman I thought was my cousin, and she was my mother?" This was surreal.

"Yes, I'm afraid so."

"You buried my mother without telling me? I stood at her casket and felt so sad because I didn't know her the way I knew Wanda and Betty and Phyllis and all your other children and thought I had done something to make her not want to be friendly with me?" It wasn't a question.

Aunt Hazel was a little nervous at this point. "Cloteel came to me when Fran died and asked if I thought she should tell you the truth. I told her that after all these years I didn't see how knowing could help you now. I wanted to tell you myself years before Fran died, but I couldn't do it. I couldn't hurt your mother, and I didn't think I should bring up the past."

A Girl Named Connie

I was not the past; I was the present. I was Hazel's first grandchild and she had allowed her oldest daughter to give up her baby. Did it occur to any of them that watching me grow up was heartbreaking?

Fran died in 1968 when I was in college. At the age of forty, she hit a tree head on, doing ninety miles per hour. According to the family, she had a stroke. "She had dropped off a kid she had picked up who was walking to school and minutes after she let him out, she hit that tree."

When Fran died, my mother was hysterical. She cried and cried. After all, this was her niece. What I didn't know was the guilt she was also likely feeling that she had allowed my mother to die without my knowing the truth. Now it was too late.

All I knew about my birth mother was that she married a man who wasn't good to her and gave birth to Brenda and then Sharon, who was two years younger than Brenda. Getting away from home might have forced her to marry this man in the first place. They divorced, and she brought her girls back to Aunt Hazel's where she lived until remarrying, and her daughters lived until they married. When I asked Brenda about those days, she said, "I honestly don't remember my childhood. It was like a fog." Fran might never have gotten over my birth and consequently, she could not straighten out her life.

"Fran was different," Wanda told me long after I learned the truth. "She kinda withdrew herself from us." Wanda was only six when all of this took place, so she grew up knowing Fran had been sent away but she didn't know why.

"Fran was a kind person," Wanda said, "who would give you the shirt off her back."

"What did you think when my mother (Cloteel) came to visit and brought this baby with her? Did you wonder where I came from? Did you ever think I might belong to Fran?" I asked.

"I just thought they had adopted a baby. I never thought that there was a connection with you and Fran. Remember, Connie, I was only six years old and nobody talked about the situation. I didn't know anything until Fran died and then Mom Bybee (I would have been her first great-grandchild) told me. I was a grown woman." She wasn't alone; no one in the family knew I was Fran's baby until after Fran died. This had been a well-kept secret within the family, but evidently not among the townspeople. How Brenda's husband knew this is still a mystery.

I felt sorry for Fran. I felt sorry for me. A lie by omission is still a lie. For a long time, I resented those who didn't tell me more than I resented Fran for being so weak that she gave me up.

Nothing made sense to me. Out of the blue, my mother decided to solve Hazel's problem by taking the baby? Did they agree not to tell me or anyone else the truth? I could not believe that someone would not have let it slip. "Mother never told us anything," Wanda said years later when I questioned her. "We knew Fran went off for awhile, but I was too little to know why and nobody talked about it."

"Did she come back as if nothing happened?" I asked.

"Pretty much. You have to remember this was a time when kids didn't ask questions."

Later, I went back to Aunt Hazel with more questions. "Who else knows?

"Everyone probably does by now." What did that mean? I wanted to ask why it was acceptable for me to come into the house as Bill and Cloteel's daughter but not as their granddaughter. I tried to be upset with Aunt Hazel

A Girl Named Connie

for allowing her husband to be so cruel to Fran, but I knew she was afraid of him. They all were.

It was then I knew that keeping the secret of my adoption was not to protect me; it was to protect Fan. I decided not to tell my mother or my father what Brenda or Aunt Hazel revealed to me. The fear of hurting them kept me from saying, "I know who my mother is, and it's fine." This time NOTHING was fine.

Fran had been dead for fourteen years by the time I knew the truth, so I saw no reason to change the dynamics of my family. Brenda and Sharon would continue to be my cousins in front of others. I was so relieved to come from my mother's bloodline that nothing else mattered. I now had roots. I didn't need public validation. Fran was my birth mother and Cloteel raised me. As for my father, I had no thoughts about him until a decade later.

I concluded that Uncle George, Cloteel, and Bill made a deal. Cloteel and Bill would bring raise me and make sure the rest of the family saw me often. That is why we visited Aunt Hazel and her children almost every Sunday; more than we visited any of my mother's other siblings. After all, the woman I thought as my Aunt Hazel was my grandmother. I was the oldest Smith grandchild, even though I was a Wilson. I was the first grandchild for Aunt Hazel and the first great-grand child for Mom Bybee. Now I understood about the lamp, and that I was nothing more than….a business transaction.

CHAPTER FORTY

In 1997, I found myself in a dilemma. I assumed my parents had adopted me by the time they brought me to Edmonton, so was shocked when I applied for a birth certificate and discovered there was no Connie Allen Wilson born on April 10, 1946. Not only was I not their child, but I was also never legally adopted.

"Are you sure?" I asked the clerk at the Frankfort office.

"Let me check again," she said. "Are you sure of the birth date?"

I wasn't sure of anything, but I had celebrated my birthday on this date, so I assumed they knew.

"As far as I know that is the right date. I was adopted."

She searched again. "I can't find any record of your birth or adoption."

I thanked her and hung up.

Then it occurred to me that maybe I was never adopted. Why didn't I think of this when my dad handed me that notarized letter years ago? All those years that I didn't want to be adopted led me to the day when I wished I had been. I was not a Wilson, which meant I was still a Smith. Why would they not adopt me?

The problem was that I could not retire without a birth certificate with the name Connie Allen Wilson on it so what was I going to do?

I stewed over this for days. Part of me thought my parents felt there was no need to adopt me since I was my mother's great niece while the other part assumed they didn't want to adopt me. I had no immediate answer or solution.

Then it occurred to me that the "home" would have sent my birth certificate to Frankfort. Since I knew my birth mother's name, I was going to go that route, hoping it might offer some legal evidence of my existence that would satisfy the state retirement officials. This time, I sought the help of another lady I knew who worked at the office of vital statistics in Frankfort. Years ago I would have given anything to have seen my birth records.

Not understanding that this certificate would not contain any information with the Wilson name on it showed my naiveté. I wasn't prepared to see my actual birth certificate from fifty-one years ago but decided nothing could hurt me now. I was wrong.

"Can you do a little snooping for me?" I asked my friend. "Would you look for a certificate for a child born to Jewell Frances Smith on April 10, 1946, in Louisville?" I approached this as if I were conducting business.

After a few minutes, she said, "I have one here in front of me on the computer screen. Were you by any chance born at the Susan Speed Davis Home for Unwed Mothers?"

"Yes, to Jewell Frances Smith," I repeated.

"Hum, you aren't Connie Allen on this document. The name on this one is Connie Ailene Smith."

Had Fran named me Connie Ailene? My parents had changed my name to Allen. I was Connie Ailene Smith; not Connie Allen Wilson. To some women that would have made no difference, but it was unnerving. To be one name and find out you have another is strange.

"Can I get a copy?" Within days, I was holding it in my hands. This paper transported me back to the day I was born to a woman who might not have wanted me or might not have known how to keep me. This paper triggered a deep sadness, and I hadn't even opened the envelope.

I sat at my dining room table and slid the document out. Since I was very young, I had longed for the information inside this brown manila envelope. My detective work had led me in many directions, but it took a mad husband in a fight with his wife to give me answers.

There it was: Registrar of Vital Statistics Certified Copy at the top of the document. I was nervous. Was I ready to look at my birth certificate? Was I ready to go back to the time when my broken mother (I assumed) was forced to give me up and watch her aunt raise me without touching me or holding me or smiling at me? Would this document tell me more than I already knew? I put the envelope on the table and poured myself a cup of coffee.

The following weekend I had a compelling desire to find the home of unwed mothers where I was born. Driving around the area, I knew it didn't look as it probably had in 1945, but what I saw was a structure that looked very much like a hospital, but outside in the garden, I stood in front of a statue of a woman holding a baby. That statue symbolized all mothers and their children, legitimate or not. I will never get that place out of my mind or the women who went there who were most likely under extreme duress and heartbreak.

Every piece of paper I had signed or form I had filled out since I was young was in the name of Connie Allen Wilson. All my school records, my driver's license, and my social security card had the name Wilson, but according to the state department, there was no such person. How could they not have made me legal? Part of me was a little miffed. Evidently, they had not wanted to adopt me. Then I left miffed and went straight to ticked off.

They could have saved all of us a great deal of unhappiness if they had been honest with me. I would not have gone through years of thinking the worst about myself and my mother. Maybe I could have helped her. I had a good life; better than hers from all accounts, so maybe she wouldn't have suffered so much if we could have been friends and I could have told her it was fine.

My problem was not solved. Nothing in this document would assist in my retirement. My dad couldn't "fix" this, and I didn't know any way to become legal other than through the courts. There was only one way to do that. Perhaps I built up my nerve because I was more than a little irritated and frankly, I didn't care much about how my parents felt at that moment. I was going to take care of my problem first instead of worrying about hurting them.

I called home and without hesitation, I said, "Mother, I need a birth certificate." I wanted to throw her back a few steps.

There was a long pause. Dead air.

"Why do you need a birth certificate?"

"I can't retire without a legal document with my name on it. I don't have one. I called Frankfort, and there isn't one in my name."

I was digging at her a little. By now she was in her late seventies, so I should have been a little softer. She and Dad thought they would never have to face me with this truth, but I could not protect them any longer.

"Let me talk to your dad. I'll call you back." I could picture the scene at home.

In minutes, the phone rang. "Sister, I have something to tell you." I stopped her.

"I know, Mother. You don't have to tell me, and it's all right. If you all would like to adopt me, I have worked out the details, and we can get this done Thursday."

"Of course, we want to adopt you." Just like that. *Of course, we want to adopt you.* Then why after all these years had they not done so?

"Then here is what you need to do." I had made arrangements down to the smallest detail. If one thing were out of order, my dad might bolt.

Before telling my mother, I had called my friend and a local attorney. "Herb, this is Connie Wilson. I need to be adopted." He was taken aback because he thought I had already been adopted. I then explained my need for legal paperwork.

"This is not something I have done," he laughed. "I'll have to check to see if someone your age can even be adopted." I was fifty-one.

He called back very soon. "Connie, it is legal for you to be adopted so we can move forward. How do you want to do this?"

"Very discreetly." He set the court date, and all I had to do was get my parents there. We would go before a judge in his chambers. This adoption would be without fanfare.

"Mother, I will be down Thursday, and we will go to the courthouse, and you all will adopt me. I will be there before Dad leaves for work." I was very unemotional about the details. I approached this as a business meeting. "Be ready when I get there to take care of this," I said. "Be sure Dad is ready." I didn't mean have his clothes on.

"That will be fine." I could hear a bit of uneasiness in her voice. To speak of what happened so long ago was difficult, but what was worse was that their secret had not really been one at all.

I made the trip home and waited to be adopted.

A Girl Named Connie

PART III

CHAPTER FORTY-ONE

MY GREATEST CHALLENGE sat in front of me, and I was losing my nerve. Dad continued to read his newspaper.

My mother slid the eggs Benedict onto my plate and turned back to the stove. I wanted her to say something, but she didn't. I ate my eggs even though my stomach was uneasy. I knew I had to make the first move.

"Dad, you know why I'm here?"

He nodded, looking off at the TV.

"I know this is hard for you, but I can't retire without one."

"I know," he said.

I did not want to agitate or say anything that might cause him to back out. He wanted no attention drawn to himself or consideration of what might people think seeing him at the courthouse. He was peculiar, and we all knew it.

"Dad, I'll come by the store a little before ten if that is okay, and we will walk over to the courthouse together."

"All right," he said as he put the paper down, folded it, picked up his hat and walked out the door. This exchange was painful for the three of us, but it had to happen.

He opened the doors of the store promptly at eight o'clock every morning and this day would be no different. After he had left, I watched the clock and Mother, and I avoided conversation.

Dad closed the store for two hours that day. He had never closed the store during the day, but he posted a sign for his customers. "Be Back Soon." The ladies were not working, and I always thought it was to avoid having to explain anything to them or have them speculate.

In an awkward silence, the three of us walked across the street, through the courthouse yard, up the steps, and into the historic courtroom. We sat in the back while all the derelicts in the county came before the judge on charges that ranged from cold checks to petty theft to domestic violence.

Not a person in that courtroom did not know my mom and dad, so naturally they cast glances as if to ask why Bill, his wife, and daughter were in the courtroom. No one said, "Bill, what are you doing here." They probably thought I was in trouble, and they were there to get me out of it. I was a little old to be in trouble.

Finally, we were called into chambers and sat nervously as the details unfolded. The judge said, "This may seem like a very unusual situation, but I assure you it isn't." He was trying to put us at ease. I knew this was not a common occurrence. Adopting someone my age was not an everyday affair, but I appreciated his effort to make this as comfortable as possible. "Who would like to tell me the story of how this unfolded?" I don't know if he *had* to know the story or just *wanted* to know the story, but I was glad he had asked or otherwise I might never have heard it from my mother's lips.

Without hesitation, my mother began. "My sister called to tell me her daughter was pregnant, and my brother-in-law would not let Fran, their daughter, bring the baby into the house, so Fran, as we called her, was going to give up the baby. Bill and I talked about it and decided that we wanted to have this baby. We had been trying, but I couldn't get pregnant. I went to my sister, told her what we wanted to do, and she agreed." All the time I was listening, I wondered if anyone had asked Fran what she wanted to do.

"We told Hazel that we would take Fran to Louisville and stay with her until the baby was born. That's what we did. We picked Fran up at the end of the road when we took her to Louisville and when it was time to come home; we brought her back to the same spot. Her mother was waiting for her at the end of the road so she could walk her to the house. Hazel looked in the window to see the baby, and that was it. We always planned to adopt Connie, but at first, we were afraid Fran might want her back, so we gave it some time and then we simply let too much time go by and it didn't seem necessary."

My dad did not speak. "Connie, do you want to be adopted?" the judge asked.

"Yes, I do."

He slid papers in front of us and I became the legal daughter of Bill and Cloteel Wilson. No one walking to and from stores, buying groceries, paying bills, looking for a parking spot had any idea that Bill and Cloteel Wilson were inside the courtroom adopting their fifty-one-year-old daughter. Most of them would have thought my parents had adopted me years ago. Some never knew I was not Connie Wilson.

We left the courthouse in silence, walked back across the grassy yard, Dad unlocked the store, and I drove back home to Louisville. For another girl in another family, this day might have been monumental. There might have been hugging or crying or some indication that it was not just an ordinary day, but not in my family. Emotions were guarded and often ignored. In some situations, the media would have captured this moment for the local paper, but that would not have been at all acceptable.

My parents had protected their secret and Mother would continue to act as if nothing had changed. However, it was on this day my adoption would forever alter my relationship with my father. He would not look me directly in the eye and was more standoffish. This awkwardness went on for a month. I had to "fix" this problem.

I think what upset him was that I now knew that I belonged to my mother's family but not to him. I never talked to him about this, but I did have an opportunity not long afterward to try to reassure him.

I came home a few weeks later and went to the store. When no one was there, I put my hand on his arm and said, "You are the only father I have ever had, and you will always be my only father." He shook his head as if to say he understood.

My lawyer filed the adoption papers, and I would soon get a copy of my new birth certificate and submit my retirement papers.

Not one time after this day did my parents and I discuss what had happened, but I could tell a difference in my dad. He looked as if he had lost me. One time when he and Mother were having one of their heated conversations, he stopped and said, "We better not do this in front of Connie, or she'll know how we Wilsons are."

"Bill, she has lived with us all her life. I guess by now she has caught on." This was the first time Dad had made me feel a visitor.

Within a year after they adopted me, my dad sold his store. I learned about the sale after the fact. Shocked and dismayed, I couldn't understand such a move. "Why would Dad sell the store? He loved the store?" I asked Mother.

A Girl Named Connie

My mother said, "He's tired. He needed to get out of the business." By her agreeing with the decision, I knew there must have been a good reason. Not that it was a good one, but I later surmised why he did it. Money.

My dad would have died behind that counter if something hadn't pushed him to do the unthinkable. His store was so famous a reporter from the *Courier* had written a feature story about him and for a while, he was an icon throughout the state. A legendary place of business closing its doors without fanfare was unusual. There was no "going out of business" sale; there was no warning. One day he was standing on the street talking to whittlers and the next he was locking his door for the final time. He would not have a reason to go to town at night to check the door.

The person who bought the merchandise did not keep the store open but moved all the items to another location. Later, the city bought the building and it is now a police dispatch center. My heart breaks each time I go back to Edmonton and see a building I do not recognize.

Never would I have dreamed of my dad selling his store, but I sure never would have thought he would have done it without telling me. I had no "last time" to walk through the narrow aisle, turn sideways to get up and down the steps, or pull a box from a stack of Nancy King underwear. In thinking this was a family business, my disappointment in not being including in the decision to sell hurt me deeply. Confident my brother knew, I was beginning to see a pattern of him becoming connected in a way that I was not. They were so tightly woven that it was hard for me to make my way inside. My brother continued to live with my parents until they both died. I was mostly surprised that he wasn't saving the store for my brother.

Under normal conditions, I might have broken out in a full-blown fit of anger. "What do you mean selling the store without telling me? Do you know what this store means to me? I didn't get to take out one single thing to keep as a reminder of growing up here." They would conclude that they never thought I would care.

My brother, as far as I knew, never knew about our courthouse date.

CHAPTER FORTY-TWO

I MIGHT HAVE CONCLUDED that God was going to ease up on me. I had been through enough drama to last the rest of my time. I spent my youth wishing to know my origin; then I found my birth mother was right under my nose but died before anyone told me. When I came to terms with that, I discovered I was not legally a Wilson and then to top it off, after I was adopted my dad sold the store I had loved all my life. What next?

Just when life was going smoothly, and I had filed my retirement papers, Peggy and I were with her family at the Smokey Mountains State Park, and she privately told me she might have a problem. "One of my breasts looks funny."

"Do you want me to look?" I asked.

"If you don't mind." She showed enough for me to see it was turning a variety of colors from blue to green and looked very infected.

"You need to see about this as soon as we get home." I didn't want to scare her, but I would have left for a hospital then. How long had she been watching this breast turn from normal to abnormal? Why hadn't she mentioned it?

Back in Louisville, her doctor immediately started her on an antibiotic, and she was told to come back in two weeks for a sonogram. "Let's get the infection out so we can see what is going on," he said. That made sense to me. When she was well enough for the test, the results detected a tiny lump.

"It is small," she told me, "and the doctor said I shouldn't worry, but he's going to do a biopsy to be sure." She was not worried, but I was terrified. "You don't have to take off from school and go with me," she insisted, but I didn't listen. I wanted to be there.

The doctor removed the lump, and she waited with confidence that it was "nothing." Peggy always faced hardships with a positive attitude as compared to my assumption that when the word "cancer" is said, nothing good was going to happen.

"I'm sure I got it all," the doctor said after the surgery. The pathology report came back as stage one cancer, which was the best news for a person to receive other than benign. Fortunately, it was contained, and he was confident he had removed all the cells and radiation would take care of the chances of it spreading. She was thrilled with the rosy picture he painted, but I saw only potential dangers.

She didn't need chemo. That was the best news he could have given and she was overjoyed. This would mean she would escape the sickness and vomiting that came with chemo treatments during this time. For some reason, I didn't trust cancer with no chemo, but this was not my family, so I kept quiet. She went to her radiation treatments and continued to work as if she was not going through cancer. Peggy was not a complainer, and none of her family ever showed a sign of defeat. They approached her cancer as if it were a minor bump in the road. I could not do that. The thought of losing her led me straight into depression, but I managed to keep a positive outlook in front of her. I was a wreck.

Within six months, her breast had swollen twice its size, became infected again and was extremely painful. The fear in her eyes scared me because it was the first time she had shown that emotion. "We have to get you to the doctor," I said.

He was baffled. "I honestly don't know what is going on, but I do know we need to do another biopsy. First, we have to get rid of the infection." *Puzzled* is not a word a cancer patient wants to hear. After rounds of antibiotics and another scan of her breast, the results were not good. That tiny lump had metastasized to her bone.

"How is this possible when it was in stage one?" she asked as only Peggy would do in her soft, non-threatening voice. I wanted to blame him. I wanted to put my hands around his neck and choke him. I wanted to yell, "YOU SHOULD HAVE ORDERED CHEMO."

"Sometimes the chicken gets out of the coup," he replied. Did he compare her cancer to a chicken getting out of the coup? I did not see the humor and neither did she.

"Who is your oncologist?" he asked.

"You never gave her an oncologist!"

"Well, we better get you one," he said, "I will schedule a mastectomy."

"YOU will not touch her again," I said.

He became indignant. "It's not my fault."

"Then whose fault is it? Don't worry; she won't sue you. She is nicer than I am."

I needed to be mad, but in addition to being upset with him, I blamed myself for not following my instincts.

"You need a second opinion," I said as we left his office. So she changed doctors. This one also recommended a mastectomy followed by chemo and more radiation. We braced for the surgery.

He took out the second lump and discovered cancer had spread to the nodes. Within the time that followed, it would eventually move to her bones and her brain.

When I told my mother and dad about her treatment, I remember Dad said, "Don't let them burn her up."

At thirty-six years old, she was facing the greatest battle of her life.

After surgery and for many weeks to follow, she was so sick she couldn't work. She could barely sit up. Her hair fell out, her muscles weakened, and her weight dropped. I tried to prepare bland food to keep up her strength, but every bite she ate came up. I felt helpless, and so did her sisters.

Then she rallied. Within a few weeks, she had more energy and mobility. She was able to go back to work, and we thought maybe she was going to lick this disease. I have never seen such bravery and determination. She seemed to be the same person she had been before cancer. Had I witnessed a miracle? God was protecting her, but He was also protecting me.

I became her cheerleader as well as her coach. Whatever she wanted to do, we did. She didn't want much. I made sure each day was without stress as much as a day in the life of a cancer patient can be. Her checkups were mostly good ones for a few years. Sometimes her levels would be too high or too low; but with medication, those could be regulated. In the meantime, life was flowing as normally as possible. She put on her wig and went to work.

CHAPTER FORTY-THREE

Sometimes a diversion is a gift from God. Peggy and I needed one, and when I received a call from Carol, I couldn't help but think this was it.

Carol had retired the same year that I did and with their children gone, she was antsy. Keep in mind, I have never been good at saying "no."

"I have a business idea," she said when she called me late one night. "I want us to open a thrift shop. I want you to be my partner."

I didn't know how I could be a partner one hundred miles away and with Peggy's precarious health, but I was willing to listen. Business interested me, but I had never been a thrift shop person.

"We'll fix up Dad's TV shop and between the two of us, we'll have enough stuff to fill it the first time. I need you to find a source in Louisville to buy clothes for us to resell." Her dad had been dead twenty years, and various businesses had been in and out of the shop, so it would be an ideal location but needed some work.

"Get clothes where?"

"We have to find a source. Maybe you can inquire where these other thrift stores get their clothes." We weren't going to be a consignment shop but a place that bought low and sold a little higher.

"I think we need to talk about this," I said and drove down for the weekend.

Within a month, we began our project. Carol, with Peggy's help, designed a layout for the store, and Guy and I hung racks and built shelves. I wasn't as interested in this business as I was in giving Peggy a new focus. She laughed with Carol as they priced the clothing and placed each piece on racks. Hearing her laugh was musical. I thought she might kick this illness as long as she was laughing.

This business would have continued longer than three years except for two things: our source for clothing was drying up, and Carol was offered a job teaching English at the middle school level. This was supposed to be an "emergency" position for one year but it turned into six. We closed the store, but today people still remember shopping at Fantastic Finds.

The best part of opening this store was the time Carol and I spent together and how involved Peggy became with the process. No matter how many miles between us, Carol, Roberta, Judy and I never waived in our friendship, and Peggy became the fifth player on our team.

During the time I was coming to Edmonton to bring clothes for the store, Peggy and I visited Mother and Dad an hour or so and then spent the night at Carol's. Mother never understood why I would prefer to stay somewhere else. How could I tell her I didn't want to be there? There was too much drama, and I never knew when tempers would flare, and that would have embarrassed me in front of Peggy.

"We have business to discuss," was always my answer.

A Girl Named Connie

As far as my mother and dad were concerned, I was living a prosperous life and a happy one. They knew about Peggy's cancer, but not the extent of it.

In my attempt to appear financially comfortable, I showered my nephew with gifts. I am positive this was to compensate for my inability to love him the way I should have. During these years, I could not say "no" to him because I had established a pattern of giving and didn't know how to stop.

So when he decided to marry, which was a total shock because I didn't know he had a girlfriend, he called me. I was always there for him if he needed me and this time, he needed me badly.

"Connie, I have a favor to ask." *Of course, you do.*

"What is it?" I tried to be cordial.

"My girlfriend wants to have a wedding, but she has no money and her parents won't give her a wedding, and she is upset. Can you help us?"

"Let me understand this. You are getting married, and you want ME to pay for a wedding?"

"Yes."

"What's wrong with her parents?"

"They don't want her to get married." I didn't know if that were true or not. Maybe they just didn't want to pay for a wedding.

I thought about this for a week and felt sorry for him, so I caved. He called me again after I had agreed to give him a little money. I had not met this girl and the reason I was footing the bill instead of James or Mother or Dad was because they were not supportive of this wedding and with good reason.

"Can we get married next week?"

"What is the hurry?"

He stalled! He was just a kid straight out of high school marrying a girl who happened to be pregnant. I wanted to choke him. I also did not want this baby to be given away.

"I'll help, but I can't do much."

Over the next few days, he called about a cake. He called about buying her a wedding dress and a ring (he had no money for a ring) and flowers and paying for a reception. By the end of the week, I had consented to finance more than just a little wedding.

To make it special for him, I even bought a bottle of champagne and two nice flutes to use during the toast. Just like a real bride and groom. These flutes had been a gift to me, so when he asked if they could keep them I should have said "no."

I knew this marriage wouldn't last a year.

Shortly after the baby was born, I began to buy gifts for him and tried to find a way to bond with my great-nephew, but doing so was impossible. He and his bride were breaking up and making up, and grandparents were intervening until finally they divorced. I never saw the child again. He is now a teenager.

My hometown friends and I are wired so differently.

"How can you not have a relationship with your nephew?" Carol asked not so long ago. She loves her nieces and nephews tremendously.

"All I mean to him is money."

"What about his son? You don't even know where he is!"

I had no response. Emotionally, I could not insert myself in these relationships, and if they came to me, I knew it was for money. The bickering and the atmosphere of instability kept me away. At least, that is what I told myself. Maybe I did not have the capacity to love. Maybe I had a hard heart. I don't know why I could not attach myself to my brother, my nephew or my great nephew, yet I became like a real aunt to Peggy's. Sometimes I felt guilty because of my lack of attention and affection.

Peggy watched me being taken advantage of but never criticized or offered advice even though I knew what she thought. She never wanted to interfere with my personal situations if they did not include her.

CHAPTER FORTY-FOUR

DURING THE TIME Peggy was in remission, we traveled with my friends to Las Vegas, a city she loved. All of us focused on her comfort and pampered her without her noticing. Pampering was not her style; she didn't know how to receive it.

 Peggy refused to rest; she wanted to walk up and down the strip, shop in the stores, and take in the lights at night. I think she knew this would be her last trip. I certainly feared it might be.

One night we girls decided to eat at the famous buffet at the Rio. As we stood in the long line, casting our eyes around, passing the time, chatting and shifting from one hip to another (before cell phones), all of a sudden I saw this punk looking kid step into line in front of a person behind me.

"Hey you, what do you think you are doing?" I yelled, pointing my finger at him. My friends turned around to see to whom I was addressing.

Carol said, "Do you know him?"

"Hell no, I don't know him, but he thinks he can walk up here and break line in front of these people and get by with it after we've been standing in line for nearly an hour." I was speaking so loudly others were turning around to look at me. At that time, we were close to having a plate in our hands.

"You get your ass to the back of the line," I said and pointed the way.

"But I'm with them people," he slurred, motioning to the couple in front of whom he had broken. I turned to them.

"Is he with you?"

Then I went up and down the line, "Is he with you and you and you?" He wasn't with anyone.

"Get out of this line and get back there," I yelled.

Some of his buddies had arrived just about the time he turned to go and looked as if they were going to whip me. I got them first, "If you know what's good for you, you'll go on back there, too." They left.

I turned to those around me and said, "I don't work as a lunchroom monitor for nothing."

Would I have done this if I had been in my right mind? Probably not, but when you are in a certain stage of grief, you fear little, and I was not going to stand by and let this boy cut line. I was looking for a fight. I wanted him to sass me; I wanted to tackle him to the ground and beat his face. I wanted to do to him what I had longed to do to Lisa.

Peggy didn't know, and neither did my friends, but I had begun to grieve for her.

"I'm glad he didn't try to whip you," Judy said. "We would all have landed in the hospital."

When the trip was over, all of us knew this would be the last time Peggy would travel with us. She was to begin a journey of her own.

CHAPTER FORTY-FIVE

By EARLY 2000, my dad had a car accident, which was the beginning of his downfall. He pulled out from a local convenient store, and a car going far over the speed limit hit him before he could get out of the way. An ambulance took him to the hospital, and Mother called me.

I rushed from Louisville and insisted moving him to Bowling Green, a larger facility with more options. "I'm not going; the insurance won't pay for it!" he shouted in ER, acting like a madman.

"Yes, it will." I didn't know if it would or not, but what I did know was that we were moving to Bowling Green.

It was there he would have his first thorough examination, at least as long as I could remember. The reports came back that his urine was bloody, and tests showed an enlarged heart and prostate trouble. He knew he had problems with his prostrate, but did not know about his heart. He assumed he had cancer. He kept saying, "I know I have cancer. I have cancer. You know I have cancer." I couldn't console this strong man.

A Girl Named Connie

"Dad, Peggy has cancer. You don't have cancer." I repeated this until he stopped declaring he had cancer and driving the nurses crazy with his insane ranting.

I stayed with Dad at the hospital for a week with him complaining about the ambulance ride being "rougher than a road wagon" and about the nurses, the doctors, and whatever else was keeping him from being at home. Dad was a "pistol" to deal with and that is why I was there and my brother was home with my mother. I could handle him at least a little. My brother could not.

When I finally took him home, he was painfully weak, and I realized that it would take a while for him to build up his strength. If he had cooperated, he might have gotten better. For some reason, he saw death in front of him and walked toward it.

While 2000 was a bad year for Dad, it was Peggy's best year. She felt well, her numbers were up, and life resumed somewhat normally, but she was never going to feel like working again so staying alive became her job.

Mother called every other day to keep me updated, but when she told me Dad didn't want to eat, I came home and forced him to go to the doctor. He was wearing me out with his childish behavior, but I wish I had sought the reason for his trying to starve himself.

"Dad, you have to eat," I begged him. He would simply say he wasn't hungry. His heart was failing, but he was too stubborn to cooperate with Mother or me. Even though he was difficult to keep alive, I saw the fear of dying in his eyes.

Within a week, he was admitted once again, but this time to the nearby hospital; and during the same time, my mother fell and broke her hip. Now I had two headstrong patients. Since they were in the same hospital, I saw no reason why they couldn't be in the same room where they would be happier. That was a mistake.

The pattern of arguing they had found so easy at home did not cease just because they were in a public place. Mother complained and Dad growled at her. He complained and she growled at him. Growing tired of listening to their pettiness, I asked Dad why he was so angry. He said, "I never thought I would be in a place where I couldn't get up and help your mother." I left the room rather than cry in front of him. They loved each other, but I had doubted it because of the way they fought and the razor edge they used against each other in the form of words.

One day, as I headed toward their room, their doctor came out in tears. I stopped her, thinking something terrible had happened to one of them. How many times does one see a doctor cry?

"What is the matter?"

"You are adopted? Right?" She was from India.

"Yes, why?" I couldn't image how she knew this since it was such a guarded secret.

"Be glad you are. I asked when you would arrive and was informed that you made no decisions because you were not blood. Be glad you are not blood." Someone had hurled insulting remarks to this lady about her speech and her being a foreigner.

What she had wanted my father to do was necessary, and I would eventually convince him to follow her orders, but I did not tell him about the episode in the hall. I wasn't sure who had disrespected this doctor so badly, but when pushed into a corner, it could have been any of them. This was the first time someone in my immediate family, to my knowledge, had told anyone outside the family that I was not blood.

For the next year, both were in and out of hospitals, and I was making weekly trips to take care of them. Retirement had come at the right time. I was exhausted but tried to reason with both of them when it came to their care. My dad did not follow orders, and mother could not make him. They battled while my brother refereed.

The weekend after he was back home once again, Dad and I had our first and last major argument, and it was about his decision to appoint a Power of Attorney.

"Why do you need a Power of Attorney? You are doing better," I insisted when he told me of his decision. My dad and his money were inseparable, but he was about to divorce it.

"I know I'm not well, and you and James will need to make decisions about money, so I may not be able to think straight, and you two will need to make sure Mother has what she needs." He had to be losing his mind; never would he have made such a move if he were sane.

I looked at him, standing in the middle of the living room floor, very ill at ease. "Why can this not wait?" He could tell by my tone that I was not agreeing to this plan.

"Because my health is not good and I know it. Someone is going to have to keep this house going, pay the bills, and take care of your mother if I can't." He was worried about Mother, but what else was bothering him?

I was frightened. This moment made me realize that Dad thought he was going to die. Giving up power over his money was unthinkable. Was he giving up on life? As long as he was able to make decisions, I did not fear losing him. Now I was overcome with despair, but once he turned over his power, he was giving up. This much I knew.

"Fine." That is all I could say. I was mad and he knew it. I assumed he was going to give all his power to James.

"I want you and your brother to both be Powers of Attorney. I want either one of you to be able to sign checks in case the other one is not here." This did not sound like my dad talking.

I must have looked puzzled. Finally, James spoke. "I'm the one here all the time. I'm the one taking care of them and sometimes we need money." He sounded like a child.

Knowing I would not win this battle, I did what he wanted. This was the first time I felt my dad had chosen my brother's wishes over mine.

With Dad's failing health, he became dependent on James to take care of Mother. He knew I would take care of him as I had been doing.

Not long after that, my dad ended up in a nursing home basically because he refused to eat. In the meantime, the guy with whom he had wrecked sued for injuries. I think Dad feared that this would result in having to pay a large settlement. Maybe that is why he made us Powers of Attorney. He was the only one badly hurt, so I never knew why they were suing. By then, Dad was in his eighties.

One day as I was sitting beside his bed, he leaned over to me and said, "Sister, I need you to get me papers to sign for no one to try to save me."

"You mean you don't want to be resuscitated? Dad, I can't do that."

His voice was weak but his purpose strong. He knew he was dying, even though I didn't. I did know that if my brother knew I had helped my father with a living will and if he weren't resuscitated, he and my mother would accuse me of helping to "kill" my father. However, in spite of what they would have said, I did what my father asked. He signed a living will, and no one knew the difference.

My dad's refusal to eat only weakened his heart and moved him closer to death. No matter how much I begged him, he would not eat a bite. "I'm not hungry, Sister." Watching a man such as my dad dwindle away and my being powerless over him was a nightmare I cannot dismiss.

During the time my dad was in the nursing home, and my mother was recuperating at home, my aunt Hazel's health was failing. I don't think any of us knew how bad she was until she entered the hospital. Her son called to tell me I needed to come, but by the time I drove down from Louisville, she had passed.

Her death was devastating. She was the matriarch of the family. Her eulogy, beautifully given by her minister, reminded us of her humble life and giving spirit. "She never amassed great amounts of money or became surrounded by the luxuries of life, but she provided what was necessary for her large family of children, not only the food and clothing and shelter they needed but something much more important-a sense of security that allowed each of them to venture forth." I thought about Fran and the fact no one knew outside the family how much the family had violated her sense of security when they sent her to that home and took away her baby.

He talked about her thirty-one grandchildren, but he was wrong. There were thirty-two. Unlike all of them, I never got to call her Granny Smith. My mother grieved for her sister. I think it took its toll on her.

In 2001, my father slipped away in his sleep. I had taken Peggy to the beach because she wanted to go one more time. I knew I ran the risk of something happening, but Peggy's life seemed to be the more likely one to end first. By now, she was much weaker than she had been just months before.

My dad promised me he would eat while I was gone. "I'll be okay," he said when I told him I was leaving for a few days. When Carol called one afternoon, I could tell from her voice that Dad was gone. My brother had called her, looking for me. I had not told him I was leaving town.

Dad's death was not unexpected, but that didn't make it less shattering for me. He had been the strongest force in my life, and when he decided to starve himself to death, no one could change his mind. He was as stubborn in dying as he was in living.

I had watched his body go from robust to frail. Mother, by now in a wheelchair, was not prepared to lose him either. I wish I had asked him why he wanted to die.

That night when I tried to sleep, I kept seeing the image of my father walking up the street to a place we called "Jot'em Downs" with me sitting around his neck and holding onto his baldhead. Even though he wounded our relationship in his last few weeks, I knew he loved me the best, but he couldn't choose me first.

The three of us went to the local funeral home to finalize the arrangements. Both my brother and mother were surprised I had prepaid the funeral. At that time, they likely thought I had done this with my money. Over the next two days, we welcomed hundreds of his customers and business associates who viewed his body and followed him to the cemetery. This later became a blur. Many people shared stories with us about the store, but no one knew the man within Bill Wilson.

A few days after the funeral, our lawyer and the man who had set up my adoption, arranged an appointment to preview the will and discuss settling the estate. I rushed this because I needed to take Peggy back home. He began to read my dad's assets, all of which he had left to my mother.

"There are two $20,000 CDs," The attorney began to read the list.

"I cashed out one of them and prepaid the funeral home for both funerals," I said. James looked startled. I had not consulted Dad about cashing

A Girl Named Connie

in this CD, but felt that if I didn't do this, I might have to pay out of my own pocket.

Our attorney continued, "There is a $50,000 CD."

"That one is gone," my brother said.

"There's another one for $34, 0000," the attorney stated.

"That one is gone, too," my brother continued.

"There is one for $55,000, too."

"It's gone," James said without blinking. I didn't question the money or lack of it. After all, the CD's belonged to Dad and had been cashed before he died, so that would have been between the two of them. Perhaps the money had been put somewhere to grow more interest. I was not blood and felt I had no right to pry.

My dad lay on his deathbed a broken man with not a penny in the bank, but I had to hope that he and James had worked out a plan for it of which I was not to be privy. Just as Dad had sold the store without my knowledge, he likely had given James the authority to cash in his money rather than have to hand it over in a lawsuit. For whatever the reason, I was an outsider by now.

I should have said, "What happened to the money?"

I should have said, "Is there money for you all to live?"

I should have said, "Does Mother know there are no CD's at the bank?"

Instead, I said nothing.

Later when I went to the bank to check the lock box, hoping to find clues about my past, everything was gone. What happened to the contents? Would I ever know? After all, I was adopted and what was in that box was not mine in the eyes of my brother.

Within months, my brother became desperate, so he hocked Mother's diamond ring. When I discovered this on a visit home, I blew up. Each time I came something was missing.

"Where did you hock it?" I demanded. He knew the location of all the pawnshops within a hundred miles.

I bought it back and returned it to her only for him to hock it again. I don't know how he got it from her, but she didn't seem to know it was missing until I returned it. The last time I bought it back, I kept it. This time, she thought she lost the ring. That was only one of many of the problems in the confines of the home where I grew up.

CHAPTER FORTY-SIX

WITHIN SIX MONTHS of my father's death, Peggy's cancer became more aggressive. After days, months, and years of suffering and getting better and then getting worse, she lost her sparkle.

Peggy now needed around-the-clock care. During the day, her mother came over and stayed with her. I was working as much as I could to support my mother. When I got home in the afternoons, I drove her around the area to get her out of the house, and we stopped for ice cream. We watched a new development progress in the neighborhood and picked out a house to watch go up from the foundation. That was the goal: to watch the floors, the walls, and the final touches finished on the house and have ice cream. That house became symbolic of Peggy's life.

She was very sick and frail and throughout each night for many weeks, she threw up. Even though I tried to help, she wanted to be left alone. I understood this, but she had to have my help. Many times she ended up in the hospital and each time I thought she would never return. I prayed endlessly for her to be well. Then later I prayed for God to take her.

During all of Peggy's sickness, my mom's health was also deteriorating. I told my principal about the situation with my mother and my good friend and that I was not going to be able to run the in-school suspension program I had taken on after my retirement. "You write a leave of absence to take care of your mother," which meant I would have a job when or if she became better. Taking care of a friend would not have held my job.

I spent my weekends in Edmonton and my weekdays taking care of Peggy. Sickness had become a way of life and hospitals my second home. My desire to become a nurse was now manifesting itself as I became a caregiver to both Mother and Peggy and became somewhat of an expert on breast cancer research and treatments.

In the meantime, not only was Peggy sick and my mother's health declining, but my dog was also growing more and more feeble. Scruffer had been my family for nine years, and Peggy had grown to love him, too. I cradled him on the side of my bed, and when Peggy told me in her weakened voice to take him to the vet, I didn't think there was a point but I did what she asked.

I held Scruffer on the porch of the clinic where he died in my arms. I have never really gotten over his death, and I dreaded telling Peggy. For some reason, I thought she might parallel his death with the prospect of her own.

I had lost my father, Aunt Hazel, and now Peggy was slipping away. Giving up on the possibility of her recovering was out of the question because she was so young and had been so healthy. When it did happen, I was inconsolable.

For days, Peggy slipped in and out of consciousness, and when she was awake, she didn't speak. She smiled in recognition, but she could not communicate. I longed to hear her voice and especially her laugh. Finally, I had to accept that she was not going to live much longer so as her sister sat with her, I sought the hospital chapel. "Please God, take her. It is time," I prayed. Two hours later she was gone. We watched her take her last breath. In a way, it was also mine.

Peggy was the light in my dark. All of my life I had sought security and acceptance with no pressure to give something in return. What would I do now?

Going back home to an empty house is dreadful, but I insisted I needed to be alone. Sitting on the edge of my bed, I thought about the future, and I saw no sunshine. For a brief moment, suicide came to mind, and those thoughts scared me.

I can't explain any of what followed except to tell it. As I was sitting in my darkness, a white figure swept across me, and a soft, warm hand that was more of a light came under my hand and held it. I sat very still in that moment and then had a major panic attack that frightened me so much that I called Peggy's sister Patty.

"Would you spend the night with me?" She came.

I was lying in bed, so she crawled in beside me without a word, and we slept as much as either of us could. There was no doubt Peggy was trying to comfort me, but it would be at least ten years before I was ever the same without her. I am not sure I will ever be the Connie that I once was.

There would be other signs from Peggy, but I admit that I did some bizarre things in the next few weeks. Peggy had a collection of reading glasses scattered about the house, so I gathered them up and took them to a studio and had them mounted and framed. Where did I think I was going to hang them?

Early on she had participated in a 5K Run for the Cure, so I framed her kerchief, her run number, and her hat. What was I going to do with that?

Probably the oddest thing I did was keep a set of pictures in the glove compartment of my car of when she was in the hospital. Why would I want those pictures? I even stuck a picture of her in the odometer where I could see it when I drove. I know now that I needed help.

I didn't remember much about the funeral. Her family took care of the Catholic service because they knew what she would have wanted. My Baptist background did not prepare me for the preparations, so her family took care of the details. Her nephew gave a powerful eulogy, and as I sat with my Edmonton friends, I could feel nothing but emptiness. I, once again, was alone. Peggy would have frowned at me, but she knew I would be a lost soul.

I asked her family if we could bury Peggy above ground. "I can't stand to think of her in the ground," I said. "Can we take off her wig? I don't want her buried in her wig." Of course, they granted my requests because they knew what Peggy meant to me.

She had given me a place to be in my otherwise confusing world. With her, I was home. With her, I did not have to pretend or explain or evaluate my feelings. With her, I never had to buy my way. I knew she had not abandoned me in death, but it took me awhile to come to terms with God.

As I mourned, friends worried about my mental state. I stopped caring about myself and functioned at a minimum. However, I had to live because my mother depended on me. She needed me. At least, I thought she did. I thought I had a reason to live. Two months after Peggy died, the principal of my school called. "It's time you came back to work." He was helping to pull me out of the grave.

After my dad died, the only use I thought I was to my mother and brother was financial, and after Peggy died, the two of them constantly asked me for more. I didn't say, "Where is all the money from the CD's?" That would have been accusatory and I didn't want to imply I didn't trust that the money had not been spent wisely. This was a touchy subject and I'm not sure how much clear thinking my mother was doing at this time.

When I came home each week, James and I went to the grocery and stocked up on supplies, foods, and whatever they needed. I set up an automatic withdrawal for the electric bill, water bill, and sent them a little money a month. What they never knew was that I was as broke as they were.

Almost immediately after Peggy's death and the issues I faced with my mother, I think I went crazy. Buying things eased the pain; things I couldn't afford. I paid $5,000 for a couch because a sales clerk in a high-class furniture store snubbed me. I wanted to replace my couch because in Peggy's final months that is where she slept and looking at it brought paralyzing memories, but not a $5,000 one. I needed to be mad at someone, so I was going to show this clerk I was "somebody" and she couldn't snub me.

When I realized my mistake, I called Carol.

"Carol, I have just done the dumbest thing."

"Well, what?" She knew that I spent when I was depressed.

I told her the story. She said, "I hope you didn't let her make the commission." It never occurred to me that she would make a commission on this sale, so I didn't win after all. I could never seek revenge and get it right.

It took me several years to pay off that couch.

Unhappy? Buy something. Credit cards were my source for those splurges because I was making no extra money during all the sicknesses. Peggy would not have been happy with my spending sprees, but that was all I knew to do.

By 2004, my mother's health was fragile. She was in and out of hospitals and nursing homes. Just one stay at a nursing home was $6,000, which I had to agree to pay because Medicare would pay for only part of her stay. I also continued to buy groceries, pay the utilities, and medical supplies not covered by Medicare. My retirement check barely made my house payment, my utilities and other obligations, but I tapped into my savings fund, used my credit cards, and borrowed from my insurance to keep their household afloat. My mother never knew that I was paying for her care, and I never wanted her to know that she was broke.

During the last year of her life, my brother made a deal to sell the house that my parents had built. I never asked why he needed to sell the house, but I suspected he was desperate because this home was his home now more than mine. Many years ago I had learned that between the two of us, he would win with Mother.

He called to ask if I would come down to sign papers. A normal sister/brother relationship would have led to a discussion of doing something this final, but I didn't say anything. I assumed we would be going to a lawyer's office, but instead we met in a parking lot and signed papers on the hood of a truck. James had made this deal with a good friend of my dad's who wrote a check to me and a check to him for each half.

What I didn't know at the time was that he had sold my dad's five dollar gold piece to the same person who bought the house. I grieved over this piece more than the house and tried to buy it back but could not afford it.

Friends have asked why I didn't fight my brother on these issues. I had a legal right to make my demands, but they did not understand my relationship with my brother. He meant more to my mother than any person alive and to fight with him would have been the same as fighting with my mother. She was in his care, and he was not physically mistreating her. What he was doing was trying to continue his life and was having a difficult time financing himself. Selling the house became a solution. I was not a player in this family any longer. I was now the adopted daughter and the outsider but held the guilt of obligation.

The agreement was that my brother and mother could live in the house as long as they paid rent of $400 a month. My mother was now a tenant in her own home, but she never knew it. She would have been humiliated.

Within a few months, my mother began calling daily. She seldom called me, but she was on a mission. "Sister, do you have my money?" she said.

I didn't know what to say. "Are you keeping it from us? We are starving down here. I need my money."

"Mother, why would I have your money?" She skipped over that question.

"We need you to send it to us." I knew her mind was failing, but those accusations were hurtful. At first, I did not react. Maybe she would forget she called. If I sent her the $20,000 from the sale of the house, it would be gone and I would still be left paying the bills.

"Sister, have you sent the money?" she asked every day that she called. She would wear me down. No matter what I said, I couldn't convince her that I did not have her money. The fuel was coming fast against me, burning down our relationship. The money wasn't worth her thinking I had stolen from her.

I realized what I had to do. I'm not sure in retrospect if this was the wisest decision, but I did not want my mother to think I would take her money. If I gave the house money to her, it would soon be gone. If I kept it, she would persist in asking me for it and lose faith in me. The last call was so hurtful that I wrote a check for $20,000, my part of the house, and mailed it to her. As I predicted, the calls began again.

I had gone back to working part-time at school and needed a second job, so I contacted one of my friends who owned a construction company. He offered me a job cleaning up behind his crew each day. He was building an apartment and my job was to sweep out the debris so the workers could have a clean working space. The pay was good, but the work was backbreaking. This job would pay their rent.

I could have stopped answering the phone and ignored her pleas, but I never stopped feeling as if I owed my mother and father. I had a debt to pay, and it broke me financially and emotionally.

CHAPTER FORTY-SEVEN

FROM 2000-2004, life was hell. I had to work as much as I could to support my mother who was back and forth in the nursing home. My brother could not work and take care of her, so I was their golden goose. He had never worked for any length of time because of his "bad back." If he had been working, she would have been in a nursing home, and that is not where she wanted to be.

By 2004, my mother could not sustain food, she couldn't walk, and her mind was rapidly fading. She was born poor, worked hard, married, lived a rich, prosperous life, and then died without a nickel. I am thankful she never knew this. I had protected her by providing the life she had known. In doing so, I was left in more debt than I would be able to overcome for years.

When my mother died, I didn't know how to feel. She had hurt me so many times with her phone calls, but I consoled myself with the fact that she was sick. Honestly, I am not sure just how sick her mind was at the time. Did she think I would steal her money?

This time, there would be two of us to make the arrangements. I let him pick out everything. He was her son and the one she loved above all others, so I took the passive approach. When he asked my opinion, I said, "Whatever you want." She was my mother, but she belonged to him.

I was an orphan again. Dad was gone. Peggy was gone. Aunt Hazel was gone, and now my mother was gone. My childhood home was gone as well.

At the cemetery, I felt sadness but also an unexpected sense of relief. All the secrets, all the lies, all the turmoil, and tension were gone. Everyone in that funeral home related to me knew that Cloteel Wilson was my great aunt and not my mother.

At the cemetery as we sat under the tent with her casket in front of us, the minister said words I didn't hear, and I listened as James sniffed back tears. While the crew prepared the grave, I stood over the grassy plot of my dad. His betrayal was the most hurtful of all.

As the crowd meandered back to their cars, I couldn't move away from the graves. I had something on my mind, and this would likely be my last opportunity. It might have seemed inappropriate, but I wasn't thinking about protocol.

With several people nearby and probably within hearing distance, I walked up to my brother and said, "You have just lost your trump card. Don't ever ask me for anything. Don't ever call me. I no longer want any contact with you." He said nothing. I had caught him off guard and also in a public place. I did not fear him when we had an audience.

I gave an advance of one month's rent to the new owner of our home to give my brother time to move. I don't know why I bothered to do that.

The last time I saw him or my nephew was at the cemetery.

I walked away with a sense of peace and a path to the future that did not include anyone named Wilson. I could not afford to love them. All that was behind me. The two who loved me as their own, raised me to be strong and confident, and for whom I had spent years trying to be worthy of their love were lying in the Edmonton Cemetery among my dad's family. The mystery surrounding Connie Allen Wilson had ended, and now the truth would not hurt anyone else.

By the next afternoon, I was back in Louisville. In a very pathetic way, I was free. My path, however, was far from clear.

My new dogs greeted me with great affection, and I played with them and cried. I could hear my mother saying, "I don't know why you want those damn dogs in the house."

Later that night as I was turning off the lights, I saw the folder lying on the dining room table that held my retirement paper. I had never put it away, which was not surprising since I used that table as a place to store important papers rather than for eating. I flipped it open, and there was the manila envelope with my real birth certificate. I slipped it out once again.

I was born to Jewell Frances Smith of Smiths Grove, Kentucky at the age of 17 and to a student from Glasgow whose name was on my birth certificate. I had no clue about my father but here was his name in ink right in front of me. Had Aunt Hazel seen this document? She claimed not to know the name of the boy but here it was.

I was born in the Susan Speed Davis Home Hospital, which was just another name for a home for unwed mothers. On this certificate, I noticed the doctor tested her for syphilis. Was this a normal procedure in all hospitals or just this one? There were two boxes for the attending person to check: one for a legitimate birth and one for an illegitimate. My box was checked "illegitimate." No one wants to be illegitimate. I didn't want to be illegitimate.

My life had been content most of the time, but was it a better life than the one Fran and this young man could have given me if they had married? I thought about the actions that led to my conception and have concluded that the story Aunt Hazel gave me was only partially true.

I'm not sure this "sin" happened without her consent, but she was afraid to tell her mother the truth. Premarital sex was unacceptable. I don't think the boy raped her as Aunt Hazel said or was she victimized. I think she loved the boy, protected him and feared for him. If her father knew she had sex, he might have gone on a drunken spree and killed him. Fran had the courage to name the father in this document and why would she take this risk if he didn't know about me? She could have left it blank or put "unknown." He had access to the birth certificate just as I did. What would have kept him from knowing about me?

Having seldom thought about the man who fathered me, I didn't reveal his name except to my best friends. Carol and Judy could not understand my lack of interest in locating him. "You wouldn't have to tell him, but at least, find out about him. You may have siblings." Later they said, "We have located a man by that name in this area." Google keeps no secrets.

I never searched for him. When I told Wanda I had a copy of the certificate and knew the father's name, she seemed surprised. She had never heard of him. "He was just some boy at a party," she said. "Just some boy" was my father.

Images of Aunt Hazel walking down to the gravel road from her farmhouse on a warm spring day to greet Fran after Mother and Dad brought her home six weeks after I was born played like a movie. I could see my mother in the front seat holding me, Dad under the wheel and Fran getting out of the back, knowing that this was the last time she would be anything but a cousin to me.

A Girl Named Connie

According to Fran's sisters, she left the home and spent those six weeks in Louisville with Mother and Dad recuperating. If that is true, then she surely held me, rocked me, touched my hands, gave me baths, and loved me.

I pictured Aunt Hazel looking through the car window at her granddaughter, but one who would never call her Granny. Then I could see the two of them turn away and walk up the hill and never look back. They never looked back. Was Fran happy to be rid of her problem or would she live regretfully?

I sat in my overstuffed chair with my real birth certificate lying on my chest and sobbed.

CHAPTER FORTY-EIGHT

AGGRAVATION AND AGITATION continued for the next few weeks as James called about clearing out the house. I had taken a few pieces that I wanted while Mother was still alive. When he called, I was not in the mood to sort through their lives.

"Connie, are you coming down here to get anything?" my brother asked when I finally answered his call.

"No, you take it all." After all, my brother was their blood, so I thought he should have what they had. Honestly, I was cutting my throat by not going through everything, piece by piece. My pride stood in the way of items I wanted so badly. I had become a master of avoiding confrontations, and he was not one I wanted to tackle. My attempt at being a martyr backfired and I was left with nothing.

Why could my brother and I never have a relationship? Dad adored me, and Mother adored my brother. I felt a little sorry that he never had a good relationship with Dad. No matter how I tried to understand the dysfunctional relationship among the three of them, I never could. They had worn me down more times than lifted me up.

One of the few phone calls I received after Mother died began with, "I was worried about you," he said. I knew he wasn't worried about me. I said, "Thank you. You don't have to worry." Then he said, "Do you know what happened to Mother's China?"

"Yes, remember I paid you $1,000 for it." He suddenly remembered. I was not going to return it to him.

I'm surprised he didn't ask about Dad's Kentucky Cluster. On one of my visits, I was sitting next to Mother while she ate and she took something out of her pocket and slipped it to me. It was my dad's Kentucky Cluster diamond. It would be mine after all.

For months, I was in a full-blown state of depression and one morning when I was especially unhappy, I looked at myself in the hallway mirror and did not like what I saw. I wanted to be someone else. I wanted to look like someone else. Prone to wrinkles at even an early age, mine were becoming more prevalent due to sorrow and stress. The years of losing family and friends had taken a toll on me and it showed on my face.

Before diving into this major decision, I had a meeting with Carol and Judy. "I want to tell you because if anything goes wrong, you will know I was doing what I wanted. If I die, I have told my Louisville friends to call Butler Funeral Home in Edmonton, and they will take care of me." They listened as if to hear dreadful news.\

"I know you will think I'm crazy, but I have made up my mind. I'm going to have a facelift."

"Oh, my goodness! I thought you were dying," Carol said relieved.

I was not vain about my looks. After my high school days of bleaching my hair and going from short to long, I settled on short and have not changed that style since college. I was not obsessed with my face; I was obsessed with the wrinkles that had attacked it.

Judy said, "Connie, you don't really want a facelift. You could come out with big lips and your skin so tight your eyes won't blink."

"I'm going to have this skin removed under my neck," I explained as I pulled out the loose flab and swished it from side to side like the skin of a chicken, "and around my eyes, the lines taken out around my mouth and my forehead, and my eyebrows lifted."

"But do you know how dangerous this is?" Carol asked.

"I have one of the best doctors. I was worried about having big lips too, but during my consultation, he said he was going to increase my lip volume but not enough to look like Angelina Jolie. I told him that wouldn't be so bad. As for the danger, I don't care."

"But you may come out looking like some of those freakish women I have seen on Oprah. Some of them look like aliens," Carol continued, naming some of the most familiar.

"I'm tired of looking in the mirror and having this haggard woman looking back," I said. Most people get a new hairstyle or a new outfit. I was having a facelift.

I went under the knife the week before Christmas and didn't want anyone to stay with me while I was in the hospital or when I came home. A couple of my Louisville friends showed up with food and were shocked at the mummy they saw. "Your face was as red as Ronald McDonald's hair. Blood red. You looked like an electric sander had stripped off the first layer of skin." Bandages covered my hair, around my ears, and under my chin. Frankly, when I looked at myself, I wondered if I had made a mistake.

I locked the doors. No one could see me except the person who brought soup and fed my dogs. I healed in silence because my mouth was so swollen I couldn't speak. Microdermabrasion took off the skin from my top lip and looked as if I had kissed a frozen light pole.

When the wounds began to heal and before I had to go back to work, it was time to visit my Edmonton friends.

At that stage, a battered wife couldn't have looked any worse. My face was black and blue and my mouth was swollen to my nose. I could see the possibilities, but they could only see the aftermath of the truck that hit my face. While they tried to see beyond the swelling and bruising, Carol's husband Guy commented quite bluntly, "You paid how much to look like this?"

I couldn't stop tinkering with my forehead as we talked. I didn't realize I was massaging my dimples until Judy asked, "Does your head hurt?"

"Not really. Just annoying. I have a screw on each side of my forehead, and sometimes they bother me."

"You have screws holding up your forehead?" The girls tried to faint when I wiggled them around.

"And one behind each ear. I think when they took my ears off, they put the right one back a little higher."

"WHEN THEY TOOK YOUR EARS OFF?" That was all they could stand. Of course, I, being a biology major, found the procedure fascinating. They found it repulsive.

After several months, the wounds totally healed, and I must say many of the wrinkles diminished. The size of my lips returned to normal minus some wrinkles around the mouth, and I could finally blink my eyes. The numbness gradually left my cheeks, and the swelling subsided. I can also no longer feel the screws, but one ear is still slightly higher than the other.

This procedure was as painful as anything I have ever been through, but when I looked at myself, I saw a younger looking Connie. Even if I didn't look younger to anyone else, I felt it. A facelift gave me temporary satisfaction but did not sooth my heart.

My friends insisted I had to do something with them rather than sit at home and mourn. Once again, I was indifferent, so I followed along with no real interest or desire to be anywhere. This particular year we went to Mexico, which I consider the land of jewelry, which is dangerous territory for me. Buying jewelry to me is like giving a pain pill to a junkie.

My friends like to say that I like "fine" jewelry so I came home with thousands of dollars of what may or not be "fine" jewelry. Not long after we got back home, the high priced watch I bought stopped working, and it would have cost more to send it back than the $150 it cost to fix it.

I bought a pair of diamond earrings that cost as much as a good used car. The clerk was more than willing to finance my purchase. That's all I needed to hear.

"Connie, you might need to think about this before you set up payments," Carol whispered as I admired my ears in the mirror. I left that store with more than earrings.

That afternoon everyone gathered in my room to see what I had bought. Showing them my jewelry gave me a high, but later that night when the reality set in of how much I had charged on my credit card and how long it would take me to pay it off, I sank into a mild depression that kept me from going to dinner. I can't explain what happened, but that need to own expensive objects continues to dwell within me. Things soothe me.

Instead of telling me I had lost my mind, they consoled me by saying that jewelry was a wise investment. I have never worn the necklace or the two bracelets, so I hope they are gaining value inside a drawer.

Not long ago I brought out the jewelry I have never worn just to remember what I was paying for each month. Ironically, I discovered along with a "precious stone" necklace and two tanzanite bracelets came various letters of authenticity. They were probably standard forms mass-produced in a back room.

A Letter of Authenticity. All my life I had been looking for authenticity. To discover that the only thing that remained authentic throughout my life has been the name "Connie." I was Connie Ailene Smith for fifty-one-years, and then once adopted, I became Connie Allen Wilson.

I was working almost every day at my school. The payments on my new face and now my jewelry pushed me to work. Without Peggy to curb my spending, I was living like a rich girl but was in debt up to my new neck.

I had also turned into quite a grump, and I knew it. My nerves were on edge, and I was quick to speak without thinking and to correct students when they might not have needed correcting. My principal called me to his office for telling a student to put his ass in the chair. "Connie, you can't say those words," he said, shaking his head.

I heard his message.

They tolerated "Miss Wilson."

Sometimes when I got home from work, friends called but I didn't want to talk. Invitations came for dinners and parties, but I did not want to do either. I didn't feel like being with others, but most of all, I didn't want to be with myself. However, my Edmonton friends insisted that I continue to go places with them even though I would have rather have been at home. They tried to keep me from sinking in my sorrow, but I was willing to drown. I had an overblown case of the "feel sorry for myself." The only place I found happiness was at school.

CHAPTER FORTY-NINE

IN 2009, I FELT A LUMP. I had avoided mammograms after Peggy died because I just didn't want to know. Of course, that was irresponsible. Once again, I called Carol, Roberta, and Judy and explained what I had found and what came next. Naturally, they wanted to drop their lives and come to mine. "I'm having a biopsy and have plenty of people here to go with me."

When my doctor came in the room when I went back for the results, I could read his expression. "Connie, the tumor is malignant." I, like Peggy, had breast cancer.

"Of course, it was. Of course, I have cancer." He didn't know what to say.

Unlike the care I thought Peggy received at the beginning of her cancer, I wanted the best possible surgeon and Carol led me to her. From Edmonton, she had researched for her mother, who had breast cancer at age 86, and through her brother, who was a researcher at UL, found Dr. Chagpar. She had saved Carol's mother's life.

However, when I called to make an appointment, she was booked up for months. I wanted her, but when she wasn't available, I was bombarded by suggestions. Everyone had a doctor to recommend, but I wasn't taking any chances. Then Chance came along at a rodeo.

My half sister Brenda's family is deeply involved in rodeos and wanted me to go with them to watch some family members participate. I had never been to a rodeo, so when I parked the car I walked along with two older ladies to the grandstand, dressed in their western shirts, boots, and bandanas and when one of them said, "How are you doing today?" I spilled my entire story of the lump, the biopsy, and not being able to see the doctor I wanted.

"Who is the doctor?"

"Dr. Chagpar."

"Honey, I have worked with her over twenty years. You get your paperwork and call me and I'll get you in." That is exactly what she did.

On the day of my first visit, Dr. Chagpar came into the room reading the report from the biopsy. "This tumor is stage one. I will take it out, throw it in a bucket, and you will be fine."

"Dr. Chagpar, I would like both breasts removed." She wasn't expecting to hear this.

I explained what had happened to my friend.

"I want both of them off," I said. However, I would like to have reconstruction surgery at the same time if I can."

I met with a plastic surgeon, and all was set to occur the same day.

On the day of my surgery, twenty plus friends showed up at the hospital. "You must have a lot of friends," the surgeon told me as she made one last visit before surgery.

"Why do you think that?" I asked, half groggy.

"I have never seen so many people with a patient." In my absence, my friends and Peggy's family had gathered like they were at a tailgating party.

This outstanding surgeon is now head of the medical school at an Ivy League university.

What she didn't know was that among this group, only one of them was related, and that was my cousin Marty Bybee (Joe's daughter) who had driven me to the hospital.

I had many friends to check on me or be at the hospital during surgery, but not family the way Peggy had had for around the clock care if I needed it. I was going to face this alone, so I thought, but I had been alone for several years now and could do this by myself. The need to control my circumstances included my treatment and my recuperation.

However, Carol and Judy announced they would take care of me. Once the surgery was over, they were going to move in for a few days and make sure I ate, slept, and took my medicine. They would field phone calls and entertain visitors. Not that I had a choice, but I would have preferred to be alone. They didn't last long.

Unlike me, they are like two whirlwinds running together in a field of sand. They couldn't sit quietly and watch TV; they ran over each other trying to whip my house into shape. Unlike my mother, I never kept every item in its place. I routinely scattered magazines over the coffee table, and junk mail and old newspapers along the hearth. I straightened up when it bothered me, but my home was not the happy place it had once been, and I no longer took a real interest in whether or not things were in their place.

"You rest, and we'll cook and take care of everything downstairs." My bedroom was on the top floor. They made a grocery list and yelled up the stairs, "You're going to be sleeping, so we're going to buy some groceries." I didn't cook. My meals at home consisted of peanut butter and crackers or a grilled cheese. I can make a mean grilled cheese and open a can of tomato soup for a delicious meal.

A Girl Named Connie

They knew nothing about where to shop but set out to find a store nearby. In the meantime, I tried to rest, but the doorbell rang one time after another.

I ambled to the upstairs window only to see a delivery boy with flowers standing on my stoop. I raised the window and yelled, "Just leave them on the steps." In a little while the doorbell rang again and this time, friends were bringing food. They couldn't leave the food on the doorstep, so I went down the stairs to unlock the door.

By the time Carol and Judy returned two hours later, I was sitting in my big chair in front of the fireplace. "Where have you two been?" I sounded like a teacher.

"We had to go to Outer Loop to find a store."

"For Hells Bells," I said as I climbed back up the stairs and directed them to the newly delivered food in the kitchen.

"Where did you get these flowers?" Judy asked.

"Delivery boy while you two were out!"

They were having a good time whisking away my dirty clothes from piles I had sorted in my bedroom the week before and carrying them to the basement to the washer and dryer. One was going to vacuum and another was doing laundry; one was dusting and the other organizing papers and magazines. One fact they missed was that a person recouping from surgery needs quiet and not an electrical storm in the house.

"Girls," I said as I made my way back down the stairs, hanging on to the railing careful not to topple over on my new breasts, "I love both of you but you are leaving tomorrow. I can't take any more of your help." We laughed until the pain overcame me. "Now, if you don't mind," I said, "make yourselves some coffee and eat some of the food brought in and then watch TV and let me sleep."

They did help change the bandages. I should say Judy did because Carol doesn't have the stomach for anything so invasive. The next day they tucked me in for my afternoon rest and headed out the door. My last words were, "Don't let Pat out the door."

Because I couldn't hear, I had no knowledge of the chaos below. My dog Pat dashed out between the girls' legs and off he went down the street. They were yelling, "Pat, Pat, here Pat." Two of my city friends drove up to bring yet more food, heard the commotion and saw Pat darting through the neighbors' yards. Deana drove her car around the corner and somehow cut him off. I could never quite see this picture, but nonetheless, she caught him and brought him home, left the food, and locked the door behind her. Finally, I had understood why Peggy said, "I need to be alone."

As I began to heal, I noticed something odd about my new breasts. They were lopsided. Having paid high dollar for these two, I went back to the reconstruction surgeon. He tried to reassure me they would "level off." They didn't and for a year I lived with them hanging in different directions.

The problem wasn't just that they were not level; they were too big. "I want a "B" cup," I instructed. When he acted as if he didn't know what I meant I should have left, but I used my hands to explain a "B" cup. He showed me samples, and I picked out the ones I wanted. He must have confused mine with those of another woman because he implanted a set that was far too large for me.

Instead of a "B", my implants were "D" cups. How could a plastic surgeon mess up a set of breasts sizes? Those breasts were too big and too heavy to carry. My shoulders were dragging me down. I was a "C" cup, so this much difference did not agree with my body, so I sought yet another plastic surgeon who redid the surgery. Going through two reconstructions was worse than the double mastectomy, and they aren't exactly right yet.

During this low point, I was convinced and quite obsessed with the idea that I should have had treatment beyond the cancer pill. I was sure I needed chemo or radiation. If Peggy had had treatment early, she might have lived. How could I not need treatment? I went back to my surgeon. "Connie, if you will feel better, I suggest a test, which you will have to pay for yourself, that is the ultimate pathology. I will send your records to California, and if they say anything different, we will follow their advice." I needed to think this over.

I called Carol that night and explained my fears and the test. "If you were me would have the test?"

"If you will live more at ease, have it."

"But it will cost me $5,000. I trust my doctor, but I don't trust cancer."

"Evidently, you don't trust her 100% so have the final analysis. After all, $5,000 is just a couch."

My doctor sent my pathology report and whatever other information necessary to California, and experts concurred that I needed no treatment other than the pill. I do believe that every cancer patient lives in fear that it will return because they didn't seek out all forms of treatment.

Roberta was the next to have breast cancer but like mine, it was in the early stages. She endured what I did, but her health continually grew worse from other sicknesses. Carol, Judy and I knew she was sick, but she had come through bad periods. She visited her father in Edmonton, and Carol and Judy were able to see her during these times. "She looks so thin," Carol reported. When asked how she felt she said, "I feel great."

She was not great at all, and we three were brokenhearted. She was with me on that playground in the sixth grade. She cried for me when she thought I was going to fall to my death on the water tower. I was a bridesmaid in her wedding. We had always been together even when apart.

She was buried in the same cemetery as her mother and grandparents were, as well as my relatives. Even though she had not lived in Edmonton since high school, this was her home. One single tombstone sits on this hillside; and every time I place flowers on the graves of my parents, I lay a sunflower on hers. She loved sunflowers.

After Peggy died and I survived, I became a staunch supporter of the Susan G. Komen Race for the Cure that was in conjunction with Oaks Day during the Kentucky Derby. I had to do something to make my survival have a purpose and alleviate my guilt for being alive.

For years, I rallied students and teachers to raise money for the cause, so they sold pink shirts, and we had a week of special activities at school. I was humbled by their cooperation even though they did not know the lady for whom I had created this tribute. We raised over $3,000 each year. Then when I was diagnosed, they turned this into a Team Wilson event. On their own, they surprised me with Team Wilson shirts they had painted and decorated. This was so overwhelming.

Oaks Day (an event prior to the Kentucky Derby) was dedicated to cancer survivors. I was among hundreds of survivors, all dressed in pink, who walked around the derby track. I wore my "Team Wilson" pink rubber bracelet that I had distributed to faculty and students.

After the walk, I had gone to the concession stand and bought drinks for a couple of us and I was holding the drinks and a racing form when I felt a slight jolt.

"Oh, I'm so sorry," she said. I was facing the Governor's wife.

"I have to be careful with these," I said looking down at my breasts. "They are brand new. I don't even have them paid for yet!" We laughed.

"I have a new set myself," she replied. I had read about her surgery in the newspaper.

"I know, but yours look better than mine." I followed her back to her seat, which was not far from mine and she relayed the story to her husband.

Times such as these I felt strong again. Someone laughing at what I said or being in the spotlight with all the other survivors, dressed in my pink suit and walking the field provided a moment of self-worth. However, just as quickly as something gave me a lift, something else brought me down. That is the way I lived for several years. Grief can be as crippling as a disease.

After the deaths of so many people in such a short time and my battle with cancer, I didn't know how to move forward. Taking care of the sick had consumed much of my time but had also given me a purpose no matter how unwelcome it was. Taking care of myself was not nearly as difficult because I had always been responsible for myself. At least, while I was worried about my health, I had a focus and a purpose. I wanted to live. I didn't know I wanted to live until I thought I might not.

By then I had given up my part-time job at Bulter High School but went back as a substitute when I was well enough. Carol warned me that I needed to rest and take care of myself, but she didn't know the depth of my debt. Every penny I had saved had gone to take care of my mother, and the expenses of my sickness not covered by insurance piled up.

The truth was that I was at home in a classroom, and I missed teaching even though I was never going back full time. I was the actor, director, and writer in the classroom. That is where I have always felt the most needed and respected, and most importantly, that was the place I was in control. I could tell the truth and be real instead of pretending I was someone else.

CHAPTER FIFTY

WANDA, WHOM I THOUGHT was my cousin but turned out to be my aunt, has always been my link to Aunt Hazel's family and continues to include me in all holidays and special events. Even though I thought she would know about her sister and that time in her life when I was born, she knew very little. However, she held a very important piece of information that would give me at least a little insight into the time my mother was in the home.

On one of those visits, Wanda disappeared into a bedroom and came back with an envelope. "I think you should have this," she said. I took the yellowed envelope addressed to Jewell Frances Smith. "This is a letter to Fran from her roommate." She didn't have to explain what she meant by a roommate. This letter was dated June after my birth in April.

I didn't want to read it in front of others because I was a little nervous about what it might reveal. Would there be something else to learn about my mother? No doubt Wanda had read this letter, so when I didn't open it immediately, she understood.

A Girl Named Connie

Once I was back in Louisville, I sat in my car outside the house and opened the letter. It was from a lady named Dee.

"How are you doing at home? Just fine are my only wishes. I went up to Susie's (I think that is what they called the home) *and Sandra, Mary, and Ailene are on the third floor now.* (I assumed that was the delivery floor, and my name must have been chosen after her friend, Ailene). *How did everything turn out for you? Ruth is heartbroken. I try not to even think about it. I miss my roommate and hope to someday hear from you. Send me a picture."* Love, Dee.

I doubt that Fran was allowed to answer this letter. More than likely, she was told to forget that year of her life and the other women who were there. Did Dee think Fran had kept me and a picture of me was her request? Maybe she was asking for a picture of Fran. Dee sounded so young.

I have thought so much about those women. Somewhere are children who belong to Sandra, Mary, Ruth, Ailene, and Dee. They would all now be my age or near it. Did their mothers hold them and rock them and nurse them the first six weeks? Were they taken away at birth so the girls would not see them and perhaps want to keep them at the last minute? Were all of the babies adopted or did some go into orphanages? Was there an aunt ready to take the baby as her own the way mine did or would the babies go to strangers? The girls were there for the same reasons and the endings were not likely to be happy ones.

Some of these children may have searched for their birth parents, and some may have never known they were adopted. No matter where they ended up, we all had the same start and the same common bond; we were illegitimate.

I wanted to know those children. Know the child Ruth couldn't get over thinking about or the one Dee tried to forget. I wonder what my mother thought as she left the hospital with me wrapped in a blanket, looking up at her with my blue eyes. What happened those six weeks while she was living with Cloteel and Bill in that apartment in Louisville? Did she take care of me? Love me?

Did she hold me on the ride home or did my mother Cloteel? Did she take one last look at me as she turned to walk up the hill to a home that offered no solace? Did her heart ache when she saw me with Cloteel and Bill each time we visited Aunt Hazel, thriving in their care? Did she compare me to her legitimate children? I have to think she didn't want to give me up or walk up that long road home.

I folded the letter, put it back into its envelope, and placed it into the manila envelope with my birth certificates. It held some of the answers to a lifetime of questions, but I would never know the details. I would never know her feelings.

Many of the Smith family would not know the truth for many years, but they would all remember Aunt Hazel reminding them that, "I was one of them." No matter how much I wanted to be one of them, it would be a long time before I knew I was. What a relief to learn I had not been the daughter of a tramp or a saloon girl or a prostitute.

Instead, I was the daughter of a high school girl who had gone to a party, drank too much, had sex with a high school boy, became pregnant and probably never told him. She was sent away to a home for unwed mothers, gave birth to a baby girl she named Connie Ailene, surrendered her to her aunt, whether willingly or not I will never know, and went back home to a secret life.

She did not go back to school but worked alongside her mother in the restaurant. By nineteen, she married a guy, had two children, divorced him and eventually remarried. By all accounts, her life was unhappy and unstable. The happy person she appeared to be to her sisters did not line up with the person her children painted her to be. I saw a deep sadness in her when I think to the distance between us I never understood.

In the end, she died a horrible death. At the funeral home, Aunt Hazel took Fran's first husband by the arm and led him to her casket, "Do you see what you did to her?" She placed much of the blame for Fran's unhappy life on him. Frankly, I don't think her troubles began when she married him. I place the blame on Uncle George for forcing her to leave home and on my mother for orchestrating the solution to what they considered a problem.

In the final analysis, I realized that I was not told the truth not to protect me, but to protect Fran. I was never told my identity to protect Uncle George and Aunt Hazel. What would an out-of-wedlock child have done for the family name? By keeping this secret, Fran could resume her life as well as get to see her baby almost every Sunday. This plan worked well for everyone, it seemed, except Fran and me.

We were strangers living as family, but we were really family living as strangers.

If only I could have said to her long before she died, "It's OK. I'm fine. I forgive you." Maybe then both of us could have had some peace.

I fell into bed and pictured my birth mother, trying to see myself in her face and feel her presence. I visualized Bill and Cloteel holding me, and Aunt Hazel smiling as if she had a secret. Peggy was there to tell me to "Let it go," and just as I was about to feel the peace I longed for, I heard a voice I recognized from long ago on a crowded playground in elementary school. "You're a-dopt-ed; you're a-dopt-ed." Then I cried my lonely self to sleep.

The End

About The Author

Carol Perkins is the author of The True Story About *A Girl Named Connie*. She is a retired high school English teacher. She is also a weekly columnist for several local newspapers and online magazines.

She also co-founded a book company, Promptly Yours, Inc. that produced writing prompts for different subject areas. She wrote six of the twelve books in the series. Carol is an entrepreneur, hosts a weekly radio show on WKNX, participates in local theater, and manages a blog for her church (www.havealittletalk.com)

Carol and her husband Guy live in Edmonton, Kentucky. Their daughter and her family live in Brentwood, Tennessee and their son and his family live in Austin, Texas, so their favorite thing to do is travel between the two.

Writing this book has been a lifelong process. "Connie and I have known each other since before entering school, and we said one day we would write her story. That day came, this is her story, and one we hope you will not soon forget."

Contact information: carolperkins06@gmail.com

Facebook: www.facebook.carol.perkins550

Made in the USA
Las Vegas, NV
05 January 2025